Else Lasker-Schüler

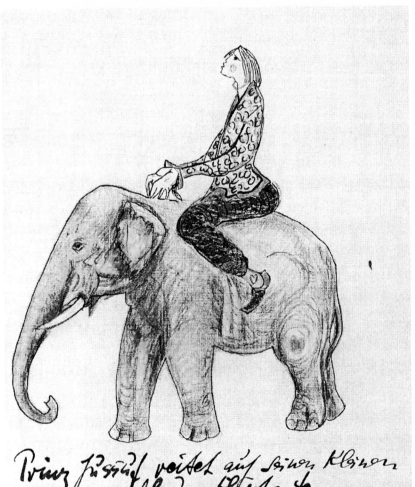

Prinz Jussuf reitet auf seinen kleinen blauen Elefanten.

Else Lasker-Schüler
A Life

BETTY FALKENBERG

McFarland & Company, Inc., Publishers

Jefferson, North Carolina, and London

Frontispiece: *Jussuf reitet auf seinem kleinen blauen Elephanten* (Prince Jussuf riding on his little blue elephant). Else Lasker-Schüler. Pen, India ink, pastelchalk on paper. Private Collection. Courtesy Konrad Feilchenfeldt.

Library of Congress Cataloguing-in-Publication Data

Falkenberg, Betty, 1929–
    Else Lasker-Schüler : a life / Betty Falkenberg.
       p.   cm.
    Includes bibliographical references and index.

    ISBN 0-7864-1460-X (softcover : 50# alkaline paper)

    1. Lasker-Schüler, Else, 1869–1945. 2. Poets, German—
20th century—Biography. I. Title.
PT2623.A76Z689 2003
831'.912—dc21   2003003663

British Library cataloguing data are available

On the cover: Else Lasker-Schüler, 1932 (*Stadtbibliothek Wuppertal, Else Lasker-Schüler Archiv*)

Manufactured in the United States of America

McFarland & Company, Inc., Publishers
  Box 611, Jefferson, North Carolina 28640
  www.mcfarlandpub.com

Contents

Acknowledgments

My greatest debt is to Sigrid Bauschinger, who encouraged me to write this biography for an English-speaking readership. Her book *Else Lasker-Schüler, Ihr Werk und Leben*, published in 1980, remains the standard work on the poet's life and work. Her current participation in the editing of the letters for the *Critical Edition* places her in a unique position to advise on numerous questions of provenance. Her willingness to share hard-earned research and to spoon-feed me special kickshaws (*Leckerbissen*) led to many serendipitous discoveries. A careful reader of the final draft, she spared me many an embarrassment. Whatever errors of fact remain are, needless to say, of my own making.

Thanks also to the friends who over the years read successive drafts critically, and made useful suggestions, among them Anita Desai, Imogene Lehman and, again, Sigrid Bauschinger. And to those who offered encouragement and advice, among them Joachim W. Storck and the late Harry Zohn.

To Hans-Geert Falkenberg who was tireless in hunting down sources and addresses for me in Germany as well as for making available to me his own files and the files of the Westdeutscher Rundfunk und Fernsehen Cologne. It was he who first introduced me to Else Lasker-Schüler through Franz Marc's *Botschaften an den Prinzen Jussuf*.

To Peter Viereck for encouragement to persevere, and for original ways of thinking about translating poetry. (And for being my first convert to the poetry of Else Lasker-Schüler.)

To Michael Hamburger for his kind permission to reprint his translation of the Trakl poem "Abendland," and for his many helpful suggestions about translating Else Lasker-Schüler's poetry.

To the Biography Seminar of New York University, where I became acquainted with the many different approaches, theoretical and practical, as well as the conundrums, of biography writing. Special thanks to Kenneth Silverman of the Seminar, who read and criticized an early draft of the manuscript, and whose suggestions I tried to incorporate in the course of re-writing.

To Henry Schneider, of the Stadtbibliothek Wuppertal, for his forbearance and help in securing the many items I requested. Similarly, to Frau Sabine Fischer at the Deutsche Schillergesellschaft in Marbach, as well as for taking the trouble to direct me to sources for material not in their own archives.

To the editors of *Marbacher Magazin 71/1995*, Erica Klüsener and Friedrich Pfäfflin, whose detailed documentation of the life and works of Else Lasker-Schüler frequently served as a road map for my research.

To the Five College Integrated Library System and Interlibrary Loan Service which, with the especial help of the Mount Holyoke (home base) staff, enabled me to track down virtually every book I requested.

To the Houghton Library, Harvard University, where I first saw the originals of Else Lasker-Schüler's handwritten postcards to Hanns Hirt.

To the Ingram-Merrill Foundation, now defunct, for providing the initial financial and moral stimulus, and to *Five Colleges, Inc.* for their continued moral and financial support in what proved to be a lengthy project.

Acknowledgment of Visual Sources

Special thanks to the Schiller-Nationalmuseum Deutsches Literaturarchiv Marbach and to Henry Schneider at the Stadtbibliothek Wuppertal, for generously providing photos and artwork of, by and relating to, Else Lasker-Schüler.

To the Berlinische Galerie for their generous loan of the photo "Die Modernen."

To the Von der Heydt-Museum Wuppertal, for providing a transparency of Jankel Adler's portrait of Else Lasker-Schüler, and to Konrad Feilchenfeldt for granting permission to use a print of a drawing by Else Lasker-Schüler that is in his family's possession, "Prinz Jussuf reitet auf seinen kleinen blauen Elephanten."

To the Museum of Modern Art in New York for permission to copy and use the Chagall drawing made for Herwarth Walden's musical setting of a poem by Else Lasker-Schüler.

To Ayala Oppenheimer at the Mishkan LeOmanut, Museum of Art, Ein Harod, Israel, for finding a way to reproduce Miron Sima's drawings of Else Lasker-Schüler as an old woman, while the actual drawings are out on loan in Germany for a large Miron Sima exhibition.

To the Bayerische Staatsgemäldesammlungen for permission to print a photocopy of the "Turm der blauen Pferde."

To the Photoabteilung der Theaterwissenschaftliche Sammlung der Universität Köln for providing an Ektachron transparency of a drawing for a stage set by Ernst Stern for *Die Wupper.*

To the Gottfried Benn Nachlass for the photo of Gottfried Benn, 1910.

To Professor Trude Dothan for permission to reproduce the drawing of Else Lasker-Schüler on her deathbed by Grete Krakauer-Wolf.

To Rafael Weiser, Director, and Dina Carter,* Librarian, in the Department of Manuscripts and Archives at JNUL, Jerusalem, for directing me to sources for hard-to-find material, and for a photo of Aron Schüler.

To Special Collections and Archives, W.E.B. Du Bois Library, University of Massachusetts, Amherst, for permission and use of photo Adolf Loos, Karl Kraus and Herwarth Walden.

And finally, to Professor Uriel Simon, for taking the trouble to go through old family albums, and select and make a new copy of the photo of his father, Ernst Simon.

Acknowledgment of Text Sources and Permissions

Grateful acknowledgment is made for permission to quote from the following sources:

To the Suhrkamp Verlag, Frankfurt am Main, for its generous permission to quote extensively from the works of Else Lasker-Schüler, as well as pertinent passages from the diaries of Bert Brecht and Harry Graf Kessler; from a Rilke letter to Sidonie, as well as scattered comments and observations about Else Lasker-Schüler in the writings and correspondence of Walter Benjamin and Gershom Scholem.

To the Klett-Cotta Verlag for the letters from Gottfried Benn to Else Lasker-Schüler cited in *Den Traum alleine tragen* and for the letter to Tilly

*Dina Carter was one of the seven people killed at Hebrew University on July 31, 2002, by a terrorist bomb. She was 37 years old and held dual American-Israeli citizenship.

Wedekind in *Gottfried Benn: Briefe. Band IV, Briefe an Tilly Wedekind. 1930–1955.* Hrsg. v. Marguerite Schlüter. Klett-Cotta, Stuttgart, 1986.

To the Rowohlt Verlag for all quotes from Klaus Mann's *Wendepunkt,* copyright 1989 by Edition Spangenberg, Munich, and *Tagebücher 1931–1949,* copyright Rowohlt Verlag GMBH, Reinbek bei Hamburg.

To the Jewish National Library, Jerusalem, for Nehemia Cymbalist's description of the poet's room (Arc. Ms. var 501).

To the Max Niemeyer Verlag for a quote from a letter, not yet published in the Critical Edition (Lasker-Schüler's letters), quoted in Alfred Bodenheimer's *Die Auferlegte Heimat,* Tübingen, 1995.

To Thames & Hudson, Ltd., for a quote from Oskar Kokoschka in *My Life,* copyright 1974.

To the DuMont Literatur und Kunst Verlag for the letter from Maria Marc (with postscript from Franz) to August and Elizabeth Macke, in *August Macke/Franz Marc. Briefwechsel.* DuMont Buchverlag, 1964, pages 146–149.

To Princeton University Press for excerpts from Holly Edward's essay, "Orientalism in Fashion" in *Noble Dreams, Wicked Pleasures,* 2000.

A word about the translations: Unless otherwise indicated, all translations are by the author. Many were done to meet the needs of the text. Others were done independently. Nearly all may be subject to further revisions.

Betty Falkenberg
May 2003

Introduction

Who was Else Lasker-Schüler? Why a biography of someone whose writings are hardly known in English?

Poet, playwright and graphic artist, Else Lasker-Schüler was a pivotal figure in German Expressionism,[1] most notably in the circle around the periodical *Der Sturm* (*The Storm*). She presided over avant-garde café life in pre–World War I Berlin much the way Gertrude Stein did in Paris at roughly the same time and was as well known for her eccentricities. In 1933, after being awarded Germany's most important literary prize, she was forced to emigrate. As an emigré, she forged her own brand of exile literature. She remained active until her death in Jerusalem in January 1945.

While Expressionist art has received much attention in recent years in America, Expressionist literature remains *terra incognita*. One obvious reason for this is the paucity of good translations. Poetry, especially, falls victim to this lack. And Lasker-Schüler's poems, simple as they may seem at first glance, are often opaque and almost untranslatable. By including samples of her poems and prose (in German and in my translations), I hope at least to give some idea of her qualities as a poet and prosaist, and to whet the reader's appetite for more.

By virtue of her activity in diverse genres—poetry, prose, drama and graphic art—and her contacts with the leading poets, painters, and Jewish thinkers and philosophers of her time, her life provides a unique vantage-point from which to view the cultural ferment of early twentieth century

Europe. What becomes increasingly striking is the cross-fertilization going on in the arts in the early years of the century.

Writing in 1912, Wassily Kandinsky remarked, "Never in recent times have the arts been closer to one another than in this latest period of spiritual transformation."[2] How many admirers of Franz Marc's exquisite watercolor postcards, first published in 1954 by the Piper Verlag in Munich under the title "Franz Marc: Botschaften an den Prinzen Jussuff [sic]" ("Tidings: Messages for Prince Jussuf"), are even aware that the "prince" in question is Else Lasker-Schüler? Or that both correspondents were highly gifted in the other's medium?

For one person to be creative in more than one art was not at all uncommon. Kokoschka, for example, known principally as a visual artist, wrote plays that are still remembered by his own poster drawings for them.

When Else Lasker-Schüler married Herwarth Walden in 1903, Walden thought of himself primarily as a musician. He was a notable pianist, and had studied composition with Zemlinsky, Schoenberg's brother-in-law. Possibly as a way of courting her, Walden composed passionate (not to say overwrought) music to many of Else's poems. When his songs were printed by the publishing house he founded in 1910, the song "Verdamnis" ("Damnation"), to her poem of that title, flaunted a woodcut by Marc Chagall as a cover sheet.

Another multi-gifted artist, Arnold Schoenberg, painted besides composing some of the most groundbreaking music of the twentieth century.[3] Not only did Lasker-Schüler draw as well as write (she supported herself in hard times with her drawings and watercolors), she inspired many poems and paintings and musical compositions.[4]

Like Gertrude Stein, her personality challenged great painters—and caricaturists. Only Kokoschka, of that inner circle of artist friends, did not paint her. When asked why not, he replied, "Because I never understood her." And Kokoschka, with his uncanny acumen, was generally credited with having a sixth sense!

Among her lifelong friends was Martin Buber, the Jewish theologian, and the fact that the friendship was strewn with nettles only added piquancy to the salad. Buber, who propounded a religion of love (the "I-Thou" relationship), revered Else Lasker-Schüler as "a true poet." Their friendship, dating from 1903 in Berlin and lasting almost up to her death in 1945, is another touchstone in the arc of German Jewish history in our century.

In 1910, Lasker-Schüler and her then-husband, the composer turned art and literary entrepreneur, Herwarth Walden, made the acquaintance of Karl Kraus, the acerb Viennese satirist and brilliant editor of the periodical *Die Fackel* (*The Torch*). This friendship was to have profound repercussions for the careers of both Walden and Lasker-Schüler. For her, it marked the beginning of one of the most intellectually rewarding and emotionally close friendships of her life.

By being active in such diverse movements as Expressionism and Dadaism, Lasker-Schüler provided a bridge between these two seemingly antithetical strands. In 1910, Herwarth Walden named his Expressionist journal *Der Sturm* (*The Storm*) after a line in one of her poems.[5] And in 1919 the Dadaist Malik Verlag (Malik Publishers), founded by George Grosz and the political activist Wieland Herzfelde (brother to the better-known John Heartfield), took its name from her Oriental fantasy novel *Der Malik*, which had strong anti-war sentiments.

How was it possible that this woman, whom Karl Kraus once described as a cross between an archangel and a fishwife, should come to play such a central role in the tumultuous cultural scene that was Berlin in pre–Hitler Germany, and again in the culture and literature of exile?

Lasker-Schüler's life spans the history of Germany from its unification under Bismarck to the collapse of the Third Reich. Her personal fate as a German Jew in the advent of Nazism makes her saga a compelling one. Some of her dearest friends, like Franz Marc, Der Blaue Reiter (The Blue Rider), were killed in World War I; others died in Russian prisons and German camps in World War II. The crucial date in *her* life—one that marked a veritable tectonic shift—was April 19, 1933, not three months after Hitler's accession to power, when she managed to flee to Switzerland.

In 1934, Else Lasker-Schüler made the first of several trips to what was then Palestine. Her third trip, in 1939, would be, for reasons beyond her control, her last. Six years later, broken and chronically ill, she died in a hospital in Jerusalem. She had been witness to two world wars and the destruction of Jews in Europe. In Palestine she witnessed civil war between Arabs and Jews and the struggle for an independent Jewish state. She was a lost soul. She did not fit in anywhere.

Despite the devastation of two world wars, much primary source material still exists, mostly memoirs and letters, including her own. Among these are the letters she wrote over the years to Karl Kraus (his to her are lost), which provide a small panoptic view of this multi-layered friendship.

In 1986, her *Briefe aus dem Exil* (*Exile Letters*), to Salman Schocken, the Jewish businessman turned publisher who shared her ambivalence to then-Palestine, was published for the first time, with commentary by Sigrid Bauschinger and Helmut G. Hermann.

In 1980, the correspondence between Gershom Scholem and Walter Benjamin came out (English translation, 1989), with its wry allusions to Else Lasker-Schüler's last years in Jerusalem. Klaus Mann's *Tagebücher*

(*Diaries*) and Erich Mühsam's *Tagebücher 1910–1924* provide intimate glimpses into the lives of two of the most psychologically complex members of her circle of friends. George Grosz's autobiography, *A Small Yes and a Big No*, and Oskar Kokoschka's *My Life*, both of which have appeared in English, are as trenchant and graphic as their authors' artwork.

Even when Lasker-Schüler is only mentioned fleetingly in a memoir, the anecdotes are so telling, the images so vivid, that they leave an indelible imprint on the brain. Picture her, for instance, an old woman in Jerusalem, walking into an orthodox synagogue during services and taking a seat among the men. When the rabbi gently points her to the women's gallery, she says, "But Rabbi, surely you don't want me to be seated among all those women?!"

Yehuda Amichai has told how he used to see her sometimes on the street when he was a boy in Jerusalem: "Her strange figure used to make us laugh...." She was, he says, "the first hippie I ever saw." Others have described her as "the first bag lady."

In Jerusalem, the National & University Library has proved an invaluable depository for Else Lasker-Schüler materials from her last years, as has the Schiller-Nationalmuseum/Deutsche Literaturarchiv, Marbach, for materials from her pre-exile years. There are official documents, which have been surfacing over the past thirty-odd years, including her birth certificate, putting to rest once and for all her own spurious claims about her date of birth. Not least are the meticulously kept Swiss police archives with their ludicrous protocols detailing her various applications for visas, and the responses with which they were met—fascinating documents in their own right that say as much about Swiss bureaucracy as they do about Else Lasker-Schüler. Much of this material has not yet been made available in English and is translated here for the first time.

As the new *Critical Edition of the Works of Else Lasker-Schüler* progresses, more and more hitherto unpublished materials surface, and our perception of the poet undergoes revisions. This project, undertaken by a branch of the Suhrkamp Verlag, the Jüdischer Verlag, has already produced five sets of companion volumes: *Gedichte und Anmerkungen* (*Poems and Commentary*), *Dramen* (*Plays*), *Prosa 1903–1920*, *Prosa 1921–1945*, and *Prosa: Das Hebräerland*. These volumes will be followed by *Briefe und Anmerkungen* (*Letters and Commentary*). The preparation of this new and comprehensive edition of the poet's work is one of the most significant and ambitious scholarly enterprises now underway in German letters.

A major Else Lasker-Schüler revival is afoot today in Germany, and not just in scholarship. She has become a cult figure, a bit like Frida Kahlo in this country, with a whole cottage industry following in its wake. Streets are named after her, and in 1995, an intercity train between Koblenz and Cologne was named the IC 545 Else Lasker-Schüler in her honor. Her poetry is read on television and by candlelight. And in Israel she has inspired both playwrights and filmmakers. She, who enjoyed telling wild tales and taking people in, would have loved it all.

What makes her so irresistible a subject are her many contradictions: a deeply religious Jew, she rebelled against doctrinaire Judaism; a staunch feminist, she saw in androgyny a source of secret power but in love a source of strength. Under the direst circumstances she produced works of enduring beauty. To her contemporaries she was an enigma. While she may remain ultimately inscrutable, we can now begin to understand the forces, internal and external, that shaped her and made her who she was.

CHAPTER ONE

Banished

"Wo soll ich hin, wenn kalt der Nordsturm brüllt—?"
("Where shall I go when cold the north winds howl?")
Else Lasker-Schüler: *Die Verscheuchte*

On an ordinary day in April 1933—the 19th to be exact—a small woman in her sixties, with dark hair bunched under a turban, rushed up to the ticket counter at the Anhalter Station in Berlin and, fixing the clerk with her coal-black eyes, asked to purchase a ticket. Still smarting from a blow delivered by an SA man (Nazi storm trooper) as she walked out of the Hotel Sachsenhof in the Motzstrasse, where she had been living since 1918, she hesitated when he asked, "Where to?"

She almost said "Dusseldorf," where she had hoped to visit a good friend at Christmastime on her way back from the premiere of her play, *Arthur Aronymus und seine Väter* (*Arthur Aronymus and His Fathers*),[1] in Darmstadt. But in the new political climate, the performance had been cancelled, and she never made the trip.

She might have said "Prague," a city she loved, and where she had friends who would look after her. In March she had written to the poet-novelist Paul Leppin, somewhat cryptically, that she hoped to be able to visit him soon. Prague, the birthplace of Rilke, who admired her, and Kafka, who did not (see Appendix 1, page 184, *Letters to Felice*), was home to an active European avant-garde. She fit in well with the bohemian café life there, and it was one of her favorite stops on her frequent reading tours.[2]

7

But what came out of her mouth that April day was "Zurich." Not that Zurich was an unlikely choice either. It was a city she knew well, and with which she had many ties and many memories, both good and bad. Whatever the reason, the ticket she purchased was to Zurich—one way. And Zurich it was to be.

Only a few months earlier, in November 1932, she had been awarded Germany's most coveted literary prize, the Kleist Prize, for her life achievement in literature, something she had waited twenty years to see happen. As a poet, playwright, and prose-writer, she had helped define the Expressionist movement in literature. Else Lasker-Schüler had been the doyenne of Berlin's literary and artistic life, the hub of an international avant-garde.

The laudatio read at the award ceremony compared her to the greatest German masters of all time. But there were mocking and threatening voices to be heard as well. The National Socialist Press had been keeping close track of the number of Jews, "half-Jews," pacifists, Bolsheviks and other riff-raff who had been walking off with the Kleist Prize in recent years at the expense of homegrown nationalists, the so-called "Blut und Boden" ("blood and soil") poets.

In its crude attempts to defame her and create a kind of chauvinist paranoia, the Nationalist press linked her name with others of her ilk who had been awarded the prize—"degenerate" types like Bert Brecht, Carl Zuckmayer, author of *The Captain of Koepenick* who later emigrated to America, and Ödön von Horváth, author of *Tales from the Vienna Woods*. Lashing out at the prize committee for its choice of Else Lasker-Schüler, the *Völkische Beobachter* (*National Observer*), under the headline "The Daughter of a Bedouin Sheik Awarded Kleist Prize!" declared: "We are of the opinion that the strictly hebraic poetry of Lasker-Schüler has nothing to say to us Germans...." Or, as the *Vossischer Zeitung* put it: "'There's no beginning and no end to Elsi's [*sic*] prose, it's not a novella, and not a novel—moreover, whatever a Jew may write, for us it is never German art.'"[3]

Nonetheless, after nearly a decade of almost no publications, 1932 proved to be a surprisingly good year for Lasker-Schüler. The Rowohlt Verlag, publishers of the pioneer Expressionist anthology *Menschheitsdämmerung* (*Twilight of Humanity*), brought out her prose collection *Konzert* (*Concert*), and the story version of Arthur Aronymus. The S. Fischer Verlag had acquired the rights for it in its dramatized form, but there was still no staged performance. Together with *Konzert*, these were among the last books by a Jew to be published in Germany before Hitler came to power.

The short prose reminiscences of *Konzert*, like the chocolate pudding with raspberry sauce recalled from her Elberfeld childhood, may be too sugary for today's reader. But their seeming innocence belies a dire need to get things down before the intact world they recall is blown to smithereens. The signs, for those who could see, were abundant. And Else Lasker-Schüler was not blind.

Nevertheless, as late as January 20 she was still looking forward, if somewhat skeptically, to going to Darmstadt in February for the postponed premiere of *Arthur Aronymus and His Fathers*. Then on January 30, Hitler was sworn in as chancellor by Hindenburg. There were those, like the recent Reich chancellor Franz von Papen, who thought that by giving Hitler the chancellorship, but within a coalition government, they had him neatly "framed in." "Famous last words," as the historian Gordon A. Craig has put it.[4]

The new political climate did not take long to make itself felt. The Nazis called for a boycott of businesses owned by Jews, who were also purged from government bureaucracies. She was not much surprised, therefore, that the production of *Arthur Aronymus* was cancelled before it saw a single performance.

One of the National Socialists' first moves once in power was to launch a systematic assault on avant-garde art altogether. In April, the first "abomination exhibitions" of "degenerate" art were held. These took place at various county museums, at the instigation of organizations like the Kampfbund fur deutsche Kultur (Combat League for German Culture). Their purpose was to inflame the public against modern art by stigmatizing it as "Jewish-Bolshevist" regardless of style, subject, or even the artist's ethnic origins. These *Schreckenskammer der Kunst* (chambers of horrors of art) or *Schandausstellungen* (abomination exhibitions), as they were called, were the precursors of the infamous *Entartete Kunst* (Degenerate Art) exhibition in Munich in 1937.[5]

Also in April, the Berlin Bauhaus, home to Moholy-Nagy and Walter Gropius, was finally closed. Lasker-Schüler had read from her poem cycle *Hebräische Balladen* (*Hebrew Ballads*) at the first Bauhaus evening in Weimar in 1919. Walter Gropius had been among those in attendance.

In music and in the theater, in universities, in business and the professions, Jews were being forced out. At the same time, freedom of the press was sharply curtailed. In May, the notorious book burnings would be organized in Berlin and in many university towns.

All of this was happening very quickly. And then, on April 19, as Else Lasker-Schüler walked out of her hotel, she is said to have been knocked down by an SA man wielding an iron rod. She was used to being harassed, and she could be defiant, brazen and fearless. She had been hurt in street fights with Nazis before. In 1931, the Nazis had demonstrated outside a movie house on the Nollendorfplatz, near where her hotel was situated, and where *All Quiet on the Western Front* was being shown. Lasker-Schüler joined a counter-demonstration, and her arm and ankle were badly hurt. She described the incident to the Prussian minister of culture: "Fists exploded like grenades."[6]

It got to the point where she cowered and held her arms over her face when she got out of a taxi in front of the Sachsenhof, for fear she would be molested by young Nazis in high leather boots.

So here she was, shaken and bruised, at the Anhalter Railroad Station, about to board a train to Zurich, fleeing for her life. The train ride from Berlin to Zurich, crossing the border into Switzerland at Basel, took a good twelve hours.

In a letter written to her Dusseldorfer friend, the journalist Hulda Pankok, and postmarked from Zurich on May 28, she says, "*Only* the heartache, the mental anguish about how one will survive, etc., and those left behind, is to blame for my not writing, my dear. I was so miserable and so shredded and starved, inside and out, but now *much* better."[7] And again on June 21: "Both my hands were half frozen and the skin all split open, because I slept hidden beneath a tree down by the lake during those first days."[8]

Five years later, writing for the first time since she left Germany to her relatives in Chicago,[9] she says, "...I have been in emigration for 5¼ years and that is a difficult assignment and barely to be endured. Dearest Ines, I have a Kleist-Prize-crowned drama, a play about peace, and in 1932 it was in rehearsal under Intendant Professor Leopold Jessner in Berlin.... Then came—H. and all of us including Jessner had to flee *over night*. Beaten, bruised and bleeding I arrived in Zurich. I lay for 6 nights in hiding down by the lake, as no one whom I knew from the War[10] was in Zurich at the moment...."[11]

But on April 20, the day after her arrival in Zurich, she had sent Hulda a postcard, thanking her for some Easter chocolates and giving her Zurich address as Augustinerhof Hospiz, St. Peterstrasse, Zurich.[12] And a few days later, on April 26, she sent a card to the French literary critic, Marcel Brion: "Cher poet verehrungswürdigster. I am here in Zurich. Very sorry, but more sorry if I have not gone to Zurich. Please write me soon, very soon! Very unfair from me?? If I ask you how is the adress [sic] of Alliance Israelit in Paris. Dear poet, will you also write there, that I am a fine poet. I come soon, I hope."[13] She gave the same return address: Hotel Augustinerhof Hospiz.

So what are we to believe? Was she so traumatized that she went straight down to the lake to sleep, too exhausted even to try to locate friends or acquaintances who could have helped her? The Augustinerhof is eight minutes from the station; it is another ten minute walk from there down to the lake. She had stayed at the Augustinerhof in the past, so she knew it well.

Perhaps she went to the Augustinerhof and was told they were all filled up but that she should come back in a few days. Then she could have given the hotel as her return address before she was actually able to move in.

In any event, by March of the following year, the legend of the lake had jelled. Writing to a woman whom she had never met, Carola Kaufmann, asking for financial assistance, she explains: "I could not, in the haste of my departure, take anything with me. I slept for days by the lake in April of last year—that's the truth!"[14]

A postcard, newly discovered among Lasker-Schüler's papers, dated 13 April 1933, and postmarked Berlin-Charlottenburg, to the lawyer Dr. Karl Schönberg, Friedrich Ebertstrasse 8, Berlin, reads, "Dear good Herr Doktor. Many many many heartfelt thanks for everything. Yours Else Lasker-Schüler. I will write at once from Zurich."[15]

Finally, among her papers in the Jerusalem archives is a notebook in which she meticulously inventoried, over sixteen pages, the contents of the suitcases, handbags, and boxes, as well as the furniture, left in the attic of the Hotel Sachsenhof, where she had been living for the past fifteen years. All the boxes were numbered. A typewriter was left with her niece, Edda, and a box of glassware was left with a third person.[16]

Knowing what she knew, seeing what she saw, was it not likely that she could have made preparations to leave long before her actual flight? Goebbels had even denounced her in public. Yet though she was prepared, in some recess of her mind, for the events that were to come, she continued to go about her daily affairs as usual. It could well have required some particular shock to catapult her into action.

In the end, does it matter whether she slept out in the open for six nights (or possibly for one?) or went at once to the Augustinerhof, whether she left Berlin in a hurry or after due deliberation? The tenor of this difficult period in her life remains unaltered. And in fact, the trauma of those first weeks in Zurich would never leave her.

In May, she wrote again to Paul Leppin, replying to a letter in which he says he envies her proximity to beautiful Lake Zurich. She writes, "What can the lake possibly mean to me, after what I have been through?" And, invoking the realm of her literary creation "Thebes," she goes on: "Where, but where is our brightly painted Thebes, all our dromedaries, camels, all our silver doves? They flap about blindly, their corals plucked from them like my heart that has been plucked out of me."[17]

In September her situation came to the attention of the Society for

Jewish Culture, which promptly paid her hotel bills, an arrangement which "was as painful as it was a relief."

Gradually, Frau Lasker-Schüler succeeded in piecing together a life for herself in the months that followed. She located her old friends in Switzerland, and she made new ones, people whom she contacted on her own behalf and on the behalf of others, artists who, like herself, had suddenly had to leave Germany.

Her days in Zurich were punctuated with exhausting trips to the free parish clinic, her arm in a sling. (Later, pus later formed in the bone and she had to undergo emergency surgery.) She had to climb endless steps in public buildings that smelt of floor wax and disinfectant. She went to the Office of Aliens, where she had to register and plead her case to get working papers so that she could publish her work, give readings and appear on radio. She had a press pass, one issued by the Jewish Press Central, Zurich, on March 1 of 1933, but that seems to have made little impression on the Swiss authorities. It didn't help matters that she had waited some months before registering at all, that she was already working (giving readings at bookshops, for example) without papers, and that the clerk noticed that she had altered her date of birth in her passport from 1881 to 1891. Neither date was correct!

Already in 1919 she had run into difficulties getting her visa renewed after spending three months in Switzerland. She claimed the woman from the Swiss Embassy in Berlin suspected her of revolutionary activities (it was right after World War I, the KPD had just been founded and the Sparticist Revolt took place in Berlin). Perhaps because her passport listed her profession as "writer," she thought, and perhaps because she was friends with such "revolutionary" types as the sexologist Magnus Hirschfeld, she was viewed with suspicion.

In "Letter to a Swiss Friend," published in the *Frankfurter Allgemeine Zeitung* on April 18, 1919, she addressed the feuilleton editor of the *Neue Zürcher Zeitung*, Eduard Korrodi, asking him, tongue-in-cheek, to please use his influence to intercede on her behalf "at the highest level." She wrote, "Perhaps you could do me the favor of asking the Herr Bundesrat [Federal Councillor], just in passing, whether I may be allowed to come to Switzerland again. I get such longing letters from the gulls of Lake Zurich, and I too long for the white birds, shrieking snow, wild brides of the North Sea, soft-feathered adventurers. Would that I were a gull! Then I would not have to wait for a visa...." As for suspected revolutionary activities, she says, "There can be no question of any such. At the most I spat at midnight in the little alleyways of your city, mostly under the supervision of my Zuricher friends...." She goes on: "As you can see, I am already in Switzerland with my thoughts; I am standing in its broad railroad station, observing with delight how the languages of all lands meet courteously together here.... Many people would like to come to Switzerland to escape the imponderable gloom, and the fact that the dance-mania has broken out in and around Berlin and spread like an epidemic ... is nothing but the natural desire to escape one's own fears. To flee [without a visa]."[18] That was in 1919.

Once again she found herself at the mercy of Swiss bureaucrats, waiting this time for a permit to remain in the country and work. Small wonder that she had to stand in line this time; the number of German refugees applying for residence and work permits had, in just a few months, skyrocketed. Apart from its resentment over the sudden influx of Jewish émigrés, the stolid Swiss bureaucracy was totally overwhelmed. Despite her renown, the fact that Else Lasker-Schüler had no credible source of independent income was a serious strike against her, and the authorities were insolent and short with her.

Before long, she learned that among the newly arrived were members of the Mann family, including two of Thomas Mann's children, Klaus and Erika. She was delighted. Klaus had just founded a periodical, *Sammlung* (*Roundup*), the first anti-fascist émigré journal. Beginning in September 1933, it was published monthly in Amsterdam by the Querido Verlag.[19]

Sammlung had the generous support of André Gide, Aldous Huxley, and Klaus and Erika's uncle, Heinrich Mann. Thomas Mann, originally on the board of editors, withdrew his support after suffering what he described as "an attack of anxiety." He feared that if not his life, his books, which were published in Germany, would be endangered. The list of contributors to the *Sammlung* reads like a roll call of German writers in exile, as well as a roster of international literati: Romain Rolland, Jean Cocteau, Benedetto Croce, Spender and Isherwood, Hemingway and Pasternak.

The magazine would prove a gadfly on the rump of the Nazis, one they were unable to shake off. In one of its earliest issues, a poem by Lasker-Schüler appeared. Originally titled "The Emigrant's Song," it was renamed "Banished," the title by which it is known today. In German, "Die Verscheucht" ("One Banished") contains the word "shy" (*scheu*), which means literally "scared off," "frightened away."

"Die Verscheuchte"

Es ist der Tag in Nebel völlig eingehüllt,
Entseelt begegnen alle Welten sich—
Kaum hingezeichnet wie auf einem Schattenbild.

Wie lange war kein Herz zu meinem mild....
Die Welt erkaltete, der Mensch verblich.
—Komm, bete mit mir—denn Got tröstet mich.

Wo weilt der Odem, der aus meinem Leben wich?—
Ich streife heimatlos zusammen mit dem Wild
Durch bleiche Zeiten träumend—ja, ich liebte dich.

Wo soll ich hin, wenn kalt der Nordsturm brüllt—?
—Die scheuen Tiere aus der Landschaft wagen sich—
Und ich—vor deine Tür, ein Bundel Wegerich.

Bald haben Tränen alle Himmel weggespült,
An deren Kelchen Dichter ihren Durst gestillt,
Auch du und ich.[20]

"One Banished"

It is a day wrapped up in winding sheets of fog.
Whoever you may meet is drained of soul.
With no more substance than a cut-out silhouette.

How long since any heart gave mine a hug...
The world's grown cold, the people pallid,
—Come pray with me—for God can still console.

Where is the living breath that from my life has fled,
I wander homeless together with the stag,
Dreaming my way through washed-out days—yes, I loved you...

Where shall I go when cold the north winds howl?
Shy beasts from round the countryside renege
And come up to your door,—and I, a heap of ragweed.

Soon tears will wash away the whole of heaven,
From whose deep cups the poets stilled their thirst—
And yours and mine.

The editing of the poem took place largely by correspondence. There were last minute changes before the poem went to press, and Klaus and Erika seemed to be racing all over Europe in those months.

In September, however, they were back in Switzerland, and on September 19, Klaus, Erika and Else Lasker-Schüler went to the movies together. Going to the movies was a lifelong passion of Lasker-Schüler's. Sometimes she went three times in one day. It was frequently a way of calming her nerves: "You sit there quietly with a quarter of a pound of marzipan potatoes and let everything go by you." If she happened to like a particular scene, she was apt to poke her companion in the ribs and murmur "Mmm."[21] This time the film was Cecil B. DeMille's *The Sign of the Cross*.[22] Klaus noted in his diary that this was "the film that inspired Göring to set the Reichstag Fire." Hardly a film to calm the nerves. His diary entry goes on to describe its effect on Else Lasker-Schüler: "She became morbidly distracted and distraught, and to quiet her nerves, she began making lovely drawings of Indians."[23]

The next day Klaus received what he describes as a "totally mad letter from Lasker-Schüler."[24] Torn between her sense of loyalty to Klaus' father, whom she revered and for whose safety she was deeply concerned, and sympathy with what he and Erika were attempting to accomplish in exile,[25] Laskar-Schüler had difficulty finding the right words:

> I beg you to understand me right, not to misconstrue this letter. I always say and write what I think. As a sign of my deepest affection for you and Erika allow me to send you these two marbles,[26] delightful glass-pushers (in the glassiest sense). Thus life pushes me around. It is painful for me to have to say this but—we cannot see one another any more. I *can* not go against my sense of honor. But I would like to give you my advice: open a cabaret that is "unpolitical." A political cabaret would not only put yourselves at risk of deportation, it could harm your two poets: Heinrich Mann and your father, who has always been so charming to me. Believe what I say.

Perhaps it was the film that had set off her imagination and her fears. But in fact the Nazis were busy drawing up lists depriving citizens of their civil rights and of their citizenship. Every member of the Mann family was on such a list; Thomas, who had won the Nobel Prize in 1929, was last.

The letter went on to make helpful suggestions about possible Swiss contacts—Korrodi, for one—but then comes back to its main thrust: "The beginning of my letter is very painful to me."[27] Klaus answered her letter the same day! (See Appendix 2 for her letter; his is not extant.)

Two days later she was writing to Klaus again: "How important that we, who no longer have a country we can call Home, stick together, and that we speak our minds—... Good luck, and all good wishes, in case we should not see one another any more?"[28]

In his book *Der Wendepunkt* (*The Turning Point*), Klaus Mann, writing in 1944 about the first phase of his emigration, describes the bohemian circle he would spend time with when he was in Zurich: "Sometimes Else Lasker-Schüler would turn up suddenly in our midst, already somewhat bizarre, sometimes frightening, sometimes wildly funny, but in every gesture, each shyly whispered or furiously murmured word, the genuine poet: talent personified, a talent of such intensity and so altogether original that in itself almost merited the name of genius."[29]

The Zurich years would be lean ones. Lasker-Schüler had never been good at managing her funds. With less than ever, a lot of her time was spent writing letters soliciting financial help. In addition, exile took a heavy toll on her health. She depended on readings to survive, but she had to cancel trips and, on doctor's orders, rest. A chronic heart condition was much aggravated by the uncertainties of her existence. There were times when she despaired and then picked up and went on. In the end she gave vent to a wish for death: "Only eternity is not exile."

But her odyssey did not end in Switzerland.

CHAPTER TWO

Saint Vitus

"I shall grow up, but never grow old,
I shall always, always be very cold,
I shall never come back again."
              Charlotte Mew:
              "The Changeling"

Else Lasker-Schüler was born February 11, 1869. A simple fact, but one that took almost a hundred years to establish.[1] As early as 1896, she had begun tampering with her date of birth. In a note accompanying some poems for *Avalun, Blätter für neue deutsche lyrische Wortkunst* (*Avalun, Chapbook for New German Lyric Poetry*),[2] she gave it as 11 February 1877. In this same biographical note, she went on to say—without, we may assume, blinking an eyelash—that she had been living in Berlin for six years and that she had studied painting in Paris and Berlin for ten years. In fact, until her marriage in 1894, she had lived in her parents' house in Elberfeld. In 1904, when her poem "Ballade aus den sauerländischen Bergen" ("Ballade from the Sauerland Mountains")[3] was anthologized, she gave her date of birth as 1876. Not one of these statements was true.

Then, in 1919, when Kurt Pinthus was busy compiling and editing the first representative anthology of Expressionist poetry, *Menschheitsdämmerung*,[4] he asked each contributor to write a brief autobiographical sketch to be included at the end. There was only one woman represented in the entire collection: Else Lasker-Schüler.

While most of the poets chose to write brief factual statements, Frau Lasker-Schüler sent in this account of herself: "Ich bin in Theben (Aegypten) geboren, wenn ich auch in Elberfeld zur Welt kam im Rheinland. Ich ging bis 11 Jahre zur Schule, wurde Robinson, lebte fünf Jahre im Morgenlande, und seitdem vegetiere ich" ("I was born in Thebes [Egypt], although I came into the world in Elberfeld in the Rhineland. I went to school till I was eleven, then I became Robinson, lived for five years in the Orient. Since then I vegetate").

She was fifty years old in 1919, and a well-known figure not just in Berlin, where she was living, but on the poetry reading and lecture circuit and through exhibitions of her watercolors, all the way from Prague to Vienna, from Leipzig to Zurich. But much as she would have wished it, she had never been to the Orient. ("Thebes," upper Egypt in ancient times, was familiar to her readers as her imaginary realm.)

Why Robinson? A considerable Robinson Crusoe cult had swept through avant-garde European literature around the turn of the century, and one reading of the myth even featured women castaways. But in a long prose piece from this same period, 1919, she states the reason she "became Robinson,"[5] and "bolted," was that she looked like the picture of him on the cover of the book. "And," she adds mischievously, "I loved adventure." Well, maybe. But one thing is certain: She would have had no difficulty in locating her ego in the male persona.

All her life, she would work over the events of her life, as if drawing with charcoal, removing a line here, heightening an image there, smudging a bit overall, until she succeeded in creating for herself and for the world an acceptable version of her history. And yet, for all the shadow play and obfuscation, the disruption of two world wars and the disappearance of many records, the date of Lasker's birth was finally established.

Her birth was in fact reported in the usual fashion, in *Die Elberfelder Zeitung* (*The Elberfeld Times*): "Geburts-Anzeige. Durch die heute Nacht erfolgte Geburt eines Mädchens wurden sehr erfreut A. Schüler and Frau. Elberfeld, den 11 Februar 1869" ("Announcement of Birth: A daughter was born this night, 11 February 1869, to the happy parents A. Schüler and wife").[6] Else was the third daughter and youngest of six children born to the couple.

Her father, Aron Schüler, was the son of a Westphalian bank manager who also ran a carriage agency. Aron was one of eleven children. After his wife's death, Aron's father remarried, and, all told, produced more children than Johann Sebastian Bach.

This family, with its entire progeny, would be the subject of a novella and play by Else Lasker-Schüler. Out of the stuff of their lives, she established for herself a rich mythic heritage. Many elements of the story, the milieu, and the circumstances of family life, are gleaned from tales her father told about his childhood. They are also grounded in historical fact. The treatment of Jews in the 1840s in the town of Geseke, where Aron was born, is historically documented.[7] *Arthur Aronymus and His Fathers* does more, however, than tell the story of her father's family. It hints at special relationships within the family, idiosyncrasies—things that can only be known at first hand, from within. Therefore it is also, at least in part, her own story.

While Else Lasker-Schüler was diligently embroidering the cloth of family history (in her play she claims, for instance, that her great-grandfather was the white-bearded Chief Rabbi of Greater Westphalia, which was stretching things a bit—he was a rabbi in the town of Geseke), she remained ignorant of a real thread of gold that would have set her mind ablaze had she but known. Since her death, it has been established that the Schülers were descendants of the famous Rappaport family,[8] which traces back to the Praguer Rabbi Loew (Jehuda Loew ben Bezalel), who died in 1609 in Prague and became legendary for his recipe for creating a golem. Loew's golem was reputed to have rescued Jews accused of blood libel, the familiar accusation that Jews used the blood of Christian children for their Passover rituals. In Else's Elberfeld childhood, such anti–Semitic myths were again surfacing.

In 1592, Rabbi Loew had an audience with Emperor Rudolph. To this day it is not known what was discussed during their meeting. Over the years, the Rabbi became a folk hero, and by the nineteenth century, published accounts of his wonder-workings began to appear. The Rabbi Uriel in Lasker-Schüler's *Arthur Aronymus* seems imbued with the Praguer Rabbi's aura.

As for the golem, it became a popular subject for novels and films, and was in fact much in vogue in the early 1900s. When Paul Wegener's film *Der Golem: wie er in die Welt kam* (*The Golem: How He Came into the World*) opened at the UFA Palast am Zoo in Berlin in 1920, one can be sure Else Lasker-Schüler, an inveterate moviegoer, was in the audience. She would also have been familiar with Gustav Meyrink's novel *Der Golem*, a spooky tale which Gershom Scholem thought "captures the collective soul of the (Praguer) ghetto."[9]

In any event, by the time Else's father was a grown man, ready to take on a trade (he was born in 1825), European Jewry could look to a very different model: The sons of Meyer Amschel Rothschild had been strategically positioned in European capitals, and were buying and selling foreign securities with redoubtable success. This early phase of industrialism, 1850–1870, revolved around credit means, and Aron Schüler, Else's father, not unlike the Rothschilds of Frankfurt, was recommending the creation of foreign gold loans and the sale and purchase of railroad and state securities to the customers at his small bank in Elberfeld.

After the crisis in the market following the boom years of 1871–1873, and increasingly in the 1880s, Else's father turned his attention to real estate, buying many properties for purposes of speculation. It would have been hard to glamorize such a profession, or professions, much less escape the stigma of philistinism in admitting them, and so Else made her father over—in her fantasy and fiction—into an architect rather than a small bank manager and real estate man.

Geseke, the town where Aron Schüler's family had come from, lies in eastern Westphalia. When Else's father decided to move to Elberfeld and start a business there after his marriage in 1857, he was able to do so without bureaucratic red tape because both towns were within Prussian jurisdiction. Otherwise, if Jews wanted to move from one state to another, they needed a special permit as Jews, one that was often difficult to obtain.

By the end of the 1880s, anti–Semitic parties had gained ascendancy in Wuppertal (to which Elberfeld belonged). Their goal, openly stated, was to "counteract the overweening influence of Jews in the German Fatherland."[10] The Schülers, however, made no attempt to hide their Jewishness from the local community. The Schüler business stayed closed on high holidays and announced the fact in the newspaper. This is not to say that they always had an easy time of it.

Local anecdote makes Aron Schüler out to be a feckless Jew rather than a successful banker and businessman. Even after his death, townspeople told how he was easily duped, easily taken in and cheated out of his rightful due. He does not appear to have been active in any community affairs though he was a familiar figure at the local pub. An incorrigible prankster, he was nicknamed "Till Eulenspiegel." Whether affectionately or derisively depended on the speaker.

Else's mother, Jeanette Kissing, on the other hand, was a respected figure in the Jewish community. She was the daughter of a wine merchant, and belonged to a well-known Jewish family. Else's uncle, Leopold Sonnemann, was active in politics and founded the liberal newspaper, *Die Frankfurter Zeitung*. When Jeanette died, the Jewish Charity organization of Elberfeld carried an impressive obituary announcement, an indication that she was a generous and important contributor to Jewish causes.

Enter the child, Else. Wearing a red dress. (Of the infant and toddler,

Opposite: **Jeanette Schüler, Else's mother (Stadtbibliothek Wuppertal, Else Lasker-Schüler Archiv).**

Else, we know nothing.) She later wrote, "I was the little girl who always wore red dresses and felt alien in my bright clothes among the other children...."[11] And again: "The Pietist children were especially piqued by the red dresses I wore. Then too I could open my eyes very wide—that looked terrific, really exotic...."[12] The little actress was clearly aware at a very early age of the uses to which she could put her penetrating coal-black gaze. And just as clearly, she had no intention of giving up her red calico dresses (whose pockets hid the hard candies her mother had stuffed into them), even if it meant enduring the cruellest taunts.

The defiant child enjoyed playing war games with the boys. Never mind that she had to play the enemy (the French, that is) as penalty because she was a girl. It was fun being a French general in command of her imaginary troops. She

Aron Schüler, Else's father (Stadtbibliothek Wuppertal, Else Lasker-Schüler Archiv).

could brazen them out and endure the nasty little verse they made up to taunt her, which they sometimes called after her on the street: "Franzos mit der roten Hos" ("Babette's got red pantelettes").[13]

But sometimes they could really try her. When she visited the Kaufmann brothers, Willy and Walter, for example, and the cook slipped her some sweets on the side, the boys made her pay, spitting into her sweetened coffee. Yes, she wept gigantic tears, as she tells us she did. Headstrong she was. Defiant. Her gaze rivets you in a photo taken when she was seven.

Opposite: **Else Lasker-Schüler in 1876, age seven (Stadtbibliothek Wuppertal, Else Lasker-Schüler Archiv).**

But her lips are trembling, as if it were only with the greatest effort that she could keep from bursting into tears. This is the thin line she walked throughout life and that made people say they didn't understand her.

Just *going* to school in Elberfeld could be a challenge. She was taunted on the way there and back. Being different wasn't easy. She didn't just dress differently. She *was* different. For one thing, she was Jewish—not a friend you could bring home if you were Catholic, or, as was more likely in Elberfeld, Lutheran.

Take Adele. She was one of those who yelled "Hepp! Hepp!"[14] after Else. But then it was Adele who "suddenly threw her arms around me in the middle of the street ... and walked with her arm linked in mine, under my new umbrella...." And Adele who admitted, when Else visited her at her humbly furnished flat, "I like you better than anyone in the class and I won't ever call 'Hepp! Hepp!' after you again."[15]

When Adele returned the visit at the Schülers' home, Else let her try on her white dress. "She grew altogether pale, she held her arms the whole time up in the air, at a distance from her thin body, for fear of getting a spot on the dress." The sentence fairly quivers with the poor child's apprehension![16] But how troubling it must have been, as well as baffling, to try to sort out the elements of Adele's ambivalence: her admiration for Else, her rejection of the "Jew" in her along with her envy of the richer girl, and Else's own desperation to find a friend. Not a very comfortable situation for either child.

School itself was hardly one of Else's favorite pastimes. Director Schornstein would pay unannounced visits to the classrooms just to check up on the children. Richard Schornstein was the principal of Lyceum West, a school for upper-middle class girls in Elberfeld. Under his tutelage, from 1845 to 1892, the school became a model for schools for girls all over Germany. He would come in puffing away on his pipe, and no sooner had he taken a seat but the answer to the math problem that had just come to her landed back in her stomach. She would swallow and sob and be told to stand in the corner.

Altogether, school was a pain. Her father agreed heartily with this view, and egged her on to play hooky. She remembered, "If my mama found out, she would punish us: no hazelnut torte that Sunday. My papa had a passion for hazelnut torte, so if she confronted him he would shrug, 'Who, me?' and pretend to know nothing about it. But he himself had skipped school regularly as a boy."

There was composition; she couldn't write an essay to save her life. Her "Friedrich the Great" essay came back with a huge "Fail" scrawled across it, "and when it came to 'Winter in the Riesengebirge,' my oldest sister volunteered to help me. I dreaded having to stay after school, it was so boring sitting in the classroom all alone."[17]

Geography? Who cared where other cities were situated? Of course, African rivers were another matter—they rhymed! And the names Senegal, Gambia, Niger or Dcholiba. Zaire and the Orange River, the Nile and Zambesi flowed from her lips like water.

Most of her teachers thought she was stupid (she says). Except for a certain Miss Kreft who would first stuff her mouth with licorice when she had something of significance to say and who had these encouraging words to say to Frau Schüler: "No, Else is not basically stupid, not really."

Yes, except for Religion, which was storytelling, after all, school had little to offer. But the story of Joseph, Joseph and his Brothers, had an incendiary impact on her imagination. It would prove to be a major wellspring of her creative life, reaching into every corner, to the point of total identification—literary, artistic, and personal. One could say she lost-and found-herself in the Joseph legend. Robinson was just a crude sketch, a mere understudy, for the true noble ancestor.

When Else's teachers reproached her for not paying attention, for "daydreaming," Frau Schüler rushed to her daughter's defense. "Joseph of Egypt," she said, "was a great dreamer, he even interpreted the pharaoh's dreams...." Frau Schüler was quick to pick up on Else's gift for rhyming. If the child was feeling down, she would play "Say the word" with her. "Chocolate," she would suddenly call out, and Else would have to come up with a rhyming word. Then they would pick up speed. "Ink: blink," and so on.

Learning to write, Else began to draw. "My letters of the alphabet burst overnight into bloom."[18] Rebuses were common in children's books when she was learning to read, and as Walter Benjamin reminds us,[19] alphabet books, which children know by heart like the insides of their pockets, drape letters in costume and bring together unlikely neighbors under one roof, say, of the capital letter "A." And the child dreams its way into their logic. For Else, calligraphy was to become a lifelong passion. Her letters to friends and others are all strewn with pictographs and hieroglyphs. And in her poem "Versöhnung" ("Atonement"), she refers to "the letters that are curved like a harp" (Hebrew letters).

It was probably with her mother that she began to read and write. And it was Frau Schüler who taught Else French, inspired by her own cult of Napoleon. (Among her more curious relics, she kept what she claimed was a swatch of the canopy on which he was born.[20]) Why that? "Napoleon Bonaparte must have looked like her, and that was why...," says Else.

Boredom was the child's most serious complaint until her mother surprised her one day with a present of buttons, buttons that were made at the local button factory. Big and little buttons, blue, green, red, yellow, purple buttons. "I laid them out in rows, four or five in a row (pentameter?) with a space between rows, on the big table, and ran my fingers over the rows in their appointed button-strophes. If I happened upon an uneven row, I would cry out, just as I react today—as if I had been physically struck—when a vowel or consonant creates a disturbance in the sound or rhythm of the poetic line."[21] Later, the buttons would get "sewn" into her poems: "They played with seashells, Abraham's small sons / And sailed their boats made out of pearl buttons" ("Hagar und Ismael").[22]

Along with buttons, she loved marbles. Squatting on the streets of Elberfeld, Else played marbles with her pals. Oh, such beautiful glass marbles. A dish of them was on her table when she died in Jerusalem.

Only half in jest did she claim to have inherited her father's incorrigible lust for play. Play was in fact a very serious matter in her life—and in her poetry. As for her father, she recalled how he would push her into toy shops so he could look at the toys himself, even as an old man. He would buy tops, marbles, and tin ducks that could waddle and quack. And in wine shops he bought miniature schnapps bottles that he would place in the hands of his little puppets, who would then act drunk and start to dance and sing. For her birthday he gave her "One Hundred Years: The Friedlander Brothers"—a toy store catalogue!

Returning to Elberfeld as a grown woman in 1912, for the 300th anniversary celebration of the town's founding, the poet visited the graves of all those beloved family members—mother, father, and a brother—who were buried in the Jewish cemetery there. Memories were re-awakened of the crumbling-toothed, slate-roofed city of her birth, with its tall brick chimneys, whose "breath poisons the air." She was speaking of the chemical works, the likes of I.G. Farben, that fouled up the air for miles around and muddied the waters of the Wupper, "A sauce for the devil." "Everything," she wrote, "was engulfed in smog." Derelict one-eyed men and scary exhibitionists followed her home from school. Sometimes she would drop her schoolbag from sheer fright.

But then there was the Schwebebahn, the suspension railway, a mass of iron coils, "a steely dragon winding its way, with its many heads and flying-spark eyes, down the black-stained river. With an ear-splitting racket the railship flies through the air over the water...."[23] And it does so still today. The Wuppertaler Schwebebahn was not built until 1901, at which time Else Lasker-Schüler was thirty-two years old and living in Berlin. But how could she, for whom time was just a silly-putty ball, resist this resonating image of the eerie monster hovering over her childhood styx?

In slight contradiction to her much-touted claim that she was unread, she does confess: "Already as a child, every book, regardless of what it was, whether *Max and Moritz* or even *Struwelpeter*, like every shop in town, was an open playground" for the imagination. What she was ever scrupulous to avoid was any admission that might brand her a blue-stocking.

But when did she first discover Dr. Dolittle? She adored *Dr. Dolittle and His Animals*. On meeting the bemonocled Edith L. Jacobsohn-Schiffer, who translated Hugh Lofting's books into German, she fell "head over heels" and at once called her "Gladdys!" But this was at the Café des Westens, during her Berlin years, not, obviously, when she was a child, when the books had not yet even been written and the Schwebebahn not built.

All her childhood reminiscences up to the age of eleven are bathed in a soft amber glow. They read like an idyll, an idyll played out under the protective wing of her mother ("Obhut" is the wonderfully religious-sounding word she uses to describe it). And throughout her long and arduous life, this mother would remain her fixed star, her guardian angel.

But when she was eleven, a cloud descended on this elysium. Else Lasker-Schüler became gravely ill with Saint Vitus' dance. By her own account, this was the reason she was taken out of school and kept at home. From then on, Frau Schüler appears to have been chiefly responsible for her education, and Else and her mother developed an even closer relationship than already existed between them. Still, one can't help wondering: Was this the shipwreck that signalled the beginning of her Robinsonade?

What books did Else read under her mother's guidance? On her own? She did have a tutor after she became ill, a kind of governess in charge of her further education, but Else claims to have learned nothing from her. We know that Goethe and Heine, Shakespeare and Schiller were read, and read out loud, at home. But when did she first discover Baudelaire?

Who were her friends in adolescence? And when did she first fall in love, and with whom? To all these questions there seem to be no answers. No documents, no diaries. She may not have vegetated, this Ms. Robinson, but she certainly left a lot of blank sheets in the book of time.

Her illness must have been very frightening, especially at its onset, which, as is usual with chorea (St. Vitus' dance), appears to have been sudden. But even this story, the story of how she became ill and was taken out of school, is shrouded in mystery. She has given us a number of fictionalized accounts, all of them factually improbable, but each in its own way revealing. And we do have a few, but not many, facts. First of all, facts about the nature of the affliction itself.

To the medical profession of the time, ca. 1890, the disease was quite well known. We read:

Chorea ... characterized by irregular involuntary movements of the muscles, chiefly of the arms, legs, face and tongue; these movements begin somewhat suddenly.... St. Vitus Dance, Melancholia saltans ... are other names ... for this disorder.

History: Choreiform troubles (at one time) generally referred to the dancing manias of a religious character so common in the Middle Ages.

Causation: Fright and strong emotional excitement.... A first attack as a rule follows either immediately or within a few days after the fright.... Slight overstrain at school, a severe thunderstorm, or a severe scolding by a parent may be sufficient to bring on an attack....

Symptomology: Involuntary twitching movements ... the muscles of the hands and fingers and of the face and tongue are most often affected.... In addition to these twitching movements there is a general restlessness of the body.... All the movements of a choreic patient are characterized by extreme awkwardness. This awkwardness and the constant jerking of the head and body are the source of greatest annoyance to the patient.... The mental calibre of choreic patients, and of choreic children in particular, is rather above the par....

Treatment: Rest, absolute rest.... Often it will be necessary to keep the mother or a nurse sitting at the bed for a few days to keep the child quiet.... While in bed, children can be pleasantly entertained ... may be allowed to play or read ... but the reading-matter should be carefully selected so as to keep the patient's mind free from all excitement....[24]

In *Konzert* (*Concert*), the collection of prose pieces published in 1932, just before Else Lasker-Schüler was forced to flee, and in which many of her childhood memories are gathered together, there is a piece called "Der Letzte Schultag" ("The Last Day of School"). It purports to be an account of how she became ill with St. Vitus' dance, and therefore never attended "the last day of school." It goes:

One day my dear mama went up into the woods. Our house was at the foot of the hill that led into the green cathedral. She did not come back for supper—there was thunder and lightning coming from every corner of the heavens,—green, then red; purple and yellow, real lemon yellow! My papa and all my sisters and brothers went looking for Mama.... I climbed up into our tower. From there I could look out on all sides. All at once I saw my dear, dear mama coming down the little mountain, looking so sad, so sad I cannot describe.... I leapt over the wooden parapet to reach my poor mother more quickly; got caught, however, in the jalousie of the lower tower window and lay there safe as in my mother's arms....

My brother carried me...—I was shaking all over—down down the
long scary ladder he had borrowed from the fire department where
he worked as a volunteer fireman—I had come down with "St.
Vitus' Dance" ... "Uncle Doctor" said: result of the fright! From
then on he called me, "Jumping Bean." I, however, knew that I had
gotten St. Vitus' Dance from something altogether different—from
the first heartache in my life, one that even the most wonderful
home wasn't able to shield me from. But at least I didn't have to
go back to school ever again. "There can be no talk whatsoever
of going back to school," the "Uncle Doctor" said, in a most
peremptory tone.[25]

If her mother really did take her out of school prematurely, as has been
generally assumed, for what reason did she do so? Was the child too delicate, too sensitive, to cope? Did she feel her artistic gifts would blossom
better under her own supervision than in the hostile environment of a
school run by martinets? Or had local anti–Semitism reached a new, intolerable level in Elberfeld?

Lasker-Schüler's Jerusalem-based biographer, Jakob Hessing, makes a
strong case for the latter. He builds on historical evidence, and on other
references in Lasker-Schüler's writings, such as those cited above, to show
she suffered as a child from anti–Semitic taunts. *Arthur Aronymus and His
Fathers* provides further evidence for this theory, as we shall see.

But these may be overlapping, rather than conflicting, explanations.
So much in life is overdetermined.

Finally, recent scrutiny of school records, plus the curriculum for
grades IX through IV (one starts with the highest number for the lowest
grade) would seem to indicate that Else in fact attended school until she
was thirteen. As it was not unusual for a girl "of good family" to end her
education at this point, no further speculation is called for.[26]

On the face of it, it would not seem to matter much whether she completed the usual course of study or not. But if she did, what image of herself was she fostering by claiming she did not? The intractable child? The
inveterate outsider? The untutored artist-genius? By concealing the fact that
she did complete the usual course of study, what would she have been
aiming to reveal?

The whole story—the jump from the tower and her landing in an
unfurled jalousie—is in no way plausible. It more than strains credulity.
Moreover, the house in which the Schülers lived in the Sadowastrasse had
no tower. So what is its purpose?

Other texts about her childhood relate that her mother frequently
sat on the balcony watching thunderstorms. A woman given to bouts of

melancholia, such moody weather appealed to her. But what would have made her go out during a storm and not come back in time for supper? Why does Else say she looked sad when she returned? Sad, not frightened or even in a hurry. And if the whole tale is an allegory, what is it an allegory about?

The image of the tower, always associated with her father, recurs in a number of different texts from different periods, sometimes, but not always, in conjunction with some manner of "storm."

In a letter to the painter, Franz Marc, later incorporated into her novel *Der Malik*, she writes, "and he [her father] built towers that threatened all the house-tops when the storm came."[27] The threat seems very explicit, and is made more so by her use of the definite article "the" before storm. The same paragraph tells of Aron Schüler's endearing and not so endearing pranks, and she keeps coming back to this menacing aspect, hinted at through the tower and storm imagery.

Another literary treatment of the traumatic event is the richly allusive "Der Wunderrabbiner von Barcelona" ("The Miracle Rabbi of Barcelona"), published in 1921, fifteen years after Barcelona's visionary architect, Antonio Gaudi, had constructed the looming belfries of his controversial Church of the Sagrada Familia, and forty-one years after the child Else's purported fall from the tower.

"Der Wunderrabbiner" is a story set in another time, Spain during the Inquisition, but with a historical background resonatingly similar to her mother's childhood years. Jeanette Kissing came from a sephardic family. The father and child in the story, however, are Aron the architect-father, and herself: "There lived a poet among the Jews of Barcelona, daughter of a distinguished gentleman, who was entrusted with the construction of watchtowers for all the great cities of Spain...."[28]

This father raised his daughter like a son. She would climb with him up to the very top rung of the ladder overlooking the city, so high that she imagined she was visiting with God. And in fact, this particular structure, with its gold cupola, had been donated by the wealthy Jews to serve as sanctuary for the miracle-rabbi. Climbing down the ladder, the little girl lost her footing and fell. But here, unlike the account in "The Last Day of School," the fall does not bring on an illness, but takes an altogether happier turn: the child falls into a mound of soft sand. The son of Barcelona's Christian mayor, who happens to be playing in the sand, thinks she is an angel fallen out of the sky and falls in love with her. As in *Arthur Aronymus*, the theme of Jewish-Christian reconciliation through love is the leitmotif. The story itself, however, has a dire, tragic end, namely a horrific massacre and destruction, from which only the two young lovers escape in a "dreamboat."

In all these recastings, the mother as an animating force has disappeared. The main players have become the father and the daughter.

Much as she will enhance the aura of the father in her prose (unlike her mother, he never figures in her poetry), he remains an ambivalent figure: on the one hand, he aids and abets her in joyous disregard of convention and in his irreverence, and on the other, he can be cross, crude, even cruel, and oddly insensitive to her feelings. Perhaps more importantly, he may have caused her mother pain—"the first grief," that even a loving home cannot shield her from.

Three scenes in *Konzert* may shed more light on Aron's character than the author intends. They all come fluffed up like cotton candy. One, called "Elberfeld in the Wupper Valley," describes a fun-loving, jovial papa:

> My papa was one of the boys. We played cops and robbers together. Together we went to the circus, but woe was me if I took too long getting dressed and we got there at the last minute and then I had to go to the bathroom, just one more time, and we missed the first act. Then he grumbled throughout the entire performance and cursed me.[29]

In this same piece, we see her father, as chief architect in a building firm, at home entertaining his "guests," workers who bring him word of impending lawsuits when roofs cave in—after thunderstorms, for instance.

> It was not uncommon for my father to bring the complaining party home with him. Then the carousing began, and lasted through the night. Beginning in the late afternoon, we heard the litigants drinking to each other, doubling up with laughter after every toast.... Early in the morning the guests were still lounging about in our lovely little garden.[30]

Oh? And what will Frau Schüler have had to say to such goings on?

In another piece, Else recalls her father taking her to the procession on the Feast of St. Laurentius.[31] And again he scolds her at the highpoint of the parade, "naughty child, you always have to go to the bathroom just when the baldachin comes into view." For all his endearing charm and good humor, this self-styled "Till Eulenspiegel" certainly knew how to humiliate her.[32]

All these tales cast a curious, oblique light on the St. Vitus' incident, for which there is no factual record, but which played a central role in the feeling life and imagination of the poet—one that was undiminished over the years. Because of the overall paucity of factual information about her childhood years, we are left to stumble about in the dark, piecing together, from the conflicting clues she gives us, a family space that seems habitable and plausible, but that may be just as fictive as the one she has concocted for us.

Moving away, for the moment, from the question of how she actually contracted St. Vitus' dance, or what immediate causes led to the sudden affliction, we may ask: What did it feel like to be a child whose movements were perceived as awkward, and who exhibited the symptoms so graphically described in the medical encyclopedia?

The story and play version of *Arthur Aronymus* both came out in the same year as *Konzert*. One of the many children depicted in this family is a little girl named Dora.

Dora first appears in the fifth scene, along with all the other children. It is Christmas morning and these Jewish children are coming back from town. The stage direction reads, "between Ferdinand and Berthold, the very fidgety Dora."

In scene seven (there are fifteen scenes in all), Arthur Aronymus has a dream. Towards the end of the dream, thunder sounds, a door falls in, and the sisters—Fanny, Elischen and Katharina—enter the bedroom, leading "a very restless Dora, who suffers from St. Vitus' dance, by the hand." (Note that here the child already has St. Vitus' dance when the thunderstorm strikes.) Arthur Aronymus lies still half-asleep in bed. Dora plops herself down on the bed. Katharina and Elischen pick her up and lay her on one of the other beds. Fanny shakes Arthur hard to wake him up and Katharina chides her. Fanny admonishes: "Otherwise you and Elischen will have to take Dora for her walk." Elischen pleads, saying they should take turns.

> FANNY: I can't hold her. I don't have the strength.
> ELISCHEN: The only one of us who's strong enough is Käthe.
> KATHARINA: It takes love, not strength, to look after our Dorle.
> *[Dora wants to say something, but because of her swollen tongue, they can't understand her.]*
> ELISCHEN: She wants to say we're always fighting about her. Our
>   poor little Dorle! *[She kisses her affectionately.]*
> KATHARINA: We should be ashamed of ourselves! (Dora nods Yes.)

As Arthur Aronymus sinks back into sleep and the girls wonder if there is something wrong with him, they hear through the open window the menacing tones of the witches' song sung by three children in the street in front of their house:

Maria, Joseph, es läutet so heiss
Bimmel la Bammel,
Wasch in Jesu Blut deck weiss,
Bimmel la Bammel!
Widerstrebt deck der Christenwein,
Bimmel la Bammel!

Zieh ding Hexenschwänzlein ein
Und erleide Höllenpein, Höllenpein
h, h, Höllenpein.
Wir aber danken Herrn Jesu Christ,
Da durch ihn unsere Seele errettet ist.

Maria, Joseph, it chimes so loud
Bimmel la Bammel,
Wash yourself clean in Jesus' blood,
Bimmel la Bammel!
You won't drink the Christian wine?
Bimmel la Bammel!

DORA (with difficulty, but audibly): I'm so frightened—

Song:

Tuck in your little witch's tail
And learn Hell's pain, the pain of Hell,
heh, heh, pain of Hell.
We meanwhile thank Lord Jesus Christ,
Because through Him our soul is blessed.

Elischen fusses over Dora, warms her hands.

DORA: I'm not going out into the garden any more.
ELISCHEN: But Dora. You have to overcome your fears.

Katharina throws her fur collar around Dora. Katharina and Elischen carry the child out of the room.[33]

Certain words leap out of this text, words that are exactly those used to describe the chorea symptoms in the medical encyclopedia. The entire characterization of Dora—"the very fidgety Dora," "the very restless Dora," or "Dora wants to say something but can't because of her swollen tongue"—have an authority about them that would almost have to have come from within, from something experienced oneself. The difficulty this child posed for her siblings, and her own perception of this difficulty, along with its attendant effects on her relationships within the family, are all so keenly felt and rendered that the "truth" of it as a description of Else's own plight as a child, rather than an imaginative leap into the mind of some sibling of her father's (none of whom, to our knowledge, was similarly afflicted), seems incontrovertible.

Both *Konzert* and the "Arthur Aronymus" treatments were written some fifty years after the fact. Else was eleven in 1880. But the terror with which the "sick" child views the outside world, and the wary knowingness with which she regards those around her who are charged with her care, seems as fresh and real to the grown woman as they must have been for the child.

And yet. There is one last morsel to be savored from Dora's plate. The older girls are talking about love trysts in the night, and when Dora tries to join in, Fanny says: "But you were sick then and fast asleep," to which Dora replies, "Towards the end I only pretended to be so sick, and danced the polka a little more wildly than I had to. I just hated going to school so...." Or as Hamlet said, "I am just mad north north-west; when the wind blows southerly / I know a hawk from a handsaw."

CHAPTER THREE

Wilted Myrtle

"The body lying beside me like obedient stone—"
Louise Gluck: Descending Figure

Between 1880, the year she became ill, and 1894, the year she married Dr. Berthold Lasker, Else passed from childhood through adolescence into womanhood. These years saw two deaths in her immediate family, both of which left her bereaved and shaken. Only so can one begin to fathom her ill-fated marriage to the doctor. In 1882, her best-loved brother, Paul, died unexpectedly at the age of twenty-one. In 1890, Else's mother, just one day after going to Wurzburg to see a specialist about a stomach ailment, died, also quite unexpectedly, at the age of fifty-two.

Paul's death came just as he was about to convert to Catholicism. It was Paul, she claimed, who had first told her the sad and wonderful story of Joseph. It was Paul, too, who kept vials filled with strange salts and acids, chemicals of every description, including cubes of yellow-green sulfur, which altogether fascinated her, a secret trove hidden away up in "the poison room" in the attic.[1] With these he would perform the most daring experiments just for her benefit. It was Paul's near conversion to Catholicism that provided the emotional well-spring for her lifelong conviction that Judaism and Christianity could co-exist in mutual respect and understanding. Even the Christmas Eve scene from *Arthur Aronymus* strains ultimately toward reconciliation.

But it was her mother's death when Else was twenty-one that left her

35

altogether devastated: "When my mother died, the moon broke apart. Once again, He, the Lord, divided the water from the land. There was lightning. Words of fire were written in glowing zigzag across the black silk of heaven's story book, a menetekel to the west wind. God is rolling through the world. His red letters struck me down, lit me up and were put out in the sea."[2]

She was still living at home when her mother died. Whether she was actually present at her death we do not know. She does not record any memories of a death-bed scene.

From all we can gather, she was a serious, well-behaved young woman at this time. She dressed conventionally, as befit a proper bourgeoise, with white lace collars, fitted bodices, and long, full skirts. There is nothing in the meager sources we possess that would indicate a radical or rebellious spirit. She appears to have outgrown any childhood rambunctiousness.

But with her mother's death she lost all her moorings. The home, until then a place of shelter, of *Gerborgenheit*, suddenly bore down on her with the onus of new domestic and emotional responsibilities.

Did she, along with her sisters, have to care for her father, as did Virginia Stephen (later Virginia Woolf) after her mother's death? In all likelihood she did. What was Aron Schüler like as a widower? It's easy to imagine him losing his grip, spending more and more time at the pub. Did the whole household resemble the Stephens' after Virginia's mother died? Everyone bustling about trying to do the father's bidding?

Whatever the case, her mother's death made Else feel like the ultimate orphan, the itinerant exile she would remain until the end of her days. "Only eternity is not exile," she would write, with increasing urgency, up to her own actual death. She never ceased to mourn the loss of her mother. In all, there are ten poems, written between the years 1902 and her own death, in which her mother's name is invoked with undiminished longing.

Who, then, did she turn to? Who were her friends after her mother's death and before her marriage? Was there anyone in her family in whom she could confide? Although she appears to have had loving relationships with her sisters, Anna in particular, there is no evidence, no letters or personal reminiscences, of intimacies exchanged. Of course, as long as they were all living under one roof, there would have been no occasion for letters. All one can do is speculate.

Certainly she would have us think it was a very close-knit family. And it probably was a strong Jewish home, held together by her mother's centeredness in it and her unfailing love. On her death, all this would fall apart.

In 1893, three years after Jeanette Schüler died, a Dr. Berthold Lasker came to Elberfeld and opened a medical practice. "Dr. med. B. Lasker,

Lasker, Else, her sister Anna, and Anna's fiancé, Lindner (Stadtbibliothek Wuppertal, Else Lasker-Schüler Archiv).

general pract., surgeon and OB." It was in the summer of that same year, 1893, that Else's sister, Anna, became engaged to the tenor Franz Lindner. Lasker was one of the witnesses to the marriage, so it would seem he made the acquaintance of the Schüler family shortly after he arrived in Elberfeld.

Because of his profession, it took some convincing for the young actor-singer Lindner to gain acceptance in the Schüler family. Else was impassioned and outspoken in her support of her sister's choice. Writing secretly to Lindner, she implored him not to cave in or abandon his hope of marrying Anna. "People say I'm spacey, and maybe I am, but I care more about Anna's happiness than my own...."[3] She sounds a bit like Carson McCullers' Frankie in *Member of the Wedding*. At the same time, it is almost as though she wanted to make sure her sister escaped the iron grip that their father and their uncle had on them now that their mother was dead. For herself, it seemed to matter less. And, in fact, in marrying Dr. Lasker, she did make a more "suitable" match, one readily acceptable to her father and her Uncle Sonnemann.

The young doctor, Berthold Lasker, came from a small town in the Neumark, in what is today part of Poland, close to the center of traditional East European Jewry. His father was a cantor in the synagogue, and his grandfather a well-known rabbi. Still, they were not Orthodox, but Conservative, Jews. Berthold got his M.D. at the University of Berlin, which held a special drawing power for Jewish intellectuals from the East. His brother, Emanuel Lasker, was to become the world chess champion. It was Emanuel Lasker who invented and legitimized the practice of utilizing one's opponent's psychological weaknesses and idiosyncrasies to defeat him.

Why the young Dr. Lasker chose Elberfeld to open a practice is unclear. Very possibly because Elberfeld boasted a famous chess club. Like his more famous brother, Berthold too was a chess buff and an absolute whiz at the game. Whatever it was that lured him to Elberfeld, during his first year there he met Else Schüler.

On December 3, the couple became engaged. And on that same day, the prospective groom participated in a landmark chess tournament, one in which he matched wits against twelve players simultaneously. An original way of celebrating one's betrothal, if not exactly flattering to the betrothed.

What was this young woman like in 1893 that made the young doctor think she would make a fitting helpmate and spouse for him?

Perhaps he saw in her a young Bettina von Arnim,[4] someone who would share his serious literary interests, if not his passion for chess, someone who would, like her own mother, host salons at their home. That, in fact, she would do for a time in Berlin, but not perhaps in the way he envisaged.

And what was she looking for in him? Did she know? It seems safe to guess that already at this time she was undergoing some drastic changes in the way she viewed the world and her place in it. Photographs taken in these crucial, but poorly documented, years show two very different Elses.

First, a decorous young woman engaged to be married, a ladylike exemplar of the upper bourgeoisie, definitely *eine höhere Tochter.* In short, an ideal candidate to become *Frau Doktor* alongside an earnest and aspiring physician who would soon move his practice to the fashionable Tiergarten district of Berlin.

As a bride she is dressed in white, with a carefully coifed floral wreath in her hair. She looks apprehensive, and there is an unmistakable twinge of sadness, if not resignation, about the eyes and mouth. She certainly doesn't look "radiant," as brides are supposed to. A year later, a very different Else, one with disheveled head, volatile mouth, and defiant bohemian dress, confronts the world—and Dr. Lasker.

Quick to take offense, her temper outbursts were beginning to be noticed, and not just by her husband.

Else as a bride, January 15, 1894 (Stadtbibliothek Wuppertal, Else Lasker-Schüler Archiv).

Her uncle Leopold (Sonnemann) remembered the sound of her footfall as she stomped into his hotel in Berlin, returning his generous gift of silver flatware, in a pique over the fact that he had signed his gift enclosure card, "Sonnemann" not "Uncle Leopold."[5]

It was in this first period in Berlin that Else began to take art lessons from Simson Goldberg, a friend of Dr. Lasker's, as well as of his brother, Emanuel, and a colleague and one-time pupil of Max Liebermann.

As an old man, Goldberg recorded his recollections of the young Else. He writes in the hindsight of his recognition of her place in German letters. Nonetheless, his observations and perceptions seem authentic enough.

> As Else Lasker-Schüler took drawing lessons from me for a number of years, and as I was a close friend of the family, in and out of their house on a more-or-less daily basis, I had numerous opportu-

nities to study the mysterious character of this extraordinary woman of genius. She was subject to psychic as well as physical depressions, and to hyperaesthesia. This condition manifested itself as borderline hallucinations. Conversations with her were always interesting, mostly pleasant, but then again over long stretches unbearable. Despite her nervous, volcanic outbursts, I was nearly always able to calm her by steering the talk to prosaic, banal subjects. Her atelier, which also served as her study, looked like a crammed junk-shop.... Her soirées were attended by the entire intellectual elite of Berlin.... Frequently when I was with Else (just the two of us) she would fall into a trance, like a somnambule, fighting off heart cramps, while her huge dark eyes rolled around with a fierce angry look,—searching. Deep furrows would form between her brows. Then she would burst into tears and say, "My God, I can't go on," and jumping up from her seat like a gazelle, reach for her pen as if to give life to her words, only then to throw herself on to the divan, exhausted and whimpering, yammering, "I am doomed forever; I can't go on!" I had the impression that she was being overwhelmed by some unutterable vision....[6]

Goldberg's is the first psychological portrait of Else Lasker-Schüler as a young woman. It is also the first mention of the heart cramps that would plague her throughout her life. There is a photograph taken in 1906 that has precisely the look that Simson Goldberg describes: piercing dark eyes, deep furrows between her brows, a fierce angry look, and an expression around the mouth as if she would indeed burst into tears. It is hard to know whether, as is frequently the case with St. Vitus' dance patients, marriage had brought on another bout with the disease, or whether her behavior was unrelated to the prior illness. Maybe marriage itself did not agree with her. She was clearly not happy.

Equally interesting in Goldberg's account is what is missing. Although Lasker-Schüler would make a considerable name for herself as graphic artist (alone in Hagen, in 1916, she exhibited 85 works at the Karl Ernst Osthaus Gallery), Goldberg says not a word about her drawing skills. Is it because his own work excels in draughtsmanship and he could not appreciate her more improvisational approach to drawing? What was the nature of his reservations?

Art lessons were not her own idea. Or perhaps she chose, by indirection, to make it appear that they were Dr. Lasker's suggestion. From the way she tells it, Dr. Lasker thought up the scheme to keep her occupied and out of his way. At first she and Simson Goldberg worked in a room off the doctor's office. But Dr. Lasker could lose his temper too, and after

Else's uncle, Leopold Sonnemann (1831–1909). Portrait by Max Schüler (another uncle), reproduced as frontispiece in *Geschichte der Frankfurter Zeitung, 1856–1906.*

a few angry clashes (the doctor would come storming out of his office to complain of the ruckus the two were raising), Else decided to rent an atelier around the corner from where they lived. Here she set up a dark room and tried her hand at photography as well as painting.

One of her earliest known graphic works (27 April 1900), is a watercolor entitled "The Lyric Miscarriage." It depicts a solitary woman, whose head is much too big and heavy for the thin reed of a body below to support it. She is standing among rankweed and bulrushes on some forsaken shore, weeping. Her thin bulrush arms hang limp to the sides of her stick-figure body, clad—incongruously—in a man's shirt, tie, and the vestiges of a jacket, which cuts across her wasp-thin waist. From the waist, a long white skirt leads the eye down to the single most telling detail of the painting: a red, red heart, centered precisely over the crotch. From the woman's face, tears are streaming, but only from one eye. The brow is knitted, and the short straight hair wears for adornment a thistle flower plucked from the shrub that the poet stands beside. A lugubrious moon, whose mournful reflection has just slipped beneath the surface of the water, looks on pityingly. In its entirety, as in its details, this painting is unlike anything else. Elements of surrealism are discernible, but it is not really surrealist. For that it is far too personal and real. What, one can't help wondering, would her teacher, Simson Goldberg, have made of it?

The studio very clearly became her own space, with its geometric-patterned Indian wall-hanging tacked up behind the divan, and over this a board or makeshift mantelpiece where she had crammed to overlapping sketches, drawings, and photographs. In front of these stood various collectibles, including figurines.

It is in her atelier, not her home, that she began to receive visitors. Her sister Anna, who had married the tenor Franz Lindwurm-Lindner and moved to Berlin shortly before the Laskers, visited her here. So did the children of her oldest sister Martha, the girls Alice and Margarete Wormser.

We see them all in a photograph (circa 1894 to 1896) on page 43 seated like birds on a telegraph wire on her daybed in the studio, the two little girls all dressed up for this visit in white

Else Lasker-Schüler, around 1896 (Stadtbibliothek Wuppertal, Else Lasker-Schüler Archiv).

dresses and high buckled shoes. Else presses her hand very tenderly into the hand of Margarete, the younger child, and bears down with it on her lap. The presence of the daybed in the studio leads one to wonder, did she spend nights here too? Given the mounting tensions in her marriage, it is certainly conceivable that she did. And mounting tensions there were. We would get to hear about them. Obliquely, of course, but unerringly.

This vibrant "Aunt Else," at home in her atelier, is hardly the same woman as the one captured in a photo taken three years earlier in which the two engaged sisters, Else and Anna, are seen with their men. Else has her arm linked apathetically through Lasker's, while Anna's arm is thrown over Lindner's shoulder. Here Anna is the intense, wild-looking one, and Else the tame domestic bird. She looks frozen into passivity. A more joyless looking couple than the Lasker pair would be hard to imagine. The doctor's expression is prim, if not grim, and worse, he appears to be altogether without humor.

Whatever led her to commit herself to such a straitjacket marriage?

Else Lasker-Schüler with her nieces, Alice and Margarete Wormser, in her Berlin atelier circa 1894 to 1896 (Stadtbibliothek Wuppertal, Else Lasker-Schüler Archiv).

How desperate must she have been, how stranded emotionally!

One of her first poems to appear in print (in 1899, in *Die Gesellschaft*) was called "Verwelkte Myrten" ("Wilted Myrtle"). The myrtle is favored in bridal wreaths, Myrtle, or Aphrodite, being the goddess of fertility.

"Verwelkte Myrten"

Bist wie der graue, sonnenlose Tag,
Der sündig sich auf junge Rosen legt.
—Mir war, wie ich an Deiner Seite lag,

Als ob mein Herz sich nicht mehr bewegt.
Ich küsste Deine bleichen Wangen rot,
Entwand ein Lächeln Deinem starren Blick.

—Du tratest meine junge Seele tot
Und kehrtest in Dein kaltes Sein zurück.[7]

"Wilted Myrtle"

You're like the gray and chilling sunless day
That lays its sinful self upon young roses.
—Lying at your side, it felt to me
As if my heart had altogether ceased to beat.

I kissed your deathly pale cheeks red,
Wrested a smile from your impassive mask.
—You trampled my young spirit dead
And then drew back inside your own cold shell.

In its form the poem is controlled and conventional: two four-line stanzas of iambic pentameter, with a strict and simple rhyme scheme. In its statement, however, it is unflinching and unconventional—shattering. The very first word, "Bist," standing alone for "Du bist" ("You are"), seems like a slap in the face, as if with it she could return the blow to her hurt pride.

She was so excited about her first publication that she wrote to her sister Anna in April telling her that all her poems had found favor with Ludwig Jacobowski, the editor of *Die Gesellschaft*, a bi-monthly. And in fact he published them all in his journal in August. She was five months pregnant, but she did not mention it to Anna at this time.

Far more mysterious than the poem "Wilted Myrtle," and more ominous, is a story she liked to tell to explain why she married Dr. Lasker. "Once, during lessons, there appeared an enormous snake on the floor of the room in which I was studying. Only years later did I find out who had put it there. It was, of course, an act of vengeance. Because once, when we were playing cops and robbers, in the excitement, I had bitten off my playmate's nose.... Since then (the snake incident), I have always had an aversion to creeping ways. Which is why I made up my mind—when I was 16—to marry a kind of marten or weasel—one that would kill snakes ... and be immune to the snake's poisonous bite."[8]

It is a very opaque passage. As an allegory it does not yield its meaning. The perpetrator of this nasty prank could easily have been her father. It was he, after all, who played cops and robbers with her, and who but a family member would have had access to her study room? Her father had died in 1897, so he could not read the tale and object. As for the nose she claims to have bitten off, let's borrow from another text, *Hebräerland:* "I laughed at the green painted cardboard nose my father wore [as a mask]...."[9]

The Freudian symbolism is too obvious to warrant more than a passing glance. But that her horror of snake-like beings stemmed from the incident with her father seems clear. And in sharp contrast to the anecdotes she tells about her father in which he is identified, this account does not need to cloak his upsetting qualities in euphemistic garb.

We still, however, know nothing about the marten-weasel as errant-knight. Unfortunately, this creature is hardly more attractive than the snake it was supposed to devour. Its family includes the polecat. It can, according to Brehm's *Tierleben* (the popular 19th century illustrated zoology encyclopedia which the Schülers surely owned), be divided into two sorts: the one, having long pointed claws; the other, more blunted. Weasels, as we know from our own folk etymology, have a reputation for being sneaky, if not exactly bloodthirsty, so these are hardly creatures one would want to snuggle up against in bed. But that, perhaps, is precisely the point.

Years later, she would regale her friends with horror stories about her marriage to Lasker. They were often so lurid as to be written off as just one more of her endless fabulations. One evening she was invited to the house of Ottomar Starke, the stage designer and feuilletonist, along with Franz Werfel and Fritz Huf, the Swiss sculptor. Starke describes the evening in his memoirs.[10] She arrived wearing a scarlet dress and high-heeled red shoes, but no one paid any attention to her, so she sat in a corner and sulked. Then, maybe to get some attention (she was in love with Fritz Huf, Starke says), she suddenly came to life, and began telling stories of how Lasker would make her dance barefoot on a floor strewn with nails. Of course they all just rolled their eyes.

But as a metaphor suggestive of some kind of sexual bondage, it seems quite fitting. She was always giving a literary twist to her emotional experiences. And Oriental spice was almost always her preferred flavor. This doesn't mean that there was no basis in fact. There nearly always was.

Whether there were actual incidents that set her against her husband, or whether, as is implied in the poem "Wilted Myrtle," she simply came to feel his coldness like the hand of death upon her, by 1898 or 1899, she had become restive and the crack in the marriage had begun to be visible to the outside world. Something else to consider, which undoubtedly played a role in her altered perceptions, was the fact that the move to Berlin from Elberfeld exposed her to new influences, new vistas opening up to her at a crucial time in her emotional and artistic development.

She had begun to publish, not just the "Wilted Myrtle" poem quoted above, but others, all in Jacobowski's journal, *Die Gesellschaft.*

This kind of "confessional" poetry was unique in Germany at this date. Clichéd love poetry by young women poetasters, yes, but poems with the strength and originality of Lasker's first offerings, no. Ten years later, in Russia, Marina Tsvetaeva would create a scandal when she published her first poems, poems that bared the same kind of raw emotion. The two women shared a rich vocabulary of sensuality and an honesty that scared off a lot of men.

One man who was not scared off by Else's intensity in these first years of her separation from Lasker, and who would uncorset her yet more, was the Berlin Vachel Lindsay, the vagabond poet and bohemian, Peter Hille, some fifteen years her senior. "You, my adorable destiny," he wrote to the burgeoning young poet, "with your hellish burning eyes! I immerse my spirit in the Stygian mists of your agonies.... Cosmic...."[11] Yes, Else lapped up the flattery and fell under his spell. In one of his more inspired outbursts, he called her "The Black Swan of Israel," a name that would stick to her for life.

Under Peter Hille's tutelage, and with her newfound self-confidence, Else Lasker-Schüler was quickly developing a public persona, but one that could infuriate as well as entice. With Peter Hille's backing, she had edged her way into Die Kommenden (The Next Wave), the literary society founded by the man who championed her poems at Die Gesellschaft, Ludwig Jacobowski, and she was soon giving readings there. But one evening, in Jacobowski's absence, the presiding moderator insulted her. The insult, as she described it in her account to Jacobowski, was in the way he announced her reading: "'Frau Else Lasker-Schüler has been requested, wie man so sagt [so to speak], to read.' This he said grinning ironically."[12]

The incident set off a fierce internecine battle within the club. The upshot was that she and Rudolf Steiner, who supported her in her pique, were told not to come back—ever. Unfortunately, it was not long before "misunderstandings" would lead to a rift with Jacobowski as well. This was a pattern: taking, then giving offense, apologizing, and then making matters worse. And it was a pattern that would persist throughout her life. Her lifelong friendship with Martin Buber would end, shortly before her death, in just such an unfortunate sequence.

But it wasn't all her doing. These were highly volatile, rebellious young people. The next club she belonged to, Die Neue Gemeinschaft (The New Club), where Peter Hille introduced her, seemed at first a kind of arcadia. The members, sometimes up to seventy people, went on outings together, gave readings out-of-doors on the shores of lakes, very much like people all over who became involved in "back to nature" movements. They also propagated radical social ideas, vegetarian lifestyles, and in general a seeming liberation from bourgeois constraints, which was what Else Lasker-Schüler was desperately seeking after the break-up of her marriage to Lasker.

It was not long, however, before she became disillusioned. Rivalries, jealousies—just like those of their bourgeois counterparts—took up much of the group's energies. She also began to sense a certain hollowness in the grand pronouncements of ideals, and by 1901 she regretted having joined The New Club. Something of their studied-dissolute appearance must have clung to her, though, because the way Kafka, and later, Harry Graf Kessler and others describe her, hippie-like *avant la parole*, sounds very much like the way the members of The New Club dressed and disported themselves.

How she earned the epithet "Black Swan of Israel" has more to do with her poetry than her appearance. One poem which may have suggested Peter Hille's conceit, and which dates from this period, is the languorous "Sulamith." Shulamite was the name of the beloved in the Song of Solomon.[13]

Lasker-Schüler's poem first appeared in the periodical *Ost und West* in 1901, then in her first book of poems, *Styx*, and again, slightly revised, in her 1913 collection *Hebräische Balladen* (*Hebrew Ballads*).

"Sulamith"

(1913 version; punctuation and line indentation
altered and simplified from 1901 version)

> O, Ich lernte an deinem süssen Munde
> Zuviel der Seligkeiten kennen!
> Schon fühl ich die Lippen Gabriels
> Auf meinem Herzen brennen...
> Und die Nachtwolke trinkt
> Meinen tiefen Cederntraum.
> O, wie dein Leben mir winkt!
> Und ich vergehe
> Mit blühendem Herzeleid
> Und verwehe im Weltraum,
> In Zeit,
> In Ewigkeit,
> Und meine Seele verglüht in den Abendfarben
> Jerusalems.[14]

"Shulamite"

> O, I came to know too much of rapture
> Too much of bliss at your sweet mouth.
> Now I feel the lips of Gabriel
> Burn upon my heart...

And the nightcloud drinks
My deep cedardream.
O, how your life calls to me!
And I expire
My sorrow in full bloom
I scatter in space,
In time,
In eternity.
And my soul burns out in the twilight glow
Of Jerusalem.

In addition to her first publications, the year 1899 saw the birth of Else Lasker-Schüler's only child, Paul, on August 24, at the Universitäts-klinik in Berlin. The birth certificate names Dr. Lasker as the father, but Else named many others, one more exotic than the next, the most eupho-nious and persistent being Alcibiades de Rouan, a Greek prince, whom she claims to have met on the street. He was so beautiful she was carried away. Alas, the beautiful prince had subsequently died. Maybe the beauti-ful prince was someone she had met on one of the club outings. Maybe he didn't exist.

No matter. She doted on this child. But Paul was also the occasion for a fair amount of guilt, or at least conflict. Her constant shortage of funds prevented her from being able to give him the kind of care she would have liked, and when she was tasting the freedom of her *Wanderjahre* with Peter Hille, who looked after the little boy?

The second entry in her prose work *The Peter Hille Book* suggests an answer:

> In front of a doorway near the town I wanted to leave Petrus for a bit—it was where my sister lived. But he stepped through the gate in the garden. And two darling little girls ran toward him—the little scamp between them had escaped their hold, and climbed like a weasel (!) up into a pear tree, right behind some squirrels.... It was my boy.... And as I stepped into the hallway of the house, the two little girls ran after me calling, "Mama Mama, der liebe Gott is out-side in the garden!" But my sister had seen us coming and looked very troubled and pensive. I knew that Petrus's majestic bearing would frighten her—and she grasped my hand anxiously: "Won't you stay with us?"[15]

Paul spent a great deal of time at Else's sister's house. So profoundly had Else fallen under Hille's spell that it didn't seem to occur to her that Anna might wish to wrest her from his mesmeric grip and recall her to her duties toward her little boy. Anna, now a mother herself, will certainly have disapproved of Else's "spiritual wanderings" with this itinerant vagabond. The pair caused a lot of raised eyebrows, even in their radical bohemian circle. Gerhart Hauptmann, in his mock-epic novel *The Fool in Christo Emanuel Quint* (1910), pokes fun at Hille, with his heavy beard and pig-eyes, the goose-down ticking of his pillow still uncombed out of his head, and Annette von Rhyn, the poetess, trotting along beside him, each totally engrossed in the other.

For the young mother in her fictional account, for Else, it was painful to have to leave her boy, but as she saw it, there was no question that she must. "I tore myself away," the passage continues, "gently embraced the two girls, kissed my madcap and followed after the magnificent one."[16]

But then Else woke up one morning and suddenly realized what was happening: "I feared for myself; he was a magician, and I ran away down the hill ... my head was a tower, I could find myself no more...."[17] The year was 1903. A year later Peter Hille collapsed in a railroad station. "The most homeless person in all Berlin,"[18] Julius Bab called him a few months after his death. Else Lasker-Schüler describes how she took care of him in his last miserable days.

It was Hille, for better and for worse, who had drawn the preliminary sketch of the literary persona that would gain sharpness of contour over the years. Name-giving was an essential part of the mystique, and he was never at a loss for epithets.

This was the time, just after the turn of the century, when a new art form was surfacing in Berlin: the cabaret. It was Peter Hille again who was instrumental in introducing her to it. With its mixture of high and low culture, theater and music, tingel-tangel and circus, it was a form that intrigued her, and for a time she even considered a career as cabarettist. Something of the circus artist, the bareback rider standing defiantly on her horse as she performs her dare-devil act, is certainly part of her nature, and one she brought to her poetry readings as well.

Her early attempts were not always successful, however. She was even laughed off the stage on one occasion. But when Hille took charge and introduced her at his own newly-formed Vorleseheim zum Peter Hille (Peter Hille's Performance Cabaret), at the Italian Weinstube, Dalbelli's, he very carefully went over every aspect of her "Oriental evenings" ahead. (He even promised her that no one would smoke during her performance.) It was here that things turned around for her.

Soon she was giving readings before large audiences. She exulted in all the extravagant guises Hille had dreamed up and magicked out of her. With her glass-bead Orientalism she conjured a world—a real tinsel Byzantium. In fact all her life she would delight in dime-store jewelry, glass rings and glorified marbles. Once on stage, she would wait till her aura had settled over the crowd, and then begin. She intoned her verses in a manner that some found mesmerizing, others irritating, and still others laughable. Even her understatements could sound overstated. She despised the "declaiming" of poetry, and was most indignant if she was accused of doing just that. Judging by the mountains of contradictory accounts, it would seem she read differently at different times, in different moods and situations.

Hille could be absurdly extravagant in his diction when praising his protégé, when it came to finding apt phrases for eulogizing her poems, he was unbeatable: "Else Lasker-Schüler is the Jewish poet. Of grand format. Say Deborah.... Her poetic soul is a hard black diamond. The black swan of Israel, a Sappho whose world has been torn asunder...."[19] Probably no one has ever outdone him in catchy epithets of adulation. More importantly, his words took hold, like advertising slogans. To this day they are used as titles for books about her as well as for blurbs for her own books.

Hille had launched her. Now there was no holding her back.

CHAPTER FOUR

1903–1909:
The Nights of Tino

*"Liebe Tino ... Schneidender schwarzer Diamant, eine
Sappho, der eine Welt entzwei gegangen ist."
("Dear Tino ... Cutting black diamond, a
Sappho whose world's been torn asunder.")*
Peter Hille

"I love the beautiful Antinous, and Onit von Wetterwehe of the silken
eye ..., and the mischievous Grimmer von Geyerbogen—and Goldwarth's
galloping mane I love too, the sunbeams on his brow ... Goldwarth, the
wildest of the musicians ... And my very fickleness worries me."[1]

Else Lasker-Schüler was troubled by more than just her fickleness. Her
sensuality frightened her. It was, in the words of the critic Samuel Lublinski, "like some wild mythic beast that she tried to flee but ultimately suc-
cumbed to."[2] It is this fierce erotic drive that marks her first collection of
poems, *Styx*. Many critics found this distasteful and wrote her off as a hysterical, overwrought woman. But more discerning people, like Lublinski,
for example, judged the poems' merits and the poet's candor appreciatively.

And needless to say, Peter Hille only egged her on. "Rejoice in your
leaping love; it is a child and wants to play."

For play there was in fact ample opportunity in those years. Die Neue
Gemeinschaft (The New Club), a group which included Peter Hille, went,

51

as we know, on day trips into the woods, where they read their poetry to one another on the shore of some beautiful lake at sunset. Nature, writ large, and with a very German tinge of mystical romanticism, suffuses all descriptions of these day trips, including her own. As part of the fun, all the participants were given fictitious names, and in the tales about them they were transmuted into legendary beings. Gerhart Hauptmann, for example, was Onit von Wetterwehe. (Onit is Tino, spelled backwards.)

Like a honey bee sampling pollen, she buzzed around these young men before settling on one, the irrepressible "Goldwarth, wildest of the musicians," as he is called in her *Peter Hille Book*.

Georg Levin (his name in real life), was the son of a Berlin doctor. A small, wiry, young man with very blond hair, he was near-sighted and wore thick glasses. He was not, by conventional standards, what one would call handsome. Intense and radiating an "irrepressible" vitality, he *was* what one calls charismatic.

In 1903 Else Lasker-Schüler was 34; George Levin, 25. They became enamoured of each other, and believed they were soulmates. In the same year that her divorce from Lasker became official, she married Levin, to whom she gave the name Walden—Herwarth Walden. It is by this name that he became famous and is known today.

Her "golden boy" had begun his career as a pianist and composer. He had studied with Zemlinsky (Schoenberg's brother-in-law) and was a winner of the Liszt stipend for piano, which enabled him to spend a year in Florence, something that surely influenced his burgeoning cosmopolitan tastes in all the arts.

Walden's interests and ambitions were indeed broad, reaching out into literature and the visual arts. He was international in outlook, and had an uncanny feel for the truly original, as opposed to the merely new, especially in painting. He launched such early twentieth-century giants as Kokoschka, Franz Marc and George Grosz. In addition, he had natural entrepreneurial talents, and the nervous, caffeine-gunned energy to realize them. In 1910, he would come to own the most influential avant-garde literary periodical in Berlin, *Der Sturm* (*The Storm*), along with the most important gallery for avant-garde art, also called Der Sturm.

Walden and Lasker-Schüler believed passionately in each other's gifts, and each was tireless when it came to furthering the other's career. Else could be quite shameless. She resorted to the most blatant flattery, writing to Richard Dehmel, who was widely regarded as Germany's most important poet, and whose poems Walden had set to music. Now she importuned him to do something for her "friend." She began her letter to Dehmel, "Meister!" and added "That you are!" for good measure.

To poets, to publishers—whoever she thought might be useful to him—
Else extolled Walden's musical talents. She could not find words enough
to praise his song settings to Dehmel's poems and, of course, to her own.
These, which aimed to express the emotional tenor of the poetry, rather
than adhere to the words themselves, she found especially wonderful. "A
poet and composer must have the same sensibility, the same spiritual core,"
she wrote to Dehmel. "And this is particularly vital today when there are
so many philistines posing as artists."³ Walden, she insisted, was a true
artist. Watching Walden improvise at the piano, "with his blond mane
flying," Kokoschka was reminded of descriptions of Liszt. One can see why
Else was drawn to him and why she was no reliable judge of his musical
gifts!

He, on the other hand, was absolutely prescient in his appreciation
of her as a poet. He kept her in mind in all his publicistic efforts, and he
was ever on the alert for appropriate public forums for her.

She needed no guidance from Hille, or Walden, or anybody else, in
the *writing* of her poetry. It was not long before she was leaving behind the
gushy Jugendstil swoonings, the hyperbolic diction, of her mentor, writing
poems in her own singular voice. She was inventing a new stanza form with
just two or three lines, not the conventional four or more, and making up
new words. She was not being overweening when she wrote to her then-
publisher, Axel Juncker, in 1906 about her new book, *Der Siebente Tag* (*The
Seventh Day*), demanding 200 marks for the first printing, and scribbling
in the margin of her letter, "Never before such poems, altogether new language."⁴

In the close Dalbelli circle, which included Rudolf Steiner, Julius Bab
and Julius Hart, men who played important roles in German literary and
intellectual life in the early years of the century, her enduring emotional
attachment to Hille was common knowledge. Having thrown off the yoke
of his influence, she was free to extol his virtues. It seemed only natural,
therefore, that her *Peter Hille Book*, written in 1906, should celebrate this
"holy gypsy" and commemorate her *Lehrjahre* (years of apprenticeship) in
his orbit. No less a free spirit than Victor Hugo had written to Hille once,
in admiration: "Vous êtes un homme!" As for our poet, when someone she
had loved died, she remained true to his memory for all time. In this case,
it was almost proof of her emancipation.

In the two or three years since she had begun to publish, she had
gained enormous self-confidence, as is evident even from her very first postcard to Richard Dehmel, written after the publication of her first book of
poems, *Styx* (1902). Dehmel, one should remember, was very influential as
well as very accomplished as a poet. "Mr. Dehmel! Have you received my

book, *Styx*. Please write to me, saying if you like my Ballade? I am Else Lasker-Schuler. Am very ill and lying down therefore card."[5] "I am Else Lasker-Schuler." Indeed.

It was at around this time, the early 1900s, when she was shedding her Wilhelmian identity, that she began exchanging the demure garb of the bonne bourgeoise for a more fanciful costume of her own devising, at least for public appearances. Around the house, on the street, she was apt to look so shabby that if she paid someone a visit, they thought she had come to borrow money from them.[6] It is not so much that she chose pants over skirts, although she does say she never liked women's clothing (especially dresses that were low-cut),[7] but rather that she sensed the possibilities for exploring the more exotic side of her nature—her Orientalism[8] (see Appendix 3)—in trousers. And while it may be stretching things a bit, one could see in the velvet jacket and wide trousers shades of the circus rider, that figure she knew and loved so well from childhood.

Undoubtedly, the sense of male power that trousers signaled, along with the freedom from conventional strictures, had a very strong appeal for her as well. Like Marina Tsvetaeva,[9] who, when she moved from Moscow to the Crimea around 1910, changed her style of dress from high heels and dresses to sandals and "sharovary" (wide boyish trousers of Turkish style). Like Tsvetaeva, Lasker-Schüler was viewed skeptically by conventional practitioners of her craft because she dealt with her own emotions in shockingly raw and honest terms. Else Lasker-Schüler was the only woman to break into the most radical artistic movement of her day, Expressionism.

If the term was to mean anything, as applied to her poetry, it had to be something very different than what was generally understood. The signature Expressionist poem "Weltende," by Jakob von Hoddis, was an apocalyptic vision of the way the world would end: through bourgeois, cosmopolitan overreaching. An impassioned social statement, it was the poem Kurt Pinthus chose to open his Expressionist anthology *Menschheitsdämmerung*.

"Weltende"

Dem Bürger fliegt vom spitzen Kopf der Hut,
In allen Lüften hallt es wie Geschrei.
Dachdecker stürzen ab und gehn entzwei,
Und an den Küsten—liest man—steigt die Flut.

Der Sturm ist da, die wilden Meere hupfen
An Land, um dicke Dämme zu zerdrücken.
Die meisten Menschen haben einen Schnupfen.
Die Eisenbahnen fallen von den Brücken.[10]

"World's End"

The hat flies off the bourgeois's pointy head,
The air resounds with screaming everywhere.
Roofers fall to earth and break in two.
And on the coasts—one reads—the tide is rising.

The storm has come, the wild seas hop
On land, to crush the sturdy dams.
Most everyone you meet has got the sniffles.
The railroad cars are falling off the bridges.

Lasker-Schüler's poem of the same title, dedicated to Herwarth Walden
in 1903, the year of their marriage, is a highly subjective meditation on love.

"Weltende"

Herwarth Walden

Es ist ein Weinen in der Welt,
Als ob der liebe Gott gestorben wär,
Und der bleierne Schatten, der niederfällt
Lastet grabesschwer.

Komm, wir wollen uns näher verbergen...
Das Leben liegt in aller Herzen
Wie in Särgen.

Du! Wir wollen uns tief küssen...
Es pocht eine Sehnsucht an die Welt,
An der wir sterben müssen.

"World's End"

Herwarth Walden

There is a weeping in the world,
As if dear God Himself had died,
And the leaden shadow that falls from the air
Weighs on us like a tomb.

Come, let's snuggle close and hide,
Life's locked up in every heart
As in a coffin.

Du! Let's hold each other tight and kiss...
A terrible yearning pounds at the gate,
And we must surely die.

She was beginning in her poems to define herself as a Jew but, like everything about her, her Judaism was totally unorthodox: defiant and humble, willful and passionate. Her poem "Mein Volk" ("My People"), written in 1905, makes the point.

"Mein Volk"

Der Fels wird morsch,
Dem ich entspringe
Und meine Gotteslieder singe...
Jäh stürz ich vom Weg
Und riesele ganz in mir
Fernab, allein über Klagegestein
Dem Meer zu.

Hab mich so abgeströmt
Von meines Blutes
Mostvergorrenheit.
Und immer, immer noch der Widerhall
In mir,
Wenn schauerlich gen Ost
Das morsche Felsgebein
Mein Volk
Zu Gott schreit.[12]

"My People"

The rock is crumbling
From which I spring
And sing my hymns to God...
I hurl myself from the path
And skid all inward-curled
Far off, alone over wailing stone
Down to the sea.

I've shoved off so far
From my blood's
fermented brew.
And still and still it echoes
In me,
When shuddering with dread
The crumbling rock
My people
Faces East
And cries to God.

In her *Hebräische Balladen* (*Hebrew Ballads*), some of which were written during this period,[13] she frequently uses Biblical materials, but in a

wholly idiosyncratic—some
might even say, heretical—
way. But a deep thread of religious "yearning" runs through
all these poems, and the Biblical echoes in her diction are
unmistakable.

Peter Hille had dubbed
her "Tino," "Tino of Bagdad."
Her second book of prose,
which came out a year after
the *Peter Hille Book*, would be
called *Die Nächte von Tino von
Bagdad* (*The Nights of Tino of
Bagdad*).[14] Her Bible-tinged
Orientalism was becoming evident in every sphere of her life.
Sometimes the two worlds,
ancient Hebrew and ancient
Arabian, came together:

"Now I am not alto-
gether poor—I have the ring
that Joseph wore when he
made himself known to his
brothers.... You may gaze long
on Joseph's ring: in each
stone you see the world of the
dead and the living; it has as
many stones as the lean and
fat kine counted together....
In Bagdad a clairvoyant told
me that I had lain for thousands of years wrapped as a
mummy, and that I am no

"Die Nächte Tino von Bagdads" ("Tino
of Bagdad's Nights"). Frontispiece by
Max Fröhlich. 1907 (Schiller National-
museum/Deutsches Literaturarchiv,
Marbach).

other than Joseph, who is called in Arabic Jussuf. I too believe that the living wander among the dead..."[15] she wrote in a letter to Karl Kraus.

The Nights is a loosely-knit collection of short prose pieces. The frontispiece drawing, by Max Fröhlich, depicts the poet as a barefoot figure
sheathed in a long loose raiment, with beads in strands that reach below
her knees. She looks as though she had strayed off the edge of a Beardsley
drawing. This Tino is a princess with a whole retinue of slaves, eunuchs,

warriors, and a palace where feasts are celebrated in her honor. And as in the court of Herodias, here too there is wild dancing and music. Waiters wear crocodile masks, and the name of the princess is engraved on the brow of the great pyramid. Of course this Tino is no ordinary princess. Her chief attribute is as Poet of Araby, author of *Ancient Arabian Sketches*.

But even as princess in this never-never land of her own creation, this Tino is no stranger to hardship and strife. "My palaces," she laments, "have gone to rack and ruin, my dromedary herds are starving, and even my doves have had their corals plucked from them."[16]

Nor is the court and realm over which she rules an ordinary one. Acts of great violence, reminiscent of Biblical scenes or scenes depicted on Assyrian friezes, are recorded here. Readers who would dismiss the poet's Orientalism as a form of escapism should heed the horrors she depicts. And remember her own horror story about her marriage to Lasker. There is Ached Bey,[17] the kalif and Tino's uncle. He lies sprawled over cushions in the palace courtyard. When he raises his enormous hand, heads fall.

There is the fakir, a fearsome misogynist who would wipe out all womankind. And even in this faraway court, love is punished, and those who have watched the naked dance of love will have their tongues bored through with stakes, while the guilty lover will be torn limb from limb and thrown under a tree in the garden. Hardly an escapist dream of paradise. Rather an arena where dream, fantasy and the heritage of Greek, near-Eastern, and Oriental mythology contend in sadistic imagery, but above all where words are made to dance arabesques and syllables sing in sounds that do not fully belong to any known language.

When she performed The Fakir herself, the greater part of the stage was taken up with a pyramid of jugs—a reference to the jugs the terrified women let fall on sight of the dreaded fakir. "In front of this, Else Lasker-Schüler, dressed in fantastic garb as fakir, under an enormous hat made of seashells, speaks without pause."[18] (For three texts from "The Nights of Tino," see Appendix 4, pages 187–189.)

The more she performed the more self-confident she became. She would order rude or unruly members of the audience to leave. It was sufficient if she disliked someone's aura. "You," she would say, "Please leave. I don't like the looks of you. As long as you are sitting there, I cannot read." It could happen that the purported "offender" turned out to be a longtime admirer of the poet. An embarrassment all around.

If the Oriental persona of Tino served as stimulus to her imagination, and was a way of exorcising her own demons, it had an additional function as well. It permitted her to make outlandish requests and seek finan-

Von Berliner   Stammtischen.

From *Der Welt-Spiegel*, an illustrated bi-weekly of the *Berliner Tageblatt*. Berlin, May 21, 1905. Caption reads: "The 'moderns,' regulars at the *Café des Westens*, at their usual tables." Else Lasker-Schüler and Herwarth Walden are at the small round marble-top table in foreground (courtesy Berlinische Galerie).

cial help from influential quarters without the humiliation of having to beg in her own name. Because she was, always, in financial straits.

Like their fellow bohemians, Walden and Lasker-Schüler lived very spartanly. A very different existence from the one Else had known growing up, and during her marriage to the successful doctor.

This new couple spent most of their waking hours in the café, the Café des Westens, to be precise. It was their home away from home. Wherever they went, whether to the café or to the movies, Else's little boy, Paul, went with them. Walden had taken on this added burden when he married Else, and treated Paul as his own child. Partly through inclination, partly through necessity, they did not entertain at home. Domesticity was not for Else, nor, at that period in his life, for Walden.

Living in cheap flats, or rooming houses, in close quarters, with no money and poor working conditions, they and their friends, colleagues, and rivals all went to the café to work, have a bite, exchange ideas, and occasionally, even blows. Patrons could run up debts for meals there, and count (up to a point) on the goodwill of the head waiter. The marble-top tables at the Café des Westens were small and round. In a photograph of 1905, the Walden pair is sitting across from each other, looking somewhat confrontational. Else is nursing a tall drink; Walden, smoking a cigarette. Her arm is on the back of her chair, as if she had just pulled away from the table, and possibly, from him, while he appears to be persisting in whatever it was he had proposed. Paul is not in the picture. Perhaps he has wandered quietly over to the dessert tray, something which he was known to do.

In 1904, Walden, in his entrepreneurial zeal, had founded the Verein für Kunst, a literary club, and along with it, the following year, a publishing house. Else was a regular performer at the Verein, and her second book of poems, *The Seventh Day*, was published by the Verein's publishing house in 1905.

But already before this date, on the basis of her magazine publications and representation in anthologies of contemporary poetry, the highly regarded critic, Samuel Lublinski, had called attention to her work: "Whosoever ... is interested in genuine modern poetry written by women, should turn not to Maria Eichhorn or Marie Madeline Freifrau von Puttmaker but to Else Lasker-Schüler, the single most notable talent in this category."[19, 20]

In 1907, two years after *The Seventh Day* appeared, she sent a copy to the still much-revered Richard Dehmel. In her accompanying letter, she calls his attention especially to the poems' "new use of language." As we know from her letter to Axel Juncker when she offered the manuscript for publication, she was very much aware that she was on to something altogether new and sensational, rhythms and syntax previously untried in German, and striking coinages that would become a permanent part of the language: *Cederntraum, Gottland, Meinwärts, Mutterheimat, Meinlingchen, Traureschenbaum, Herzkirschen,* and more. They can be translated, but only by circumlocution and elaboration.

The early years with Walden were heady, productive ones. Then, in the summer of 1907, she began work on her first and in many ways most lyrical play, *Die Wupper*. She claims to have written it in one fevered night.

Set in her childhood Elberfeld on the Wupper River, it creates a poetic pastiche of life there, with its working class and upper-middle class families interacting and clashing, along with three lugubrious tramps, Long Anna, Pendulum Fritz and the glassy Amadeus, whose sexual quirks and other vagaries are sympathetically portrayed. Other people's eccentricities were never altogether alien to her. In her own eyes she was always the Outsider.

The play has the same two-layered quality in prose that characterizes many of the poems, as previously mentioned (see "Weltende"): on one level, it floats as pure lyric fantasy, in a dreamworld; but equally, it builds on the stark reality of social and industrial turmoil, and is unthinkable without this. *The Wupper* found a publisher in 1909, but was not performed until 1919, when Max Reinhardt chose it for his Junges Deutschland Theater.

Walden was meanwhile trying his hand as an editor, working at different theater, literature and art magazines. He repeatedly ran up against opposition from his conservative employers, and was eventually fired for what were perceived as his radical authorial proposals (Strindberg, for example). And his unbending principles: he would, for example, brook no advertisements in his pages. He later moved away from "radical" aesthetics to radical politics, only to die in Soviet Russia, a victim of the very system he had idealized.

When Nissen, his employer, fired Walden from his job as editor, Else did everything to enlist public sentiment for her husband, even though this incident came at a time when their marriage was

Else Lasker-Schüler, 1906. A handwritten inscription on the back of the photograph reads, "To the poet René Schickele* and the brave sixth-former [high school senior] Anna Schickele, with love" (Schiller National Museum/ Deutsches Literaturarchiv, Marbach). *René Schickele was a friend of Rilke's and editor of *Die Weissen Blatter.*

already faltering. Feeling strongly that Walden had been wronged in the lawsuit Nissen brought against him, Else wrote to their new friend, the acerbic Viennese publicist Karl Kraus. She wanted to persuade him to use his considerable influence to expose Nissen's high-handed ways in his journal *Die Fackel.* Kraus's method was a devastating one: death by quotation. In her let-

Else Lasker-Schüler, 1906. Atelier Becker, Berlin. The handwritten inscription to René Schickele on the back reads, "I love you" (Schiller National Museum/ Deutsches Literaturarchiv, Marbach).

ter to him, she depicts Walden as utterly guileless. Altogether incapable of flattery, a born victim. This was probably true of him at the time. Later he would become an accomplished "wheeler-dealer."

Kraus, in any event, counting Nissen fair game in his safari against philistines and other predators, proceeded to demolish him in the pages of *Die Fackel.*

More importantly, he decided to provide Walden with the means to strike out on his own. Without the financial help and invaluable guidance of Karl Kraus, it is doubtful whether Walden's *Sturm* would ever so much as lifted off the ground. Kraus even contributed a few "feuilletons" to the early *Sturm* issues, but persistent misprints, ever a bugaboo for Kraus, made him withdraw.

Easy as it is to say what drew the Walden couple together, it is not difficult to see why the marriage could not hold. There were good, practical reasons for trying to make it hold. While they did not start a printing press, like Virginia and Leonard Woolf, they worked together on many projects, literary and artistic. Walden also continued to write music to Else's poems, and he seems to have been a kind father to her boy.

Two passionate natures, they were, for a while at least, "ein Herz und eine Seele." Still, a smooth, easy-going marriage it was not. Rather, it was tense, rough and stormy. Given Else's volatile temperament alone, how could it have been otherwise? Not to mention her jealousy, which she was the first to admit. And who, after her mother, could love her enough?

Perhaps, one would have to concede, all Else's personal relationships were doomed to be white-capped and choppy. Alfred Döblin (author of

Berlin: Alexanderplatz) who had been friends of both Walden and the poet since the Dalbelli days, tells of visits to the young couple, during which he witnessed, with no little astonishment, Else's terrible temper outbursts. She was, he says, "beautiful, passionate, brilliantly gifted—and intractable."[21] Simson Goldberg would only have nodded ruefully in assent.

When the marriage began to fall apart, she accused Walden of having deceived her from the start. To Karl Kraus, who was at this time as much Walden's friend as hers, she fumed: "I am so furious, so furious, I have shot to smithereens every chair every table every bedboard every wardrobe chest with a pistol. There is no end to the way I was lied to, from the start."[22] The pistol was very likely a toy pistol, won in a shooting gallery at Luna Park. She spent more time than one might think at the amusement park!

But Karl Kraus was one of the few people in her lifetime with whom she risked intimacy of this kind. She knew she could trust him not to use her confidences against her.

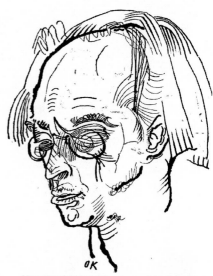

Menschenköpfe / Zeichnungen von Oskar Kokoschka
III / Herwarth Walden

Pen and ink drawing of Herwarth Walden by Oskar Kokoschka. From *Der Sturm*, volume 1, number 22, July 28, 1910 (Schiller National Museum/ Deutsches Literaturarchiv, Marbach).

In this instance, she seems not to have realized how badly her emotions had unhinged her. She was being neither fair nor honest with herself and certainly not rational.

Does it not count that she had lied to Walden? About her age, for one thing. Or had she lived with this "white lie" for so long that it would not have occurred to her?

And what about her old worry, her "fickleness?" From various remarks made over time, it would appear she took a very selective, if not self-serving, view of this failing. It was all right for *her* to become infatuated, she proclaimed. After all, she told Walden, the romance is over: "We can no longer surprise each other." And she seemed to relish "confessing" her passing "crushes" to him. In most cases these were just that: one-sided "crushes." But she could not forgive him any breach or infraction. She demanded absolute loyalty, the kind she exacted, and could only get, now that her mother was gone, from the subjects of her imaginary realms, first as Princess of Bagdad, and then as Prince of Thebes.

The year 1909 was a watershed in Else's creative life as it was in Walden's career as publicist. The meeting with Karl Kraus in June of that year resulted in the founding, the following year, of Walden's own journal, *Der Sturm*. For Else, it meant the beginning of a long and intimate friendship with one of the great polemicists and sharpest intelligences of the first half of the twentieth century. Karl Kraus, whose poisoned quill was feared by all Vienna's bourgeois presses, singled out the poetry of Else Lasker-Schüler for the highest accolades. He became her most vigorous champion. At times, he served also as her chosen confidante, as we have just seen, in matters private, as well as literary and public.

In addition to trusting him, she respected his judgment, and could listen to his criticisms because she knew they stemmed from that blend of unimpeachable intellectual rigor and deepest empathy such as she had known in her mother's home, and rarely since.

But, like God, Kraus could be implacable and inscrutable. He appeared to be ready to do anything for her, raise money, publish her poems, and assure her claim to posterity. But when she tried to enlist him in *her* chosen causes, she could meet up with stubborn resistance. He was, in all things, his own man.

There was the case of her revered friend, Johannes Holzmann, the anarchist schoolteacher, imprisoned in Russia. Else fought for his release from Russian prisons up until his death in 1914. Kraus, contrarily, refused to take up his publicist's sword for him.

From the days of the original Peter Hille circle, when she had been the object of his veneration, to the time when she came to idolize him, Holzmann had been a powerful presence in her life. Though she considered him too "pure" to allow herself any physical fantasies about him, she was hardly immune to his dark good looks.

Writing in 1909 to the English-German scholar, Jethro Bithell, whom she had never met, she talks about a *Trauerlied* (funeral ode) she has "written for a prince—he is dead or en Siberien [sic]." It is Senna Hoy (her anagrammatic coinage on Johannes Holzmann). Referring to his uncertain fate in Russia, she says that sometimes late at night she feels compelled to open the door to her house: "Senna Hoy's shadow wishes to come in."[23] This is a reference to a poem by Heine based on a Scottish ballad, Sir William Ratcliff, in which the dead man's ghost comes back to haunt the living, as in *Hamlet*.[24]

Uncanny visions and apparitions haunted her over the years, and for

Adolf Loos, Karl Kraus and Herwarth Walden around 1910. Loos (1870–1933) was the famed Viennese architect renowned as the arch-enemy of ornamental frills. He and Karl Kraus were good friends. To Kokoschka, Loos was both friend and mentor. Else Lasker-Schüler wrote of him, "Viewed from the side his head resembles the skull of a gorilla; when Loos turns to face me, the round, light-brown gorilla eyes probe me piercingly. They are dangerous, they perceive differently, from strange swift depths" ("Adolf Loos" KA 3.1 page 123f, photograph from Special Collections and Archives, W.E.B. Du Bois Library, University of Massachusetts Amherst).

the most part have a negative, unsettling effect on her. Sometimes they seem connected with a preternatural prescience about actual events.

It is curious that both her correspondence with Karl Kraus and Jethro Bithell began in the month of August 1909, actually within days of each other. To both men she makes reference, obliquely and (to Karl Kraus) not so obliquely, to her marriage difficulties. Was she trying to forge other bonds? More solid, less emotional? It would be interesting to know if she did this consciously, or merely as an instinctive survival tactic. Of course, in the case of Bithell, there was a cogent occasion. In August, Bithell, then a lecturer in German literature at the University of Manchester, was editing his little volume *Contemporary German Poetry*, which would contain nine poems by Lasker-Schüler.[24] "ELS," he wrote in his introduction, "is one flame of chaotic passion, consuming and consumed."[25]

Ecstatic as she was about being translated, and appearing (along with Frank Wedekind, Stefan Zweig, and Richard Dehmel), in an English-language anthology, her personal troubles kept breaking through the cracks.

To Bithell, she compares her tattered heart to the torn dresses of tramps that hang about their knees. She wrote to him almost every day. Mad, manic word-riots in her inimitable English: "Dear Earl of Manchester," she would begin. Or "Large Boy," or even "Dear Sire. I can't more speak englisch, all is fly out my head away. But I understand jour card something and I send 3 poems for jour Antologie. i hope jou love them."[26]

Again: "Jethro Bithell, meine Schläfen sind schon Hohlen, darin man Roulette spielt" ("My temples have become caverns in which roulette is being played").[27] "I would like to meet you, King of Manchester, but I am afraid you will be disappointed, I am so broken."[28] She says she would like to come to London, but fears "you would be ashamed of me.... Damn it all! I am in bad shape tonight—I don't want to go out on the street, but *write to you*, I will write you everything, the ocean lies between us like a rushing chasm—I am terribly frightened—no one knows how black life is and yet everyone talks about being afraid (since I have become fearful) and they roll their glass eyes like the movable eyes of dolls."[29]

So while the years 1903 to 1909 were eventful and satisfying years in her life as a literary figure, toward the end they marked the ostensible demise of her marriage and a deep bitterness and sense of betrayal within. To the outside world the couple made an effort to keep up appearances. Walden, in particular, was anxious to give the impression of "business as usual." But, as we can also see, Else was beginning to send out signals, such as her letters to Karl Kraus and Jethro Bithell, that all was not well.

CHAPTER FIVE

1910–1912: Storm Years

"Brause dein Sturmlied Du!
Und lösche meine Feuersbrunst."
("Let loose your stormsong you!
And quench my passion's rising flames.")
Else Lasker-Schüler: Dein Sturmlied

New faces were constantly arriving on the scene in Berlin. If they were artists, no matter where they came from, they gravitated to the Café des Westens. Here, the Waldens, now at separate tables, held court. Many of the newcomers were destined to become world-famous artists and writers.

One morning early in 1910, a droll and penniless young artist stepped off the train from Vienna by way of Munich, and headed straight to Walden's *Sturm* office in the Halensee. Straight, that is, after stopping off at a barber shop so as not to make too wild an impression. They had met only briefly in Vienna, and Oskar Kokoschka was not even sure if Walden would remember him. Walden's office was situated five flights up, at the opposite end of the *Kudamm* from the café, "in a house that stood out among the prosperous new buildings around it like an island of poverty...."[1]

Not only did Walden remember Kokoschka, but the two at once hit it off. Kokoschka moved into Walden's rooms behind the *Sturm* offices—the Walden couple having separated by this time—and the two men lived like starved church mice, surviving on biscuits and tea during the week, and gorging themselves on meatballs and free bread at Aschinger's on Sun-

Trier

Sturm readers, Café des Westens, 1910. Drawing by Walter Trier, Berlin (reproduced in
Willett, Expressionismus, Kindler 1970, source
unknown).

day. Meanwhile Ko-
koschka turned out
brilliant revolutionary
drawings and designs
to adorn the pages
as well as the covers
of Der Sturm for years.
Issue number 20 of
the journal is devoted
almost entirely to
Kokoschka's play Mör-
der, Hoffnung der Frauen
(Assassin, Women's Hope).
Nor did Koko-
schka escape Else's
scrutinizing gaze. She
eyed the gawky young
man with more than
casual curiosity, and confessed to seeing the young artist "as if through a
magnifying lens, a giant." Or more mysteriously: "a silent Hindu, dedicated
to his high calling. His lips are sealed."[2]

About his painting she could wax elegiac. "His princesses," she said,
were "hothouse marvels; you could count their filaments and stamen." But
beneath the human likenesses of his astonishing portraits lurks, "just thinly
veiled, an ur-animal smell."[3] She responded both to the menace and the
exaltation.

Alas, she only embarrassed and alienated him with her encomiums,
what he called her "fulsome" praise. Asked about her years later, he replied,
"Else Lasker-Schüler was a Bohemian princess who lived in the belief that
she was the prince of Thebes. Although she wrote about my pictures in fulsome terms—perhaps because of it—I never really understood her and could
never draw or paint her."[4] For the portraitist credited with a sixth sense,
this is an extraordinary admission.

Kokoschka tells of "an unforgettable trip along the Rhine with her
and Walden." This, remember, is in 1910, when the Walden couple was no
longer living together.

"We set out with a huge package of copies of Der Sturm, which they
stuffed through letterboxes along the way, to publicize the magazine.... We
must have presented a rather strange spectacle, like a circus troupe. Else Lasker-
Schüler as the Prince of Thebes in voluminous Oriental trousers, turban and
long black hair, with a cigarette in a long holder. Walden no less bohemian

than his wife, peering around sharp-eyed through his thick glasses, with his birdlike head, his great hooked nose and his long yellow hair, wearing a worn frockcoat, the inevitable stiff upright collar and pointed yellow shoes."[5]

They were roughed up by students who didn't like their weird bohemian get-up. When they got as far as Elberfeld, Else's hometown, their money gave out, and they had to return. But they had accomplished their mission and, once things were set in motion, word of the journal spread, not just in Germany, but to Paris and beyond.

If Kokoschka did not become "one of the men in her life," it was surely not because she was unreceptive. He did nonetheless exert a palpable influence on her graphic artwork.[6]

That the break-up of the Walden marriage was acrimonious we know from *her* accounts, not from Walden. Else was not emotionally prepared to be cast aside for a "blond goose," the woman Walden met while he was on a short trip in Sweden, and whom he would marry right after his divorce from Else Lasker-Schüler. The fact that the couple continued to function publicly as a team only complicated the matter. And Walden's disingenuousness created awkward situations. Once, the two made separate arrangements to meet with Franz and Maria Marc at the same café at the same time, totally oblivious of the other's plan. (See Chapter Six, "Blue Rider.")

For Walden, keeping up appearances went hand in hand with collaborating professionally with the poet Else Lasker-Schüler, a component in their relationship which continued to play a significant role in both their lives. Perhaps he felt something of the fool, after going to such lengths to keep up appearances, to be confronted in public with his lie, as in the unexpected confrontation vis à vis the Marcs, or to learn that his wife had been confiding in their mutual friend, Karl Kraus, since things had begun to go wrong. But then again, perhaps not. It might make him seem the nobler of the two. Since even good friends of both, like Alfred Döblin, were familiar with the extreme, volatile nature of Else's temperament, she would have had a hard time marshaling support in her defense. She certainly *felt* alone.

Karl Kraus, to whom she had confided, "I am so furious, so furious, ... the way I was deceived from the beginning..."[7] was sympathetic, but kept up a friendly professional relationship with Walden. The Marcs, less urbane, less cynical, went out of their way to be kind to the rejected Else.

There is a certain irony in the fact that *Der Sturm* did not begin to appear until 1910, just when the marriage was breaking up. The very first issue, in fact, must have come out within days of her letter to Kraus. Yet in its first two years of publication, *Der Sturm* printed more poems by Lasker-Schüler than by any other poet.

Moreover, Walden seems to have taken a genuine interest in her affairs, especially if he felt she was being abused by the philistine press against which he himself was forever waging war. When a Hamburg newspaper, the *Rheinisch-Westphälische Zeitung* printed—without her consent—her poem "Leise Sagen" ("Say It Softly"), with the comment, "total softening of the brain, we can hear our readers say softly,"[8] Walden urged her, against Karl Kraus's advice, to bring suit. It was, if nothing else, a breach of copyright law. The case dragged on for months, with Walden providing running commentary in the pages of *Der Sturm*. The newspaper at first prevailed. It was this incident that sparked one of her most famous essays, "Lasker-Schüler contra B. und Genossen": "Since a number of dailies have created something of a stir about my poem, 'Leise Sagen,' and declared me a mental case, a party has formed on my behalf to effect the total retraction of this dangerous contention, making legal use of every counter-indication they can muster. The result is that I am being observed not just by a psychiatrist: but by myself as well (I wish I could bill myself for my time)...."[9]

After two years of relentless agitation in the pages of *Der Sturm*, Walden succeeded in getting a verdict in her favor, and she was compensated for damages.

While her private life fell apart, her poetic gifts soared. With the composition of the poem "Ein alter Tibetteppich" ("An Old Tibetcarpet"), she set a milestone. This is the poem that Karl Kraus seized upon when he called Else Lasker-Schüler the strongest and most uncompromising lyric presence in modern Germany. He reprinted it (with permission from her and from Walden) from *Der Sturm* just three weeks after it had appeared in Walden's periodical, an unprecedented act. *Die Fackel* appeared in Vienna, *Der Sturm* in Berlin. And as Kraus had been instrumental in launching *Der Sturm*, there could be no question of impropriety or hard feelings.

"Ein alter Tibetteppich"

Deine Seele, die die meine liebet
Ist verwirkt mit ihr im Teppichtibet

Strahl in Strahl, verliebte Farben
Sterne, die sich himmellang umwarben.

Unsere Füsse ruhen auf der Kostbarkeit
Maschentausendabertausendweit.

Süsser Lamasohn auf Moschuspflanzentron
Wie lange küsst dein Mund den meinen wohl
Und Wang die Wange buntgeknüpfte Zeiten schon.[10]

"An Old Tibetcarpet"

Your soul that loves my own
Is worked in with it in the Tibetcarpet.

Strand in strand, the lovestruck colors
Stars that wooed each other sky's day long.

Our feet rest on the precious treasure
Stitch for stitch a thousand stitches wide.

Sweet Lama's son on sweet-sultan throne
How long now has your mouth been kissing mine
And cheek to cheek since color-knotted time began.

Like another great poem, Goethe's "Über allen Gipfeln ist Ruh," "Ein alter Tibetteppich" is deceptively simple (and virtually untranslatable). She might not have appreciated the comparison. "Oh, Goethe," she once quipped, "he could be awful; rhymed 'Wipfel' with Gipfel'" (like rhyming "love" with "dove"). What makes "Ein alter Tibetteppich" so remarkable, as Karl Kraus was quick to note, is the way the sounds of the words are not merely onomatopoeic but seem to be one with the meaning of the poem. We do not have to extract the figure from the carpet; the figure *is* the carpet.

In 1910, a number of poems began to appear, mostly in *Der Sturm*, which would later, in 1913, be gathered under the title *Hebräische Balladen* (*Hebrew Ballads*). Among these was "David and Jonathan," a lifelong favorite of Walter Benjamin's.[11]

"David und Jonathan"
(Mit dem Schall eines spieluhrartigen Instrumentes vorzutragen)

In der Bibel stehen wir geschrieben
Buntumschlungen.

Aber unsere Knabenspiele
Leben weiter im Stern.

Ich bin David,
Du meine Spielgefährte.

O, wir färbten
Unsere weissen Widderherzen rot.

Wie die Knospen an den Liebespsalmen
Unter Feiertagshimmel.

Deine Abschiedsaugen aber—
Immer nimmst du still im Küsse Abschied.

Und was soll dein Herz
Noch ohne meines—

Deine Süssnacht
Ohne meine Lieder.[12]

"David and Jonathan"

"And it came to pass ... that the soul of Jonathan was knit with the soul of David, and Jonathan loved him as his own soul."—I Samuel 18

(To be recited to music-box tones)

In the Holy Book our names are knit together
With brightly-colored threads.

Still our boyish games
Live on in the star.

I am David,
You my playmate.

O, we dyed
Our white rams' hearts red.

Like the buds on the lovepsalms
Under Sabbath skies.

But, o, your parting gaze—
You go and go again in silence with a kiss.

And how shall your heart fare
Without my own—

Your sweetnight
Without my songs.

The year 1910 was very busy for the poet on the poetry reading circuit and in cabaret. On one occasion she shared the podium with the brilliant young poet Georg Heym; on another, she was billed together with Karl Kraus, and his architect friend, Adolf Loos, as well as with Alfred Döblin, and Herwarth Walden. And wherever she went, she created a *furore*.

In March she wrote to Max Brod, trying to cajole him into joining her in what she envisaged as her Oriental act:

Dear Prince of Prague.... If you promise not to tell anyone, I will explain my plan to you, and if you want to carry it out with me, then either I can come to Prague or you can come here, Abba, and we'll rehearse together. I speak Syrian. After all, I've spent half my life in Asia, I've translated my works, which are set in Asia and Africa, into Syrian. I want to come on as a Syrian, with my magnificent nose-ring and fabulous cummerbund. Then, after I've read my "Fakir," I'll play on my bagpipes, blow my great-grandfather—the sheik's—trumpet, play the flute and beat the drums. But I have to have someone to translate as I go along—into French— Then on to London.... But I don't know if you'll want to do this, being yourself a poet, my dear prince....[13]

That she was altogether serious about this venture is evident from other letters written during this period. She describes the plan, with all its bizarre features, to Jethro Bithell, saying this time that René Schickele, the close friend of Rilke, was translating her "Syrian" poems into French, and that she had found a terrific dancer to accompany her. As there is no account of this particular extravaganza having actually taken place, perhaps one of her more prudent friends talked her out of it. Of course, she was quite capable of running the whole show on her own. Her manuscripts are full of markings for pauses and stresses. In her letter to Brod, she claimed that an English professor had already translated the pieces into English, undoubtedly meaning Bithell himself, which may well have been the case.

There are many reports of such "performances." She frequently tried to enlist friends as "extras" of one sort or another. The stage designer, Teo Otto, describes a reading she gave many years later in Zurich:

The whole thing had very little to do with a poetry reading in the usual sense. It was "absurd theatre" before its time. She began by building up a lectern for herself, taking a fat book, putting a cigar box on top of it, and laying the book she would read from on top of that. Then she realized she had forgotten something, snapped open her handbag, rummaged around in it till she came up with a dog collar to which was attached a small bell. That was especially important to her. Only the candle was lacking now. While she searched for the candle, the thing she had rigged up on the lectern collapsed. We [the actors Kurt Horwitz, Ernst Ginsberg, and himself] were all prepared to run up to help her, but we were secretly hoping she hadn't noticed us, because she had asked us to sing out with her when she came to the line, "Was kommt dort von der Höh?" ["What's coming from up there?"], in the poem, "Methusaleh"—and we hoped she had forgotten. Her manner of reading was very strange. She underlaid the poems with a unique set of sound effects.... For the poem, "Joseph is Sold," her Caravan Ballad,[14] she took the dog collar, and made the little bell tinkle as if it were a caravan going through the desert.... Then she hummed, "Aha ha aha ha," sounded the bell again, and drew out the tones....[15]

Even when she was not performing, she was performing, taking her friends "for a ride." Tilla Durieux was one of Max Reinhardt's most beautiful and gifted actresses. She married Paul Cassirer, who would become Else Lasker-Schüler's publisher in 1919. In her memoir *Ein Tür steht Offen,* Durieux writes:

> One day Else expressed the wish to get to know Berlin's highlife nightlife. She was at this time already separated from her husband and had become quite adventurous. She now wanted to be taken to the more classy nightclubs to see what they were like. As she kept stressing how important it was for this to be a truly elegant occasion, we put on evening dress, and were therefore no little taken aback when she showed up wearing a long red peasant blouse. On her head she wore a Turkish fez. A plaid blanket was thrown over her shoulder, and in her hand she carried a small overnight bag. I was ready to turn back, but she explained that she wanted to go as an "exotic traveler," and that she wouldn't speak German, this despite the fact that it was the only language she knew.
>
> Paul Cassirer, at first somewhat perplexed, put on an amused grin, and off we went, with our Traveler, who only spoke to us in whispers, and otherwise used words like "Gurri-murri, schnarri-darri." In this manner we went the rounds of all the well-known nightclubs, much to the amusement of both guests and waiters. And Else was delighted, completely convinced that she had been taken for "the stranger of distinction"....[16]

How to explain this all-consuming fascination with Orientalism that began with her taking on the persona of Tino of Baghdad? Was it part of a Jewish sub-culture that sought its roots in what she called the "wild Jews" of the Old Testament? Was it her way of distancing herself from the perceived philistinism of "modern" (diaspora) Jews?[17] Or was her Orientalism part of a broader fascination with the mysterious East that was already flourishing at the end of the 19th century, and held her non–Jewish peers and contemporaries—Oscar Wilde, Victor Hugo, Ruth St. Denis et al. (see Chapter Four)—in its thrall?[18] Given the kind of tinsel Byzantium she adored, this seems more likely. In any event, in the years up to World War I, Oriental exoticism came more and more to take over her life, her legend and her work.

Sometimes it seems as though not a day went by but that one of the circle of bohemian friends was getting embroiled in some private or public battle. Most of the drama was enacted at one or the other of the cafés. The respective periodicals lost no time picking up the torch (*Die Fackel*). Café des Westens was the first to get the name "Café Megalomania." But others soon acquired or boasted the dubious distinction.

Litigiousness ran rampant. Nor was physical assault uncommon. Even so wincing an aesthete as Karl Kraus could turn around and punch someone in the nose if provoked.

Some battles were carried on, or carried out, primarily if not exclusively in print. But just how universally the café and the periodical were perceived as a single entity can be seen from a cartoon in an early issue of *Der Sturm*, in which a feisty woman with a cigarette hanging out of the corner of her mouth sits at the round café table, between two arty-looking men, one feverishly scribbling away, the other engrossed in his copy—or the café's copy—of *Der Sturm*.

In the spring of 1911, Else Lasker-Schüler spent some time in Munich, going to her beloved cabaret, the Simpl (short for Simplicissimus), and to the two bohemian café hangouts, Café Bauer and Café Stefanie. She was often in the company of the well-known Berlin feminist Eliza Ichenhaeuser, and together they went one evening to the Simpl. There they ran into the anarchist writer Erich Mühsam.[19] Mühsam was infatuated at this time with the young, beautiful and outrageous Emmy Hennings,[20] who was performing that night at the Simpl.

Following the first of the "Commandments of Cabaret Life," posted at the Simpl, Else and Eliza arrived late and presumably sat down noisily. The seventh commandment read, "If you're a woman, then criticize the dress of the performing *artiste* loudly and smartly." Here, too, Else did not lose a beat. But just the sight of Else Lasker-Schüler was enough to make Emmy hysterical. Complaining to Mühsam that "that jealous megaera" had insulted her in Berlin, calling her a whore and threatening to throw vitriol in her face, she said she could not perform with "that woman" in the room. Insults between the two women flew back and forth, and despite Mühsam's efforts to placate them, the whole affair got totally out of hand. Else complained to Mühsam, calling Emmy a sex-mad seamstress, in whose mouth the *majesty* of her name had no place. Unfortunately, as Mühsam wryly remarked, Emmy was not the tamest either. She tried to forbid Lasker-Schüler to attend performances at the Simpl. When this didn't work, she arranged for a telegram to be delivered to Lasker-Schüler at the Café Bauer, telling her she was urgently needed at home. After a reassuring phone call home, Else wrote to Karl Kraus, "'Something is rotten in the state of Denmark.'"[21] The whole affair had escalated, in Mühsam's words, "into a comic grotesque."[22]

One should not underestimate the importance for Else of being treated deferentially—as an artist, a genius, and a princess. Or, from this time forward, prince. She did not suffer slights lightly, especially after the humiliation of her divorce. Writing in 1925 about the period in her life after her separation from Walden, she says, "In der Nacht meiner tiefsten Not erhob ich mich zum Prinzen von Theben" ("In the night of my deepest despair I raised myself to the rank of prince, Prince of Thebes").[23] The underlining of the word "majesty" in her letter to Mühsam is revealing. The year 1912 saw the official end of the Walden-Lasker marriage, and Walden's marriage to the "blond goose," Nell Roslund.

In 1912, the *Briefe nach Norwegen* (*Letters to Norway*), originally serialized in *Der Sturm*, came out as an epistolary novel, *Mein Herz* (*My Heart*). Unlike her previous works in fiction, all of which, we may recall, were highly fantastic, exoticized versions of events, *Mein Herz* sticks very close to actual events. Painfully so. In fact, Karl Kraus criticized the book for failing to transmute the biographical material into the stuff of fiction.

On the surface it is a jaunty romp through her solitary weeks in Berlin, while Walden is up north being entertained by friends and meeting his future wife, weeks spent mostly at the café, chronicling the usual wild goings-on there, including, for all the world to read, her fatal infatuation with the young medical intern and poet, Gottfried Benn. "I'd like to be a gray-velvet mole and toss up a storm in his armpit and burrow there ... a mosquito playing in front of his face ... a bee, then I'd buzz around his navel. Long before I met him I read him—his Morgue poems lay on my bed: horrific masterpieces, dreams of death ... cemeteries wander into hospital sickrooms and plant themselves before the beds of the suffering.... His every line a leopard's bite...."[24]

Beneath the surface of her high-spirited café *klatsch* (gossip-mongering), just barely disguised, lay the pain of the break-up of her marriage to Walden and her implacable jealousy and hatred of the "blond goose."

It is difficult, even at this remove, not to sympathize with Else in her dislike for Nell Roslund, a pretentious woman, very uppercrust, who boasted of the soirées and teas she gave while she was married to Walden, which furthered his career as gallery-owner and impresario. She herself, she confesses, had had no background "in the arts." Decades after the break-up of her own marriage with Walden, Roslund still needed to justify her role in "rescuing" Walden from his marriage to the mad, "opium-addicted" Else. She claims Walden was afraid Else would attack her, Nell, physically. Nell, of course, discounted his fears, yet wrote,

> But soon thereafter, I had to concede his fear was justified. One morning, it was in the winter of 1913, having some matters to attend to in my modest household, I came in late to the office—and happily so for me. There I found a weeping, frightened secretary, and Walden, white in the face, trying to calm her. He said Else Lasker-Schüler had stormed into the office, where the secretary, who happened to be blond like myself, sat at the typewriter. Lasker had pulled a revolver out of her pocket, when Herwarth, alarmed

by the clamor, and Else's voice, came in, just in time to knock the weapon out of the raging madwoman's hand. He brought her home, still ranting and raving. By the time I got in, he was back. Else Lasker-Schüler had heard that Walden had married a blond Swede; she assumed that it was me in the office.[25]

Else may have been impulsive and slapped the faces of people she could not stomach (she once slapped a publisher in the face, in the foyer of the theater, and said of it, "I felt an archangel was guiding my hand..."[26]), but it seems highly unlikely that she would have come to the office in the Potsdamerstrasse, armed with a real gun, with the intention of shooting Nell. And why does Nell feel obliged to tell this story? Merely to show the terrible consequences of Lasker's unfortunate—addiction? No value judgment intended, of course. Just an explanation, if one were required, of Walden's leaving Else for Nell. This *idée fixe* persists. When Nell, the well-behaved, well-coiffed, gentile lady, saw Else Lasker-Schüler on the street in Ascona, after Lasker's emigration to Switzerland, she said of her, "A bent, old woman who looked as though she had been scooped out like a gourd. Her addiction had undoubtedly made a wizened witch of her before her time."[27] Her addiction, of course. Goebbels would have thanked Frau Roslund-Walden.

And Else would have seen right through the hypocrisy, the self-deception of Nell's claim that she and Herwarth had to avoid the café out of fear of her, especially as Nell prided herself on making home such a cozy place for Walden that they hardly ever went to the café, whereas the undomestic Lasker-Schüler had forced him to spend most of the years of their marriage there. If Else was jealous of Nell, Nell was equally so of her.

Into the emotional vacuum that followed the divorce, a vacuum that felt to her like an abyss, stepped the eponymous "Giselheer, the Barbarian"—Dr. Gottfried Benn. He had just published his first volume of poems, *Morgue*, and was still an intern, when he began to frequent the Café des Westens, where Else Lasker-Schüler presided over her table of "regulars."

⚜ ⚜ ⚜ ⚜ ⚜

CHAPTER SIX

⚜ ⚜ ⚜ ⚜ ⚜

Blue Rider

> *"Nie sah ich irgendeinen Maler gotternster und sanfter malen wie ihn. 'Zitronenochse' und 'Feuerbuffel' nannte er seine Tiere..."*
> ("Never have I seen a painter paint with such divine earnestness and gentleness. 'Lemon -oxen' and 'fire-buffaloes,' he called his animals....")
> —Else Lasker-Schüler: An Franz Marc

At about the same time that she drew the young Gottfried Benn into her orbit at the café, Else Lasker-Schüler made the acquaintance of Franz Marc, a Bavarian painter and founding member of Der blaue Reiter (The Blue Rider), a Munich-based Expressionist group of artists.

Had the paths of the painter-poet Franz Marc and the poet-painter Else Lasker-Schüler not crossed when and as they did, the history of twentieth-century art and letters would not be quite the same—not that either influenced the other in their chosen medium, but the way their artistic sensibilities acted on each other was profound and, in its way, unique.

The years 1910 to 1913 marked the flowering of the Expressionist poem and the Expressionist painting. In Munich, the group around Kandinsky and Franz Marc known as the Blaue Reiter formed the center of avant-garde activity, in a movement marked as much by its idealistic theories and its bold ventures into "total art" as by its Expressionist mode. The brief period is remarkable for the number and quality of theatrical and musical compositions staged, composed, and with librettos, by one and the same per-

78

son, or by artists working so closely together as to be almost one creative spirit. Into this framework, Else Lasker-Schüler, with her multi-faceted talents, fit perfectly.

In Berlin, the new art forms found a lively forum in the pages of Walden's periodical. Started on a shoestring, *Der Sturm* was destined to become *the* Expressionist journal for serious literary and artistic endeavor.

Two years after its founding, Herwarth Walden, whose eye for art was at least as fine as his ear for music and poetry, opened a gallery next door to the periodical offices. Its opening exhibition in March 1912 featured works by the Blaue Reiter group and Kokoschka. Whether it was his eye for great works of art, or as Paul Klee maintained, "a good nose for smelling them out" ("there's something wrong. He doesn't really care for the pictures. He just has a good nose for smelling them out,"[2]) his instinct was infallible. Like the periodical, the gallery soon became the most coveted venue for aspiring young artists.

The *Sturm* gallery attracted avant-garde artists not just from Berlin, but from all over, including Eastern Europe and Russia. Futurists and cubists, along with Expressionists, soon exhibited there.

Franz Marc, who lived far removed from the hustle and bustle of Berlin, in a tiny Bavarian village called Sindelsdorf, was "a portrait painter of animals." He felt his way into their interior lives with intense, visionary empathy, which is not to say that he and his circle of artist friends were oblivious to the drawing power of the Metropolis for their careers. Marc was among those who had exhibited at the opening *Sturm* exhibition in March. In December he was planning a visit to Berlin with his wife, Maria.

Marc had read Lasker-Schüler's poem "Versöhnung" in an early issue of *Der Sturm*, as well as in her collection *Meine Wunder* and had been so moved by it that he had attempted to capture the spirit of the poem in a woodcut.

"Versöhnung" (for which one possible translation is "Reconciliation,") happens also to refer to the Jewish Day of Atonement, Yom Kippur. It is a day on which one asks forgiveness, not just of God, but of anyone to whom one has, knowingly or not, given offense. The holiday also happens to occur in September, the month of the poem's second printing in *Der Sturm*.

"Versöhnung"
Es wird ein grosser Stern in meinen Schoss fallen...
Wir wollen wachen die Nacht,

In den Sprachen beten,
Die wie Harfen eingeschnitten sind.

Wir wollen uns versöhnen die Nacht—
So viel Gott strömt über.

Kinder sind unsere Herzen
Die möchten ruhen müdesüss.

Und unsere Lippen wollen sich küssen,
Was zagst du?

Grenzt nicht mein Herz an deins—
Immer färbt dein Blut meine Wangen rot.

Wir wollen uns versöhnen die Nacht,
Wenn wir uns herzen, sterben wir nicht.

Es wird ein grosser Stern in meinen Schoss fallen.[3]

"Reconciliation"

A great star will fall into my lap.
Let us keep watch through the night,

Pray in tongues whose letters
Are carved like harps.

Let us make up tonight—
So much of God spills over.

Our hearts are children
Non-nodding with sleep.

And our lips long to kiss.
What holds you back?

Does not my heart border on yours?
It's your blood colors my cheeks red.

Let us make up tonight—
If we hold close, we won't die.

A great star will fall into my lap.

In the summer of 1912, Walden had asked Marc if he would send him some woodcuts for *Der Sturm*, and in response, Marc sent him one he had made for "Versöhnung." He sent it off at once, and in September the poem appeared for a second time in *Der Sturm*, this time alongside the woodcut.

Marc's woodcut depicts a female figure praying, and a dog, whose head is bowed as if also in prayer. Strong lines define the shapes and figures that round out the composition which suggests a wheel with spokes, or rays of light.

Deeply touched by this evocation, Frau Lasker-Schüler had written to

Franz Marc's 1912 woodcut "Versöhnung" for the poem by Else Lasker-Schüler of that title. On the cover of *Der Sturm*, September 1912. 20 × 25 cm (Schiller-Nationalmuseum/Deutsches Literaturarchiv, Marbach).

Marc on the ninth of November, expressing her gratitude for his wonderful rendering of her vision. The letter addresses him as "Most worthy Painter" and says she would like to visit him when she comes to Munich. It is decorated in her customary fashion with drawings and calligraphic embellishments. She asks, "What made you chose 'Versöhnung' to illustrate? Are you too so woefully lost as I am, that I have no path left only the abyss."[4] It signs off, "the impoverished / Prince of Thebes" [comet drawing] (Else Lasker-Schüler). Below the signature there is a drawing of a city with palms and crescent moon with the caption "Thebes (old Temple area)."

On November 1 the divorce between Lasker-Schüler and Walden became official. Later that month he married Nell Roslund. Lasker was ill with a high fever during this entire time.

It was in these weeks of illness that she sent off a second letter to

Franz Marc, disclaiming the first as a forgery and demanding that he send her the letter with her alleged signature. Twice before, she writes, some evil person has written letters in her name, and forged her signature. Then she goes on: What poem? What woodcut? Why, she doesn't even subscribe to *Der Sturm*! What's more, she has forbidden its editor (Herwarth Walden!) to print anything of hers or so much as mention her name. Finally: "Ich kenne nur **zwei** *Gemälde?* von Ihnen gelbe Kuh, blaue Reiter" ("I know only *two* paintings of yours yellow cow,[5] blue rider")....[6]

Such sudden, seemingly inexplicable reversals were something she was notorious for among her friends. Frequently she reacted to an imagined insult or threat and would make an abrupt about-face. And sometimes, as with Emmy Hennings's spurious telegram calling Lasker back to Berlin so she would be rid of her, she had reason to be suspicious. In this instance, given her distraught state of mind in these weeks, it is also conceivable that she had simply blanked out on what had come before with regard to the poem and the woodcut.

Marc was thirty-two years old, and was just becoming recognized as a painter. After years of emotional turbulence and a disastrous liaison of his own, he was at last to be married to the steady, caring Maria Franck. He was looking forward to meeting with Walden in Berlin. It was important that he take on the challenge of the metropolis, "the demons of the city." Walden, for his part, thought very highly of Marc's painting, and was eager to gain him for his new stable of gallery racehorses.

Despite Walden's attempts to make the divorce sound civilized and friendly, it was anything but that. Walden even paraded his new young wife-to-be at Lasker's uncontested stomping grounds, the Café des Westens, as well as at Café Josty. Else's sense of humiliation, added to her proverbial dread of being abandoned, must have been nearly intolerable.

Although Franz Marc could not know the source or take the full measure of her grief until he came in person to Berlin, he must have intuited her distress when he received that strange follow-up letter. In a "Versöhnungs" gesture truly worthy of her poem's Biblical resonance, and tactfully ignoring her rebuttal, he wrote a second time, just before he was to leave for Berlin. This time he reached for a blank postcard, and on the back, made a pen and ink drawing, "Der Blaue Reiter mit seinem Pferd" ("The Blue Rider with His Horse"). The verbal message was brief: "The Blue Rider presents his Blue Horse to Your Majesty. Greetings from my wife. Yours, Franz Marc."[7] Not a word about the woodcut, the poem, or the *Sturm*.

The ploy worked. The gauche charm of the drawing, the mock-ceremonial tone of the message totally won her heart.

This time, when the beautiful painted postcard arrived, Lasker replied at once, sending her letter to the Berliner *pension* where Marc was staying with Maria in anticipation of his meeting with Walden.

Picking up on his signature appellation, "Der blaue Reiter," she had determined what she would call him, and *only him*, henceforth. This, despite the fact that common parlance had already established the designation "Blaue Reiter" for the group (of which he and Wassily Kandinsky were joint founding members). Casting Marc alone as the Blue Rider was definitely an affront to Kandinsky.

But Lasker couldn't stand Kandinsky. She thought him a prig, and would always refer to him, even in direct address, as "Professor." The badge of "artist" she would not grant him. Her dislike for Kandinsky extended to his predilection for Bavarian glass paintings, which hung in great profusion in his home, and which he reproduced in all their maudlin naiveté in the *Blaue Reiter Almanac.* How right she was in her feeling about Kandinsky's proclivities time would show.

No, for her the Blaue Reiter would always and only be Franz Marc. In her epistolary novel *Der Malik,* she makes him her Biblical half-brother, Ruben, a conceit which conceivably had its genesis in Marc's actual Jewish ancestry (he was part French Calvinist, part Jewish).

When the Marcs arrived at the Café Josty for their scheduled meeting with Walden, and by separate arrangement, with Lasker, they were surprised to find the couple seated at separate tables. The Café Josty was in the Potsdamerstrasse, near where Else had moved in early September. It happened that she, too, had asked to meet the Marcs at the Josty, ignorant of the fact that they were to meet there with Walden at the same time. For the Marcs, this arrangement, to meet both of them there, seemed altogether natural. They knew nothing of any discord. This was part of Walden's public relations policy.

When they arrived, they were altogether perplexed. With Walden was his new bride, Nell Roslund, the "blond goose." It was a moment of great embarrassment and consternation for everyone, and for Else, of great pain. Franz Marc, learning the truth regarding the state of the marriage, and hearing Else's version of events, was at a loss.

Seeing how run down and sick she was, the Marcs invited Lasker-Schüler to take the train with them back to Sindelsdorf and spend a few weeks recovering in the Bavarian countryside. But the quiet did not agree with her. The wide open spaces, which the Marcs thought would be a balm to her troubled spirit, only unhinged her more.

She could not have been an easy guest to have. Did she, one wonders, insist on sleeping in a reclining chair, which was her wont at home? Did she keep them up all night talking, or reading from her poems? All her life

"Virgin Welcoming the Descent of the Holy Ghost." Upper Bavaria, first half of the nineteenth century. Watercolors and oils and gold. Painting on glass. 28.5 × 22.6 cm (courtesy Heimatmuseum Ober-ammergau Inv. nr. 269). Murnau, on Lake Staffel, was a center of this cottage industry. Kandinsky and Gabriele Münter lived in Mur-nau and bought great quantities of these paintings which then hung all over their apartment. Kandinsky reproduced eleven such in the first *Blaue Reiter Catalog*, and for a time the style and vivid colors of these paintings were an important influence on some members of the group.

she dreaded being alone at night. This was true of her up into old age. In Berlin, she went out to the café. In Jerusalem, Schalom Ben Chorin tells how he visited her the day she arrived, and how, when night came, she beseeched him not to leave her. One can get a sense of what it must have been like for the Marcs from Franz's cryptic P.S. to Maria's letter to their close friends, August and Elizabeth Macke: "If August is putting on weight again and becoming too complacent in his ways, you might prescribe a fortnight of Else Lasker-Schüler for him—that should do it. But all joking aside, she is a prodigious person."[8] (See Appendix 5, pages 189–191 for full text of letter in translation.)

After two weeks of restless stirrings at Sindelsdorf, she went to Munich for a brief *kur*. Here she remained till the beginning of February when she returned to Berlin. When the Marcs visited her in Munich (she had rented a room in the Pension Modern), they found her at a table engaged in a furious battle with tin soldiers.[9]

She appreciated the Marcs' many kindnesses. They introduced her to their friends and fellow artists of the Blaue Reiter: Jawlensky, Marianna von Werefkin, Kandinsky, and Gabriele Münter. While she could not wait to get home, she came away feeling a strengthened bond, a need to reach out and draw Marc deeper into her private fantasy world.

When she was back in Berlin, she wrote

> My dear, dear, dear, dear Blue Rider Franz Marc. You ask how I found everything when I got home. Through my dormer window, I can reach out into the night and touch a little black sheep, one that the moon watches over; if I had such a playmate then I wouldn't be so alone. My hole in the wall is actually a corridor, a narrow *allée* without trees. I own roughly 50 birds. True, they live outside, but in the morning they all sit outside my window and wait for me to feed them. Let anyone say anything against the birds! They are the highest beings, they live between God and the air, we live between earth and the grave. My hole in the wall is a long and scary coffin. I am terrified every night to lie down in my coffin. For weeks now I have been taking opium, then the rats become roses, and in the morning the tiny colored sun motes fly around like angels in my coffin space and dance across the floor, dance over my shroud, painting it all kinds of colors. O I am weary and sick of life.... All my garlands hang down in shreds from my heart....[10]

But if this first letter dramatizes her depression, the second is quick to make amends. In fact she chides herself for having written such a melancholy epistle. In the interim, two things have raised her spirits. First, her book, *Mein Herz*, has hit the bookstores and is being advertised everywhere. Second, she has started taking a new medication for her nerves, something called Neura-Lezithin, "the original, the one with the rhino head in the ring," so that whenever she hesitates in conversation, or begins to stammer, "the rhinoceros brain steps in and responds for [her] with astonishing, not to say alarming, good sense..." with the result that editors no longer dismiss her as a raving maniac, denying her assignments, nor will "Herr X be able to write about my screaming hysterically in the café, something he anyway picked up from vicious sources...." The letter skips and jumps ahead, savoring Marc's latest postcard drawings, his little sheep in a meadow, in all their exquisite detail. "If I were a hurdy-gurdy, and a cripple did the cranking, he would grow limbs from the sheer joy of the dance. And I'd like to turn a somersault, Blue Franz, because we say Du, and not Sie to each other...." Another drawing, King Jussuf's "Three Panthers," evokes these reflections: "Over all animals the wildcats are sovereign. The panther is a wild gentian, the lion a dangerous delphinium, the tigress a furious glistening yellow maple. But your beatific blue horses[11] are so many neighing archangels and they gallop right into paradise, and your llamas and does and calves recline in consecrated groves. Your pastoral creatures smell of milk. You raise them yourself on cream.[12]

What strikes one reading—and seeing—the letters and drawings of their correspondence is the way the amazing criss-cross of their talents was furthered by the exchange. We know that Lasker-Schüler supported herself over long stretches with her artwork; we may be less aware of Marc's literary ambitions and his considerable gifts in expressing himself forcefully in verbal images. Marc had studied philology before becoming a painter, was an avid reader, and wrote beautiful letters, notably, the *Briefe aus dem Feld* (*Letters from the Front*) to his wife Maria (and to his mother) from 1914 to 1916. These letters and postcards encouraged each to stray further beyond the borders of their chosen medium into new unexplored territories on the other side.

The Marc–Lasker-Schüler correspondence had another curious double character. On the one hand it was a spontaneous and intimate outpouring of emotion, for Else, in particular; at the same time, it was a conscious literary and artistic endeavor. She managed this sleight-of-hand with great finesse. It was a gift she utilized in her poetry too: she could be simultaneously passionate and cold, inside and out, often with a self-ironizing gallows humor that left the listener stunned. In one of her most intimate letters to Marc, one intended, notwithstanding, for publication, she wrote of her hopeless passion for Gottfried Benn, to whom she had given the nickname "Giselheer." Giselheer, the Barbarian. He had been quick to jilt her and she wrote to Marc: "If he could see me like this, he would love me, he likes everything that's dead...."

She could also wring things out of her unhappiness that were designed to make people laugh. In this same letter to Marc, she makes up an imaginary exchange between herself and Dr. Benn (Benn was a gynecologist and dermatologist as well as the "Morgue" poet), as if she were a patient of the doctor's and had consulted him for a cure for her lovesickness. He tells her that the hole in her heart could be repaired with a single stitch. (Benn could be very cruel; he was not one to mince words.) She goes on with her report, saying she has great confidence in the doctor's medical opinions: "He maintained that I had invested Giselheer with my personal fantasies, that I barely knew him.... When I think how he drew a line under my coat as if I were a doll with patent leather shoes—If my City [her Thebes] were to learn of all this (the *humiliation*), my honorable paschas, my ministers and my trusting people—I could never become kaiser."[13] In another letter to Marc she complains, "People are forever sticking potatoes on the prongs of my crown."[14]

By assigning fictitious roles to her friends and lovers, and to herself, she could exercise control over her universe, and take on the demons of an unruly existence. In the same way, she would wage mock battles with tin soldiers.

It is hard to believe she was not physically attracted to Marc, whose erotic appeal all but leaps out of every photograph of him from this period: he was tall, dark, with a striking aquiline profile, and beautiful sensitive eyes that stared out at the world with an animal shyness. Yet she seems to have made a point of not acknowledging any attraction she may have felt. Undoubtedly she sensed from the start the close bond between him and Maria. She was always careful to include Maria in her greetings when she wrote to him. And when she writes, "I kiss you," she is quick to add, "your hand." Maria was not insensitive, however, and doubted the sincerity of Lasker-Schüler's "love" for herself. The relationship would make her increasingly uncomfortable over time.

In a letter of September 1913, Lasker-Schüler felt obliged to correct an impression she feared to have given of herself as a *sexueller Mensch*, protesting they don't really know her, that her feelings lie "much deeper." Whether this will have reassured Maria is doubtful.[15]

On the sixth of August, 1914, Franz Marc went off to war. She wrote him such ardent letters that his wife grew nervous. She even tried to cross the border into France to visit him! And she sent him little knick-knacks which she mistakenly thought would cheer him: a little glass dog, a music-box, and bonbons, "which I hate." At Christmastime she sent a miniature Christmas tree and a blue, N.B. blue, table-runner.

On the face of it, nothing could seem more unlikely than the friendship between Franz Marc and Else Lasker-Schüler. Their outward lives could not have been more different. Whereas Lasker-Schüler had gravitated toward a totally unordered bohemian existence in the big city, spending her days at the café, Marc, with his wife Maria, lived out a bucolic idyll in a tiny Bavarian *Dorf*. But both inhabited fantasy worlds, realms that each could enter and enhance, to the enrichment of both. And both possessed talent in the other's chosen craft.

The Blue Rider correspondence lets us follow the steps in the process of mutual nourishment, while making clear that each followed the natural line of his own development. During the entire time she corresponded with Marc, Lasker's drawings show less stylistic similarities to Marc than to Kokoschka, Kirchner and Klimt.[16] Marc's own drawings would evolve, over the course of their correspondence, into ever more abstract cubist color symphonies.[17]

The way the cross-fertilization did work was remarked upon already in 1913 by Klabund: "The art of Else Lasker-Schüler is closely related to that of her friend, the Blue Rider, Franz Marc. All her thoughts have wondrous colors and slink about like painted animals. Sometimes they step out of the woods into a clearing like shy red deer."[18]

Marc's second postcard to Else Lasker-Schüler is the original (and only surviving) draught of "Der Turm der blauen Pferde" ("The Tower of the Blue Horses")[19, 20] A detail hardly ever remarked on are the small stars and crescent moons on the heads and bodies of the horses. These were the personal emblems of Else Lasker-Schüler, emblems with which she adorned her face and garments in her myriad self-portraits as Jussuf (as in her postcard drawing of 1 November, 1913). The inclusion of these in Marc's painting are like a secret hieroglyph and show how deeply and reverently he had entered her spiritual world.

Her poem "Gebet," written after Marc's death, is dedicated to him, as is her epistolary novel of 1919, *Der Malik*, set in her imaginary Thebes. Lasker had always harbored very strong anti-war feelings. These come out with passion in *Der Malik*, especially at the end, when the great warrior Ruben is killed in battle and Jussuff kills himself for grief. In *Der Malik*, Ruben is Marc, Jussuff's half-brother.

In April 1914, Marc wrote his last postcard greeting to Else Lasker-Schüler before he was inducted into the army and sent to the front in August. The correspondence from then on was sporadic, and subject to Marc's increasing sense of distance to the poet.

On March 4, 1916, Marc wrote home from Verdun: "L. (Dearest), just think: ... yes, this year I will be coming home to my undefiled home, to

"Der Turm der blauen Pferde" ("The Tower of the Blue Horses").
Franz Marc's New Year's greeting for Else Lasker-Schüler, 1913. Watercolor and gouache, painted on a postcard. 14.3 × 9.4 cm (Bayerische
Staatsgemäldesammlungen). The postcard is the only surviving draft
in color of Marc's famous painting, "The Tower of the Blue Horses."
The painting, which was once in the Nationalgalerie Berlin, is considered lost since the end of the Second World War.

you and to my work. Amidst all the boundless images of horror and destruction among which I now live, this thought of homecoming has a kind of halo around it. Keep these for me, my home and yourself, your soul and your body and all that is mine, and belongs to me...."[21]

That same afternoon, at the foot of a hill near Verdun, Franz Marc, a cavalry officer in the Bavarian Battalion and Field Artillery Regiment, rode off on his tall horse to reconnoiter a hidden path for the transport of ammunition. In less than twenty minutes his faithful horse returned riderless, covered with blood.

On March 9 in the morning edition of the *Berliner Tageblatt*, a piece appeared by Lasker-Schüler commemorating the Blue Rider in a prose epitaph and short poem. "The Blue Rider has fallen," it began, "a great Biblical figure, on whose shoulder hung the scent of Eden." (See Appendix 6, pages 191–192 for the full text.)

At one time Else Lasker-Schüler hoped to publish the whole Blue Rider correspondence, complete with both their drawings, a hope that was never realized during her lifetime. One offer she rejected out of hand, so ignominious were the conditions. For the editors of the periodical *März*, the artistic ideology of the "Blaue Reiter" school was so odious, they would only agree to publish the letters if the name Franz Marc was omitted. Needless to say, Lasker-Schüler would not even consider this.

The fate of the cards and letters over the decades is a checkered one, and reflects both personal and historical vicissitudes.

In 1919, three years after Marc's death, at a time when Lasker-Schüler's finances were being more than usually strained by the illness of her son, she saw no other way out of her debts than to offer the cards for sale to the Berlin Nationalgalerie. So in 1919, the director of the National Gallery of the "Staatliche Museen zu Berlin," Ludwig Justi, acquired the entire collection of Franz Marc's cards, 28 in number, and in 1920, 23 of the Lasker-Schüler drawings.

It was not long, however, before she came to regret her action. When she tried, in 1921, to buy them back, claiming that she had had no right to sell Marc's drawings in the first place, as they were left to her son as well as to herself in Marc's will, and adding that if she had found a single human being who would have lent her the money to help pay her son's doctor's bills, she would never even have considered selling them. She claimed further that there had been 29 cards, and one of them was now missing! Getting nowhere with her appeals, she asked a lawyer to represent her. Neither this nor the earnest intervention of a friend, Elfriede Caro,[22] who said Else Lasker-Schüler was so upset over the matter that it was to be feared she would kill herself, was to any avail. "The picture-card drawings of Franz Marc, acquired through purchase from Frau Else Lasker-Schüler, have entered the possession of the state, and can therefore not be returned."[23]

In 1937, the works of both artists came under the designation "Degenerate," and accordingly were confiscated by the Nazis.

Then, in 1939, a painter-collector couple, Sophie and Emanuel Fohn, in a serendipitous coup that involved an exchange with the Nazis for some German Romantic paintings, managed to acquire 22 of the Marc postcards and six of the Lasker drawings. With this exchange, the collection was salvaged. In 1965 the Fohns bequeathed their holding to the Bavarian Staatsgemäldesammlungen, with the proviso that the works never be loaned, removed, or even moved, from their permanent place in the museum.

The remaining six drawings by Marc and seven by Lasker-Schüler had been returned after 1945 to the National Gallery in Berlin, part of the then–DDR.[24]

An exhibition of the entire exchange, postcards, letters, and drawings took place for the first time in 1987, in the Staatsgalerie moderner Kunst, Munich. It was curated by Peter-Klaus Schuster, who also edited the accompanying catalogue, published by Prestel Verlag. Unlike so many sagas of confiscated artworks that have recently come to light, this story has had a happy ending.

CHAPTER SEVEN

Café Megalomania.
The Pauper Prince

"Der hehre König Giselheer
Stiess mit seinem Lanzenspeer
Mitten in mein Herz."
(*"The great king Giselheer*
Thurst his steely spear
Straight into my heart.")
        Else Lasker-Schüler: Gottfried Benn

No matter how often or how vehemently the poet protested that she was fed up with the café, she was always quick to add that of course this didn't mean she intended not to go there any more. It was for her, as for so many of her ilk, not just a home away from home. "A launching pad," is what she called it in a letter to her English friend, Jethro Bithell, "our stock exchange," "where you go to clinch deals."[1]

She may have complained of the huge debts she ran up at the café: "one with the waiter at noon for a paradise chicken with applesauce, and one with the waiter at midnight for a schnitzel with french fries and a vanilla ice-cream with red currant sauce...."[2] But never mind. The café was where it was at, where she had to be, sick or well. "I was sick, but me they carry in, bed and all."[3] She was often sick, and always lonely, despite the facade of wit and good humor she presented to strangers.

92

Just how important a part in the lives of its habitués the café played can be seen in the drawings and memoirs of nearly all those who frequented it in the first decades of the century. As the painter Ludwig Meidner[4] notes, it was hardly the most elegant café on the Kurfürstendamm—it was, in fact, quite nondescript—but you could order a cup of coffee or a glass of beer for 25 pfennige, and sit around till 5 A.M. without being approached by a waiter to order anything more.

So of course, if you were looking for Frau Lasker-Schüler at any time of day or night—after noon, that is—this is where you would go to find her. Like Gertrude Stein at Les Deux Magots in Paris in this same period, Else Lasker-Schüler held court at the Café des Westens. She was a good ten years older than the up-and-coming Expressionists who chose her as their icon. They did not know this but felt her as a presence nonetheless.

How did she pass the time there? If it was still early in the day, she might be writing a letter, or drawing, or reading. Very often her arm would be in a splint. She was forever injuring her hand, probably suffering from what we now call "carpal tunnel syndrome."

It was a quiet time and one she cherished. Until the others started straggling in. How long did she stay? She hated going home at night. "A pity," she writes to Karl Kraus, "when dawn breaks, or someone looks at his watch. Dreadfully unpoetic that.... Time must laugh himself sick."[5]

It was one such day—or night—that Gottfried Benn, the young dandy and medical student who had just published his first collection of poems, *Morgue*, found himself drawn into the poet's orbit. The publicist Kurt Hiller recalls Benn "gravitating" to Lasker's table at the café. All his life Benn seemed to prefer older women. In Lasker-Schüler's case, the difference happened to have been greater than he realized—seventeen years.

In one of her first letters to Franz Marc, a correspondence which began at just about this time too, Else writes, "You, Blue Rider, I want to tell you something private, but don't tell anyone, not even Maria." This correspondence, remember, despite its private nature, was ultimately meant for publication. "I've fallen in love again, but really. His name is Giselheer [the name she gave to Benn]. He is straight out of the Nibelungen."[6] "Giselheer, der Heide [the Barbarian]," is what she called him in a poem, "weil er so ein Barbar ist" ("because he's such a heathen"). In her eyes, he was a great raptor, haughty and disdainful.

What drew her to him, apart from ineffable chemistry, was their common hatred of pollyanna cant. She also could appreciate his preoccupation with things "unmentionable" like death and disfiguration. This comes across in a funny-sad, self-lacerating comment she made to Marc when

Benn retreated: "I am so wretched, I even look dead. If he could see me like this, he would love me, he loves everything that is dead."[7,8]

Another thing Lasker-Schüler shared with Benn was a pet peeve: neither could stand Kandinsky. Kandinsky had a sentimental streak, philosophized too much, and covered his walls with "primitive" Bavarian glass paintings.

Despite all their shared anathemas, Benn was quick to extricate himself from the affair. Casting Else off as inamorata, he never ceased to be in awe of her as a poet. Nor was he loath to acknowledge his debt to her publicly.

It was her own words that thrummed in his mind when he formulated this dedication for his 1913 collection *Söhne* (*Sons*): "Ich grüsse Else Lasker-Schüler / Ziellose Hand aus Spiel und Blut" ("I salute Else Lasker-Schüler / Aimless hand in play and blood").[9] This seemingly obscure phrase can be traced to her own *Briefe nach Norwegen* (*Letters to Norway*), where she uses the hand metaphor to contrast her own temperament with that of Karl Kraus. Kraus's hand, drawn and painted many times by Kokoschka, she sees as a diplomat's hand, one that is sure of its purpose. She likens its splayed fingers to a mongolian umbel. By contrast, hers is a hand that seems without aim or purpose, but that is liable, in play, to turn bloody.

Benn had taken the trouble to decode the passage and use it in an oblique "salutation." It is this coded dialogue that typified their exchanges, hidden references that only they could understand, that lends a peculiar piquancy to their aborted romance.

That first letter to Marc, describing her new love, goes on with this curious, cloaked passage: "My city of Thebes is not exactly edified." She proceeds to berate her city, "a fanatic Islamic priest."[10] Benn, like Marc, was not Jewish. But he was one of her truly great loves, and she would remain passionately in love with him long after he withdrew his amorous affections from her. Which was very shortly. In fact, her very next letter to Franz Marc must report that her new love is already extinguished in the heart of her lover, "like a Bengal Flame."[11] Benn bridled at the thought of being possessed by any woman. And after her signing herself in a note to him, "Your flesh-eating flower,"[12] he might well have feared being consumed by her. The paths their lives would travel could not have been more diverse. And yet among her few possessions found in her trunk in Jerusalem after she died was a small bundle of memorabilia. Among them was a copy of Benn's text to Hindemith's 1931 oratorio *Das Unaufhörliche* (*The Never-Ending*), with this inscription from Benn: "To Else Lasker-Schüler, the great lyric genius, in friendship and admiration 18/xi/31 Gottfried Benn."[13]

The immediate drama of the love affair had been amply played out on paper. First, the complementary love poems. Then, like an elegant duel between two knights of the shining word, each countering and feinting, both in top form. Finally, it became bloody. Benn was unremitting. Else, truly devastated, importunate. Even as she resigned herself to the reality, she continued to write heartbreaking love poems to him. Poems that, in print, were an embarrassment, for all their intimacy and "excess." And he responded with the same clinical coldness that made his *Morgue* poems so original and so shocking. But wait. Does not even the most passionate love poem lose its purely "confessional" aspect once it has been worked over as a poem? Benn himself makes this point when he calls attention to "das lyrische Ich," the "lyric I-persona," not to be confused with "the confessional I" in Lasker-Schüler's poetry.

In her last poem to him, "Höre" ("Hear"), she writes, "Ich bin dein Wegrand. / Die dich streift, / Stürzt ab" ("I am your hedgerow, / that curbs your path, / —falls off").[14] To which he replies, "Keiner wird

Top: Gottfried Benn. Drawing by Else Lasker-Schüler. In *Die Aktion*. volume 3, Col. 639 (Schiller-Nationalmuseum/Deutsches Literaturarchive, Marbach).

Bottom: Gottfried Benn around 1910 in Mohrin, near Frankfurt an der Oder. 9.4 × 7.1 cm (Schiller-Nationalmuseum/Deutsches Literaturarchiv, Marbach).

mein Wegrand sein. / Lass deine Blüten nur verblühen. / Mein Weg flutet und geht allein" ("No one will hedge me in. / Let your blossoms curl up and die. / My path runs over, and I walk alone").[15]

Nor does it end there. She picked up on this "Wegrand" motif in one of her late late poems of exile: "Ich liege wo am Wegrand"[16] ("I lie by the side of the road"), sounding again one of her eternal themes, abandonment—long prevalent in her poems way before her years of literal exile.

It may—or may not—be surprising to learn that long after intimacy between them had ceased, they stayed in touch and remained friends. It was Benn who stood next to her, at the gravesite in 1927, holding her arm, when the son whose life she had been unable to save, died of tuberculosis and was buried. What greater token of friendship could one imagine? But in 1933, after promising to come to her aid if ever she needed him, he let her down. Benn was a complex individual, and his relationship to Nazism was, up to 1937, to say the least, regrettable.

When she was told, shortly before she died in Jerusalem, that Benn had joined the Nazis in the early 1930s, she could only shake her head. "I can't comprehend it. What times...."[17]

In 1952, Benn gave the keynote address at an Else Lasker-Schüler memorial celebration at the British Center in Berlin. It is an extraordinary speech, proceeding from pained personal reminiscence to unequivocal poetic judgment. In trying to unravel the threads of her quixotic personality, Benn unwittingly divulges, and only by indirection, his own lack of civil courage: "Those who were of a mind with her conceded her right to her exhibitionism, but they didn't want to be identified with it or with her. A strange process and a tragic one."[18] It is the same thought as is expressed in his description of her—decked out in the tackiest baubles, and him ashamed to be seen on the street with her. It is as if after her death their roles had been reversed, and Benn became the wooer.

"Höre" remained one of Benn's favorite poems over the years. Moreover, in that same 1952 eulogy to Lasker-Schüler, he quoted the last stanza: "Fühlst du mein Lebtum / Überall / Wie ferner Saum?" ("Do you feel my being / Wherever you go / Like a distant hedge?").[19] To which he made this startling belated reply: "I have continued to feel it over all the years, through all the divergent paths and wrong turns of my life."[20]

It is safe to say that during her own lifetime she never stopped loving him.

The year 1912 was almost unparalleled for Lasker-Schüler as a year of performance and readings: Zurich, Vienna, Cologne, Dresden, Munich were all on her calendar. These readings were an important source of income.

She often sought to expand the reading performances into cabaret acts, as we have seen elsewhere. The travel also afforded her an opportunity to cement old friendships, and make some interesting new acquaintances.

But just how desperate, sick and angry she was after her divorce comes through in almost every letter she writes. She was especially disappointed and aggrieved that influential people whom she knew on the committee for the prestigious Kleist Prize did not award it to her in 1913. It would have paid an honorarium of 1000 marks. Kleist, she said, would certainly have given it to her! (She was eventually awarded the Prize in 1932, less than a year before she was forced to emigrate.)

Of the three people on the committee to whom she wrote, Richard Dehmel was the one on whom she heaped the bitterest reproaches. After all, they had known each other since her earliest Berlin days, she was a great admirer of his poetry, and as the most esteemed of the early Expressionist poets, he could have used his influence on her behalf. She could not find words enough to berate him. Winding up her diatribe, she said, "Where I have no money—am alone. Herwarth Walden has fallen in love with a stupid unthing with curls (*eine Lockenundame*), with long hanging pearl earrings [here, one of her inimitable drawings] I am divorced as of two weeks ago."[21]

In July she wrote to Karl Kraus: "Surely you know that Herwarth and I have been going our separate ways for a long time—I don't see him at all and we are each man for himself."[22] A few days later she writes again: "No one writes to the Prince of Thebes any more.... Tell me the truth, Herzog [Duke],[23] you can't stand me any more.... My look is so black that no one talks to me.... My voice too rumbles like a dark sea without a shore. No human being can take comfort in my word. I won't wince if you can't stand to have me around. I myself can barely hold together, no bridge to any soul."[24]

But then, in the very next sentence, she announces, "Very soon a publisher will be publishing a fine, carefully selected broadsheet of my poems— I would like to dedicate it to you—like this: 'A present to Karl Kraus.'" She asks him to please accept it. "Not out of devotion. Not out of some drop of blood.—*aus Revanche* [in Return]." To have Kraus as advocate of her poetry was no mean claim. The fourteen poems are the original group, *Hebräische Balladen* (*Hebrew Ballads*), and came out as a book in 1913,[25] with the dedication: "Karl Kraus zum Geschenk" ("A Present to Karl Kraus").

Among the poems in this selection are "Tibetteppich," "Versöhnung," "Mein Volk," and "Jakob." In one of the letters she wrote to him in these days, she makes allusion to a drawing she had done of a Jacob resting before the ladder—"half buffalo half serpent. He is resting from tending his flocks."[26]

"Jacob"

Jakob war der Büffel seiner Herde.
Wenn er stampfte mit den Hufen
Sprühte unter ihm die Erde.

Brüllend liess er die gescheckten Brüder,
Rannte in den Urwald an die Flüsse,
Stillte dort das Blut der Affenbisse.

Durch die müden Schmerzen in den Knöcheln
Sank er vor dem Himmel fiebernd nieder
Und sein Ochsgesicht erschuf das Lächeln."[27]

"Jacob"

Jacob was the buffalo of his herd.
When he stamped with his hooves
The earth flew up under him.

Howling he left behind the piebald brothers,
Ran into the jungle to the rivers,
Stanched the blood where apes had bitten him.

Wearied from the pain in both his ankles,
He sank down in a sweat beneath the sky,
And from his bullock's face was born—the smile.

Else Lasker-Schüler claimed not to have read the Zohar when she wrote the poem. But the image of the last line bears a striking resemblance to a legend of the Cabbala: "When the steer smiles, the lamb is born." She did say the image overwhelmed her when she wrote the line.

In January 1913, at about the same time that Franz Marc organized an art auction, whose proceeds were to go to the poet, Karl Kraus advertised in the pages of *Die Fackel*: "The poet Else Lasker-Schüler lives in circumstances of extreme poverty. Her difficulties with meeting the barest necessities of life have become so serious that the undersigned circle of friends and admirers feel obliged to appeal to all who share an appreciation and understanding of this poet's work,—so beyond the grasp of the fashion of the times—to join us by showing your support. Contributions...."[28] The undersigned included Selma Lagerlöf, Adolf Loos, and Arnold Schoenberg.

The years following the separation and divorce were marked not just by monetary constraint but by deep emotional turmoil. The aborted love affair with Benn. Other deaths, not just her sister's, but deaths which, owing partly to their bizarre circumstances, haunted her, and increased her sense of incomprehension, of being alien to the ways of the world.

To say that she felt alien to the ways of the world is not to say that she did not try to negotiate, to deal with and act upon, the world.

There was Johannes Holzmann,[29] one of the young acolytes of the Peter Hille circle whom she dubbed Senna Hoy, and whose tragic fate became the subject of many of her poems. But not only the subject of her poems. With his long black cape and boots, Holzmann looked the part, and indeed was, something of an *enfant terrible*. When they met, probably in 1904 or 1905, Else Lasker-Schüler was already the doyenne of the old Peter Hille group.

Karl Kraus. Brush, pen and ink drawing by Oskar Kokoschka, 1909. Appeared in *Der Sturm*, number 12, May 19, 1910. Else Lasker-Schüler likened Kraus's splayed fingers to a Mongolian umbel (Schiller-National-museum/Deutsches Literaturarchiv, Marbach).

While Holzmann was a schoolteacher by profession, his radical anarchist views, which he aired in his periodical *Der Kampf* (*The Struggle*), frequently got him into trouble. When anarchist groups in Zurich and Paris wrongly accused him of being an informant, he went (a second time) to Russia to clear his name and to protest slavic pogroms. This time he was arrested by czarist police who accused him of engaging in "revolutionary activities."

For seven years he sat in prison. Eventually it became clear that, albeit for different reasons, neither government wanted to see him freed.

Then, in November 1913, having got nowhere writing to the authorities on his behalf, Lasker decided to go herself by train to Russia. Although she traveled with Holzmann's brother, it was a brave and totally unheard-of thing for a woman to do. After a harrowing journey, she found him wast-

Else Lasker-Schüler. Photograph Atelier Bender, Wuppertal. Reproduced in *Saturn*, volume 3, number 4 (special Else Lasker-Schüler issue) (Schiller Nationalmuseum/ Deutsches Literaturarchiv, Marbach).

ing away in the prisoners' ward of an insane asylum four hours from Moscow.

Lasker's trip came at a time when her own funds were miserably depleted. Despite the flurry of readings that took her all over central Europe, the divorce from Walden had left her financially ruined as well as emotionally devastated.

As a single mother, with a frail child, she was under additional pressure and strain. She worried continually about the boy's future. Paul required special care, care she could not hope to give him at home. She was living, and would always live, from this time on, only in furnished rooms. The boy was sent away to the Odenwaldschule, a beautiful Landheim school in the Odenwald, but which cost 600 marks for every academic quarter. That was just tuition and board. The 500 marks that she received for the manuscript of *Hebräische Balladen* she sent at once to the Odenwaldschule for tuition. In addition, there was clothing and outings. (She could never have managed this alone. An anonymous donor helped with tuition. This anonymous donor turned out to have been none other than Ludwig von Wittgenstein.)[30]

Many admirers and friends had tried to come to her rescue in these years, 1910–1914. Karl Kraus published appeals for contributions in *Die Fackel*, placing them in prominent full-page notices. Franz Marc organized and contributed paintings to an art auction for her (among these was "Traum," a painting he made expressly for the auction, and which was inscribed, "For the Prince of Thebes from Fz. Marc").

The tale of her precarious journey, by train to Moscow, the ensuing odyssey, the horrors she encountered when she finally tracked Holzmann

$$\mathfrak{H}\,e\,b\,r\,\ddot{a}\,i\,\mathfrak{f}\,\mathfrak{d}\,e\quad \mathfrak{B}\,a\,l\,l\,a\,b\,e\,n$$
$$\mathfrak{von}$$
$$\mathfrak{E}\,l\,\mathfrak{f}\,e\quad \mathfrak{L}\,a\,\mathfrak{z}\,\mathfrak{k}\,e\,r\,\text{-}\,\mathfrak{S}\,\mathfrak{d}\,\ddot{u}\,l\,e\,r$$

$$\mathfrak{A}.\quad \mathfrak{N}.\quad \mathfrak{M}\,e\,\mathfrak{y}\,e\,r\quad \mathfrak{V}\,e\,r\,l\,a\,\mathfrak{g}$$
$$1\qquad 9\qquad 1\qquad 3$$
$$\mathfrak{B}\,e\,r\,l\,i\,n\,\text{-}\,\mathfrak{W}\,i\,l\,m\,e\,r\,\mathfrak{z}\,b\,o\,r\,\mathfrak{f}$$

Cover design by Else Lasker-Schüler for the first edition of her
Hebräische Balladen, 1913, H.M. Meyer Verlag (Schiller-National-
museum/ Deutsches Literaturarchiv, Marbach).

down, are preserved in the letters she wrote to Karl Kraus at the time, and
nowhere else in her writings with such immediacy and detail. (See Appendix 7, pages 192–193.)

Why, one way wonder, in view of his refusal to become personally
involved in the case (he remained oddly silent about the affair in *Die Fackel*),
did she choose him to confide the painstaking account of her Russian journey?

Else Lasker-Schüler had met Karl Kraus in 1909, when he and Walden were contemplating a joint publication. From 1930 until his death in 1936, Kraus published the most controversial periodical to emerge from the dying Hapsburg Empire. He was an arbiter of justice and clean prose. The best means of unmasking a hypocrite, he showed, was simply to quote him verbatim. This is what he did repeatedly in *Die Fackel*. If Karl Kraus would take up the pen in the cause of that "romantic rowdy," Johannes Holzmann, she felt, it would have enormous weight.

She was right in characterizing their different "hands." His was a steely cast of mind; hers an unruly "intuition." But when she was angry or despairing, it was to Karl Kraus that she turned. However, Karl Kraus did not let others dictate his "causes" to him.

Equally futile was her attempt to enlist Martin Buber, whom she had known from her earliest Peter Hille days in Berlin. Buber did not come forward. Only Franz Marc took the matter, and with it, her efforts on Holzmann's behalf, seriously. The painter Marianne von Werefkin[31] was a friend of Franz Marc's. She had relatives in high places in Moscow. Using her influence, an initiative was undertaken. However, through no fault of theirs, all efforts to save Holzmann failed. His health deteriorated, and when Lasker-Schüler finally got to see him, he lay with high fever in a cell surrounded by raving madmen. The scene remained engraved in her memory.

What it must have done to her own health just to make the journey! Then, on arrival, she had to climb up eight flights of stairs, go through eight gates to eight towers, each guarded by armed soldiers. And then the shock of seeing him so emaciated and near death. He was 31 years old when he died. It was her belief that when he knew there was no more hope for a reprieve, he took his life.

Finally, when she came back home, totally devastated and exhausted, she was met by malicious gossip. In some quarters it was even suggested that she had never really gone, but was merely spinning another self-dramatizing and self-aggrandizing yarn, myth-making *à la Lasker*.

It is no exaggeration to say that during the entire seven year period of Holzmann's incarceration, Lasker-Schüler was haunted by his fate. Already in 1909, she had written to her English friend Jethro Bithell in Manchester: "Sometimes I must open the house door late at night, the [Senna Hoy] shadow wants to come in. I believe the Siberian prince is Sir Ratcliff..."[32] (the mad hero of Heine's verse-drama tragedy).

One reason why she was unable to lay the episode with its horrific end to rest was that she felt a gnawing guilt that she hadn't done enough in all the years he was in Russia. This comes through in the agonized letters she wrote to Kraus.

After Senna Hoy's death, Fran Pfemfert, the editor of the influential monthly *Die Aktion*, which had published much of Lasker's work, and was more politically oriented than *Der Sturm*, became involved. Pfemfert suddenly wanted to print essays by Holzmann, the very ones Lasker had hoped he would print for the two years prior to Senna Hoy's death. In these and related issues, it would appear from what she says that Pfemfert was prevaricating. "But Pfemfert's sudden drinking, the noisy stepping into the foreground, swimming as it were in the very blood of a dead friend, designating himself as the ever true and faithful one,—all that makes me wild,"[33] she writes to Karl Kraus.

In the end, she draws in her talons, in light of a greater aim: to insure the publication of the Holzmann essays. Moreover, she is making a genuine attempt to be fair, even as she portrays him to Kraus in her letter: "...not a very distinguished person, but not very happy either ... kids himself...."[34]

Else Lasker-Schüler: "Self-portrait of the Prince of Thebes in battle head-gear." Below, in her handwriting, in parentheses: "In the possession of the Blue Rider Franz Marc." In *Saturn*, volume 3, number 4 (special Else Lasker-Schüler issue) (Schiller Nationalmuseum/ Deutsches Literaturarchiv, Marbach).

It almost seems to have been her fate to become involved in tragic lives—and deaths—that were a source of torment to her for months, sometimes years. These experiences invariably wore her down physically, and left her emotionally drained.

All her life Else Lasker-Schüler loved going to the movies.[35] From its beginnings, the new medium with its new technology fascinated her. Film, as an industry, with full-length features, didn't really take off till after the first World War, but already before then, the full-length feature *Quo Vadis* was shown in Berlin, and she herself had a chance to try her own hand at script-writing. It was all something of a lark.

On one of her trips to Leipzig, on a wintry day at the beginning of 1913, she was sitting with some friends in Wilhelms Weinstube, a gathering place for young Expressionists, when someone suggested they go to Dessau for the day. And for want of something better to do while they were there, they wandered into what turned out to be a particularly awful silent film.

There were a few real movie houses already in 1913, but this was one of the old-time "fleabox" affairs, where schmaltzy shorts were shown, very often in the back of an abandoned store or warehouse. The film they saw was called *Lady Glane's Adventure*. The picture was accompanied not just by the ubiquitous piano player of the silent film epoch, but there was a man who commented on the action as it happened, pointing to the screen with a class-room pointer. When they came out, and were able to stop laughing, they had a serious discussion about the misguided attempt of the silent film to imitate the technique of the novel or the stage, instead of making use of the new technology of *moving* pictures. Wouldn't it be fun to try their hand at it?

Kurt Pinthus, who would edit the definitive anthology of Expressionist poetry in 1919 *Menschheitsdämmerung* (*Twilight of Mankind*), was one of the group that day in Dessau, and it was he who had the idea. He told them all to go home and write a script. It should be set in an interesting, preferably exotic, milieu, it should have hands-on action, there should be surprises, something spectacular, something that could pack an emotional punch. Among those who got to participate in this exercise were Walter Hasenclever, Max Brod, Albert Ehrenstein, Lasker-Schüler, and Pinthus himself. Dutifully, they all went and did their homework. Then he collected the pieces they wrote, and published the best ones in a *Kinobuch* (movie scripts).

Under the title "Plumm-Pascha," Else Lasker-Schüler delivered a piece that would have made Cecil B. DeMille's eyes glaze over. It appeared to be a by-product of *The Nights of Tino*, in which there was also a Plumm-Pascha piece, but this "Plumm-Pascha" was a very different dish of tea. The "Plumm Pascha" of *The Nights of Tino* is a sweet fairy tale, which begins with a little boy, "Pull" (her son, Paul), riding around on a white elephant outside the palace at Baghdad. But the Plumm-Pascha film script begins: "At the command of Plumm-Pascha, the grand vizier of Upper Egypt, the last priests of a sect of the steer-headed god Ptah are being burned at the stake. A crowd jeers the victims, throwing stones at them, but until they are totally burnt to ash, the martyrs hold their little idols with their bull-heads upright out of the flames."[36]

Interesting milieu? Something spectacular, with hands-on action? Packs an emotional punch? All of the above. Although it came out late in 1913 (Kurt Wolff's Leipzig firm published it), *Das Kinobuch* was dated 1914. Historically, it is of great interest to preserve the earlier date, not only because of the outbreak of war in 1914, but because it was the earliest attempt in a genre that would one day take over the entertainment industry. And to think it was all done as a kind of lark, without any thought of commercial gain. Unfortunately, the authors never had the opportunity to see their projects realized on the screen.

The summer of 1914 also saw the publication of *Der Prinz von Theben* (*The Prince of Thebes*) by Kurt Wolff's publishing house Verlag der Weissen Bücher, Leipzig, with three color prints by Franz Marc. The following year the same publishers brought out a new, greatly expanded edition of *Meine Wunder*. But *Der Prinz von Theben*, along with the high-spirited little Plumm-Pascha piece for the *Kinobuch*, were her last publications before the outbreak of the war.

Karl Schmidt-Rottluff's drawing of "The Prince of Thebes" in *Der Sturm*, volume 3, number 93, page 759 (Schiller-Nationalmuseum/ Deutsches Literaturarchiv, Marbach).

CHAPTER EIGHT

1914–1918: War Years

"Was it for this the clay grew tall?
—O what made fatuous sunbeams toil
To break earth's sleep at all?"
                    Wilfred Owen: Futility

One evening in the spring of 1914, Else Lasker-Schüler and the sculptor Fritz Huf got dressed up just for fun: he, as a Dutch fisherman in sackcloth, she in a working man's smock. Thus attired they proceeded to have a boxing match. We do not know who won; we do know that on the morning after, she sat for her portrait in clay. She hoped he would coax out of the clay an image of Jussuf, the Theban prince, "hard as stone, unflinching, sovereign, pious, star and sickle-moon, on her brow."[1]

According to her own verdict, and to the enthusiastic response of her son, Paul, who wrote to Huf that he had never seen such a colossal head of his mother as Huf had made, he must have succeeded brilliantly. Alas, the sculpture has disappeared. It would be reassuring to see her looking so defiant, so high-spirited still.

But in August of that year war broke out in Europe. In the words of the historian Gordon A. Craig, "most Germans believed ... that their country was the victim of a brutal assault...." The declaration of war "released a heady excitement that swept the whole country...." The mood in Europe "was a curious compound of uncomplicated patriotism, romantic joy in the chance of participating in a great adventure, and naive expectation that,

106

Gesammelte Tonwerke

HERWARTH WALDEN / Zehn Gesänge

Verdammnis / Werk I / Dichtung von ELSE LASKER-SCHÜLER

Verlag DER STURM Berlin W 9

Cover drawing by Marc Chagall (1914) for Herwarth Walden's musical setting of "Verdamnis," Else Lasker-Schüler's 1902 poem (courtesy Library of the Museum of Modern Art, New York).

somehow or other, the conflict would solve all of the problems that had piled up during the years of peace."[2]

Not so for Else Lasker-Schüler. She was way ahead of many of her male friends (and that included Franz Marc), who, in 1914, in their misplaced idealism, believed that a war would have a cleansing, regenerating effect on society.

From mid-July through September she was staying in Munich. It was where she witnessed the outbreak of the Great War. During this period she was arrested four times on the street for provocatively flaunting *Galakriegsschmuck* (gala war decorations).[3] The fact that she went out dressed as the Prince of Thebes in a bright silk turban made her an object of suspicion. Her attempts to "camouflage" herself by draping a German flag around the turban surely did little to allay these suspicions.

While in Munich, she happened to cross paths again with Emmy Hennings. But this time instead of vitriol, it was a soothing boric—actually acetic—acid solution, *essigsauerer Tonerde*, that Else Lasker-Schüler administered. Here is Emmy Hennings' account, from *Ruf und Echo* (*Call and Echo*), her memoir of 1953. (She had been warned by the police on the street to break up an anti-war demonstration.)

> I began suddenly to weep heftily, and a stream of tears was all that separated me from total misery, for which I had no name more. *Weltschmerz* hung in the air, as we were in a world war.
>
> Die Dichterin [the poetess] Else Lasker-Schüler happened to come along, saw me weeping, asked me why, but that was asking too much. The poetess was very kind to me, took me with her to the Café Stephanie and ordered some apple cake with whipped cream for me. I began to feel a little better, but my left eye was very swollen and hurt; Else Lasker-Schüler asked to have a napkin and a bowl of cold water brought at once.
>
> Yes, and some *essigsauerer Tonerde*. Then she ministered to me, and wanted to bandage my eye, but I said it wasn't worth it, I was sure to be beaten up again, if not today then tomorrow. "No, please," I said, "I have to look the world in the eye. Although it's true that even through a bandage one can see what's happening today."
>
> The poetess herself wore a beautiful brightly-colored silk turban, that showed off her black hair marvelously, beautiful and interesting, like a dream out of the Orient, but the rest of what she was wearing didn't look like her at all: a wide sash with the German flag emblazoned on it, thrown over her shoulder like a legionnaire's decoration or a rifle-club emblem.
>
> I asked: "Dear Prince of Thebes, are you so bang-up patriotic that you have to walk around in the clear light of day so decked out with flags?" "Otherwise," she replied, "I'll be taken for a foreigner, possibly for a spy. I can't risk that. I bought myself a Bavarian cummerbund, at Tietz's. Look. Want to show it to you right away. Waiter, would you please take away the water bowl and the boric

acid. Thank you. We've already been served. How do you like the sash? A bit more discreet, no?" "Chic," I said, just to be nice, while she made preparations to adorn herself with the second sash as well. "One dare not say it out loud," she said, speaking in anything but hushed tones, so that every one in the café would have had to have heard what she said, "but, believe me, we (the Germans) were not victims of any assault, one just mustn't say it out loud."[4]

In truth there was nothing she would not dare to say out loud.

Tales of sightings of Frau Lasker-Schüler at the Café des Westens in the years of the Great War all have a melancholy ring to them. They are still surrounded by the hush of awe, but there is more murmur of outward signs of depression, neurasthenia.

The café itself continued to be the center of the literary and political avant-garde. Foreign artists and journalists knew where to direct their steps if they wanted to meet with their German counterparts in radical thinking. Already as a student in Leipzig in 1914, the Spanish Resistance fighter, Marxist publicist and diplomat Alvarez del Vayo knew of the Café des Westens, and in 1916, arriving in Berlin in the midst of war, that's where he headed. "The bohemians of Berlin," he observed, "despised the war."[5] This was certainly true of Lasker-Schüler. He recalls the frequent police raids on the café, the searches for deserters and members of the opposition.

The chemical binder for all these café radicals was not a shared ideology. Unlike the unswerving Marxist del Vayo, they held very different world views. What they did share, and here Lasker-Schüler was among the most vocal, was their contempt for the bourgeoisie. That band of petty philistines! It was this hatred of the bourgeoisie and its crass material values that turned the café into a breeding ground for radical politics, not the other way round.

The banal psychological explanation for bourgeois-baiting as revenge against parents who tried to squeeze their offspring into a conventional mold simply does not hold up for Else Lasker-Schüler. Although she was brought up in an upper middle-class home, with an assimilated German-Jewish cultural background, she saw it as a nurturing home, one that made her feel "shipwrecked" on losing it after her mother's death. But, like Robinson, once she had to fend for herself, she began to shape the tools of survival according to her own rules.

That meant that neither as a woman nor as a Jew would she ever accept an assigned role. After her divorce from Walden, she never lived in her own home, only in boarding houses and hotels. Her standards and tastes, however, remained unchanged. While deploring her lack of funds, she would state categorically, "Having small change is worse. I was not brought up *en miniature*."[6] This after consuming some fresh salmon with butter sauce that her lawyer friend, Hugo Caro, treated her to at the café.

In addition to its resident artists like Lasker-Schüler and Walden, or foreign visitors like del Vayo, the café attracted a host of young people just out of school, eager for a whiff of bohemia. Walter Benjamin was such a one. "This was the time," he wrote of 1914, "when the Berlin cafés played an important part in our lives.... And let there be no mistaking: the headquarters of Bohemia up into the first years of the War was the old Café des Westens. Our world was a different one from the emancipated crowd that surrounded us there.... Once, Else Lasker-Schüler drew me over to her table...."[7]

Benjamin was, and would remain, over the years, somewhat ambivalent about her. Irritated by what he saw as her "vapid, hysterical" mannerisms, seeing her surrounded by sycophantic youths, laughing at their stupid jokes, he was almost as put off by her as Kafka. Still, many years later, writing to Scholem, he will recall her poem "David and Jonathan" as one of his all-time favorite poems. Unlike Kafka, he could acknowledge her genius as a poet even when she got on his nerves.

Also present at the café that day when Lasker called Benjamin over to her table was her young admirer, Wieland Herzfelde. Wieland, the brother of John Heartfield (political satirist and inventor of photomontage), was himself just a youth at the time. Later, he became the editor of the influential periodical *Neue Jugend*. Herzfelde was, and would remain, one of her staunchest followers and an intelligent reader of her work.

Not just the smoke film settling on your shoulder, but the decibel level at the café could give you a headache as the night wore on. During the war years this must have set a new record. There were, for starters, two competing contingents: the literary coterie, around Lasker-Schüler, and at home in Walden's *Sturm*. They might be outshouted by the more political, *Aktion* crowd led by Franz Pfemfert. Because they were less blatantly activist, they were accused of being a-political by the others. But it is one thing to be oblivious of events and another to feel alien to them.

Else Lasker-Schüler was frequently faulted for her unworldliness. One has only to look at the names of those people she celebrated in her essays to see how mistaken this notion was and to get an idea of her world view: Karl Kraus, of course; Doktor Magnus Hirschfeld, the sexologist; Franziska Schultz, the pioneering feminist who opened a home for "wayward Magdalenes," to name but a few. Among her Munich friends was the well-known feminist Eliza Ichenhaeuser. There was certainly nothing unworldly about her stance on issues that mattered.

It had been Pfemfert, the editor of *Aktion*, whom Lasker-Schüler had tried, unsuccessfully, to engage in the Senna Hoy affair. The two groups, *Sturm* and *Aktion*, were not really enemies, but now, in wartime, they could find themselves at loggerheads. Moreover, Lasker-Schüler was turning away from *Sturm* because of Walden and his new entourage. Herzfelde frequently acted as mediator between them.

After corresponding with her as a young student, and attending a reading she gave in Frankfurt, he finally met the poet in Berlin, at the Café des Westens. It was in April 1914, four months before the outbreak of the war. He walked her back to her place and recorded his impressions:

"She lived in a garret that had little to recommend it, being in no way cozy and much too high up; still it contained some very lovely objects: glass chimes ... a table full of tin soldiers and elephants and oriental jewels. (Whether or not they were real, I didn't even think to ask.) On the walls hung posters, drawings by Franz Marc, as well as her own, and those of her son, Paul."[8] Wieland, like Benjamin, was just a kid out of high school— just a few years older than her own boy—and he quickly fell under her spell.

With war a daily reality, the furrow between Else Lasker-Schüler's brows grew deeper. Wieland Herzfelde was not the only young man she would ask to see her home. Franz Jung, a young writer in those days recalls:

> I ran into her frequently at the Café des Westens. She sat alone much of the time, as if abandoned by all. She was grateful for any friendly word that came her way. Else Lasker-Schüler had lost all contact to the world around her and to events in the world at large. The War must have been something totally unimaginable and incomprehensible to her. Sometimes she would ask me to see her home. I recall a typical old-time Berlin room, with a small raised area by the window where people in the good old days would keep their plants and flower pots. It was this spot in which she chose to sit, in a simple cane chair, looking out at the street and into her own world, the camel paths through distant deserts, the thousand year-old realm of the Prince of Thebes. She would murmur to herself and give herself over to her painted dreams or she would recite poetry or read aloud from letters that she had thought to send by courier but never had.[9]

Her dark mood breaks through in letters as well. It was, in fact, to Franz Jung that she wrote, "You have so many friends, and they all love

you. I only have people around me who want something from me." And
again: "I cannot begin to tell you how sad I am.... Why *should* anyone want
to see me; I would run away from myself."[10]

Nevertheless, she appears to have retained her sense of humor, and
could pepper her letters with a strong dose of self-irony. Writing to Martin Buber, after a particularly overwrought argument she had had with him
at his house,[11] she says, "If you were to listen to me talk all day long, you
would realize, since I talk *only* about myself, that one should read only *my*
poems—if any, if one invites me to be their guest. I know you value my
honesty."[12]

Buber's reply is characteristically Buber: "I think one should be more
concerned to listen to what others are saying rather than whether *they* hear
you." ("Ich meine, man sollte sich mehr darum bekümmern, wie man die
Welt hört, als wie sie einen hört.") The letter begins, however, with a genuine expression of his feeling for the poet: "Dear and Revered One" ("Liebe
und Verhrte")—"You would try in vain to diminish by even a single iota
my feeling for your person" ("Sie würden sich vergeblich bemühen, meinem
Gefühl für Ihr Dasein auch nur ein Fünkchen zu nehmen").[14]

One evening the left-wing publicist, Kurt Hiller, was seated at a table
near the Lasker entourage at the café. The year was 1915. Hiller was a fascinating figure in his own right. He belonged more to the activist-*Aktion*-
wing, and was outspoken in defending his rights as a homosexual,
something quite daring at the time.

The group around Lasker-Schüler included the young Herzfelde,
whom she called Roland, because he was such a brave and loyal soul. George
Grosz, who was a close friend of Wieland's, remembers: "Standing up for
his friends was second nature to him. If anyone showed lack of respect for
one of them, it might lead to a slap in the face and a little beating up....
One time a well-known literary figure made a joke at her (Else's) expense.
Wieland threw him out of the Café...."[15]

Whatever happened that night left wounded feelings all around. Both
men—Herzfelde and Hiller—were eager to give their own account of what
transpired.

Herzfeld:

> On a day in April 1915, Else Lasker-Schüler sat at her table at the
> Café des Westens. She was holding forth about the virtues of a
> young poet whom none of us yet knew. [It was Hans Adalbert von
> Maltzahn, who was serving as an officer in the army.] She portrayed
> the young man as an impoverished aristocrat who had the interest
> of the Jews at heart, even though he himself was "fair-skinned" and

handsome. [Yes, she was infatuated with him.] In the midst of her rhapsodizing, she was called to the telephone.

Taking advantage of her absence, Kurt Hiller began to speculate about what kind of chap this young fellow might be, only to interrupt himself with these words: "Ach, what difference does it make, she just got off at the wrong floor." This remark, along with the accompanying obscene gesture, enraged me. I got up and rebuked him in a loud voice, saying I would slap his face, but not till tomorrow, so he shouldn't think I was just acting on impulse. I then challenged those at Hiller's table to get up if they felt as I did. At which point Hiller found himself sitting alone. The next day of course the café was jam-packed as never before. Hiller appeared at the appointed hour with two bodyguards. Before he could even speak, I had knocked off his hat, which then rolled into the gutter.[16]

Some forty years after the fact, Hiller too felt obliged to give his own, somewhat sanitized, not to say sanctimonious, version of the incident:

Among her acolytes at the marble-top tables at the café, in the middle years of World War I ... was Wieland Herzfelde ... at which time I had a confrontation with him at the revolving door of the famous café.... A few days earlier, I had solicited, from the friends seated at my table, opinions regarding the poetry of Else Lasker-Schüler, with regard to the three elements common to all great poetry: the sensual, the spiritual and the cerebral, whereby in the poetry of Lasker, despite the glory of the first two, the third element is altogether lacking.[17]

This judgment notwithstanding, Hiller had published Lasker-Schüler's poetry in his own exclusionary Expressionist anthology, and was not basically inimical to her work. Once again, he was a complex human being with many sides to his nature. But he also made an effort to separate his aesthetic judgments from his personal likes and dislikes.

At any rate, after the incident with Hiller at the Café des Westens, the Lasker crew, which had more or less established the café as their headquarters, were asked not to frequent it any more (at least this is one version). They moved to the Romanische Café, where they regaled one another for a long time to come with the tale of the Hiller-Herzfelde rencontre.

That the poet dealt with Hiller's affront cavalierly in conversation does not mean that it had not wounded her deeply. This is evident from a letter she wrote to Karl Kraus in April 1915.

"I wouldn't trouble you in these times of death with such trivia, but you should know, because my spirit has been crushed. Yesterday I went to see my lawyer again about Kurt Hiller, who keeps persecuting me although I can think of nothing I have done to harm him. [Was she thinking of Hiller's homosexuality, which others used against him?] Now Hiller said in Wieland's presence: Dr. G. [a doctor from Vienna] should not have been put away in jail, rather Lasker-Schüler. Dr. G. at least is not a public threat like Lasker-Schüler ... and he added something so filthy that I don't even want to repeat it, I can't bear to see it written—of me, the Prince of Thebes.... I must go on writing my poems, but I am totally devastated by these external things...."[18]

Again, we see Else turning to Karl Kraus, and in the most disarming, child-like way, letting down her guard. Knowing how severe he was in his judgments, she must have felt that, like her mother and like Franz Marc, she could trust him. He wouldn't mince words with her, so if he called her to order, well, she would think about it.

On the night of November 3, 1914, Else Lasker-Schüler came rushing into the café, and announced that Georg Trakl[19] had sought her out in a dream, saying that he was going to kill himself.

Else had met the young Austrian poet (he was 17) in March of that year. Trakl had traveled from Salzburg to Berlin to visit his married sister, Margarethe Langen, a concert pianist, who had become ill following a miscarriage. The two poets met just one single time.

Trakl was another young man who cut a very romantic figure. Dark, melancholy, victim to an early drug addiction, with a known suicidal bent, he was a cult figure in artistic circles. He was in fact one of the most interesting poets to come out of the Expressionist movement. And one of his most famous poems, "Abendland," is dedicated to Else Lasker-Schüler. The first two lines of this poem sound like something she could have written: "Moon, like a dead thing / Stepped out of a blue cave...." (See Appendix 8 for the original and a translation by Michael Hamburger). The one meeting between them had a tremendous impact on each. Whenever Else wrote to their mutual friend, Trakl's patron, Ludwig von Ficker (von Ficker was the editor of a periodical published in Innsbruck, *Der Brenner*), she inquired after Trakl's well-being.

In May 1914, she wrote saying she wondered why Trakl hadn't written to her: "I never thanked him enough for the dedication [to "Abendland"]."[20] The poem had appeared in three different versions, in three different places, all with the dedication to Else Lasker-Schüler, and all in the month of May. It was one month after Senna Hoy's death, and in her letter to von Ficker, she says that both Senna Hoy and Trakl will figure in her forthcoming book *Briefe und Bilder* (*Letters and Pictures*).

August 1914, the outbreak of the Great War. Trakl leaves civilian life to join the Medical Corps of the Austrian army as a lieutenant. He had trained as a chemist, and after the battle of Grodek, close to a hundred wounded soldiers were put in his charge. Because of an acute shortage of medical supplies, he could do nothing for them but watch them die. Out of this experience came his famous poem "Grodek." It also brought on a nervous breakdown.

After trying to take his own life, Trakl was removed to the garrison hospital nearest Grodek, in Cracow. Here he was confined for observation in a cell with an officer who had gone mad after weeks of thinking he would be executed as a deserter. Trakl himself lived under the same delusion. The parallel to Senna Hoy's situation in a psychiatric prison in Russia is striking.

On October 25, von Ficker visited Trakl in his hospital ward. Together the men wrote a postcard to Else Lasker-Schüler, Trakl asking her to visit him there.

But it was on the night of November 3, according to friends gathered at the café, that Else Lasker-Schüler came rushing in to announce that Trakl had sought her out in a dream, threatening to kill himself.[21] Two weeks later his family received official notice of his death—in the night of November 3.

When Lasker learned of this death, and the circumstances surrounding it—he had died of a self-administered dose of poison—she was beside herself. She telegraphed von Ficker: "Am in despair would have come to Cracow but card not received ... where funeral I weep Jussuf."[22]

Then she sat down and wrote a letter to von Ficker:

> It is night. I must write to you—if I had had any idea—I would have gone at once to Trakl in Cracow. The card [that the two of them wrote, asking her to come] has still not arrived. I am so horrified, no words. I got a heart cramp right away and still can't breathe properly.
>
> Now I ought to go to Georg Trakl's sister; I brought her flowers and was with her for a long time, but I was not able to tell her the painful news which is why I ask you to tell her for me. Also—that she should feel free to say whatever she wants to me. I found her at once so moving and that pained me so today. I cannot write any more only I want to tell you again how inconsolable I am, the only comfort was in your letter that there is someone like you still there, my dear Landvogt [squire]. Greetings to your Swede and the two children. Your poor Jussuf.[23]

The card arrived on November 13.

For a brief period, Else Lasker-Schüler became totally absorbed in the affairs of Gretel Langen. But this relationship would soon turn into a nightmare.

To von Ficker once again: "I spent half the night with Trakl's sister, who is so inconsolable that I didn't want to leave her." Else's sympathy extended so far that she tried to help arrange for the transport of Trakl's body back to Austria so that he could be buried, according to Gretel Langen's fervid wish, on home soil. And yet again: "The poor sister. I can't tell you how she suffers."[24]

It is at this point that one begins to feel Else Lasker-Schüler is at the breaking-point herself. Quoting again from a letter to von Ficker: "Just this morning the card from the hospital arrived. Mailed from Cracow on 25. X. and received only today. I would have come at once as sure as I am Jussuf...."[25] Now everything comes tumbling down inside her. The premonition that she didn't follow, the awful thought that inadvertently she let a friend down, whose death she might have prevented. Years later, in 1926, when von Ficker sent her a picture of Trakl along with a volume of his poems, she thanked him, saying, "I certainly don't wish to be presumptuous, but, had I dared, I could have made him happy."[26]

The war itself, hailed by so many young innocents, was for her from the start an unspeakable horror. To von Ficker she exclaimed, "All the soldiers who are yet to fall! Many have already come back demented, deranged."[27]

As for Gretel Langen, her sympathies were about to undergo an abrupt reversal. Actually the trouble had begun a year earlier. Trakl had asked Else Lasker-Schüler to convey a message to his sister, but

> Frau Langen sent me away at the door! with shameless excuses! Nevertheless I went back now for Trakl's sake. I had a good talk with the sister too good despite her being repugnant to me ... there's not a true word in all of Frau Langen. She denounced her husband to me, etc. and talked in a terrible way about Jews to a friend of mine, the brother-in-law of Louis Corinth.[28] This woman with whom I sat up all night has no right to abuse me. I cannot stand these hypocritical ... vain conceited creatures.
>
> Nevertheless I forwarded your letter to her and already today received a shameless reply from *Herr* Langen. More than once I have overcome my distaste. This woman with her humorless philosophic romanticism.... She persecutes me out of sheer jealousy ... And still I went there and invited her for Georg Trakl's sake. This drinking is all an act (imitating her brother), and her "pain" was repugnant to me.... Please don't believe a word she says. But for your friend's sake I beseech you to stand by her....

Please don't think ill of Jussuf. [In the margin]: I would never
have written all this ... but for the enclosed letter! This woman had
a real outburst—in the café—because a composer asked me for my
poems. Immediately she began to rant and pour abuse on the Jews,
in front of my acquaintance.

Finally the dart hits home: "Did Trakl have such views about Jews too?
I have to know. I am a Jew. Thank God."[29]

Once more, on December 9, 1914, Arthur Langen wrote to the poet,
forbidding any further correspondence between the two houses. Lasker-
Schüler sent his note on to von Ficker, but not before scrawling on the
back, "I think I will go mad."[30]

This sad turn of events made it impossible for Else Lasker-Schüler ever
to write about Trakl again. "It is all her—Frau Langen's— fault," she states
boldly. Among Frau Langen's more offensive utterances was this one: "the
Jews should all be packed off to Asia." "This, [again Lasker-Schüler] at a
time when thousands of Jews, fine artists among them, are dying fighting
in the War...."[31] This sentiment would be captured in a poem in 1917, "Der
alte Tempel in Prag" ("The Old Temple in Prague").[32] Here are the first two
of its three stanzas:

"Der alte Tempel in Prag"

Tausend Jahre zählt der alte Tempel schon in Prag,
Staubfällig und ergraut ist längst sein Ruhetag
Und die alten Väter schlossen seine Gitter.

Ihre Söhne ziehen in die Schlacht.
Der zerborstene Synagogenstern erwacht
Und er segnet seine jungen Judenritter.

A thousand years the temple's stood in Prague,
But it was crumbling to dust and had earned its day of rest.
The old fathers had closed up its gate.

Their sons go forth in battle now.
The worn-out temple star revives
And blesses its young Jewish knights.

We do not know whether Else Lasker-Schüler was aware of the alle-
gations about incest between Trakl and his sister—given the kind of gossip
that circulated in her artistic circles, it is not unlikely that she did—but
this was of no concern to her. What was crucial was whether Trakl shared
his sister's repugnant racist views. Knowing how close they were, this was
a most unsettling thought. The fact that she had met Trakl only the one

time gave her little to go on and meant that she would forever be plagued by doubt.

Her poem to Trakl, "Georg Trakl," taking as its starting-point his appearing to her on the eve of his death, ends with these lines:

> "Sein Schatten weilte unbegreiflich
> Auf dem Abend meines Zimmers."
> "His shadow lingered, strange, mysterious,
> On my bedroom's eventide."[33]

Shadow. Shades. Shades of Senna Hoy. In both instances, trying to work good, she became embroiled in battles of far broader scope, battles that she could not decline, and that left her with a sense of powerlessness against the forces of evil in the world and her nerves too frayed to deal with other blows.

The war took the lives of some of her closest friends. Not just Franz Marc and Trakl. Alfred Lichtenstein, author of poems, short-stories and satires, died in September 1914 from wounds suffered during the attack on Vermandovillers on the Somme. Hans Ehrenbaum-Degele, who had printed many of her poems in the journal he co-edited, *Das Neue Pathos*, and whom she had dubbed "Tristan," was killed in Russia in 1915. Peter Baum, a poet from the Peter Hille circle, originally from her home town, Elberfeld, was killed in battle in 1916. Hugo Caro, the lawyer who had represented her in her dealings with publishers, and who sustained her through hard times during the separation from Walden, died while serving in Döberitz.[34] She commemorated each of them in prose essays and/or poems.

Apart from these personal losses, the war years hardly improved her financial situation, and in 1916 and 1917, friends again tried to find ways to help her. If she was wearing a clean shirt, it was frequently threadbare from repeated washings. George Grosz could not get over the fact that when he visited her, she came to the door in slippers that were pasted over with paper because there were holes in them.[35]

Scribbling in a sketchbook a draft of a letter he was planning to write to their mutual friend, the sculptor Milly Steger,[36] in the summer of 1916, he wrote:

> Have just come from Prince Jussuf (I'm not a very sentimental fellow, but something has to be done here). I'm writing to you ...
> because I know that despite the misunderstandings that have come

between you and the Theban throne, that Kaiser Abigail (Jussuf) has always spoken very fondly of you. Maybe you know some well-to-do family in Hagen who would be willing to give a few hundred marks. You know as well as I do how proud Prince Jussuf is—the best would be if the prince is not informed ... the best would be to telegraph the money to the Pension Bayreuth, Nürnbergerstr. 62/ Postamt 50 Berlin W. poste restante.[37]

He adds that unfortunately he himself is unable at the moment to help out. (See Appendix 9 for a poem to George Grosz.)

And always hanging over her head was the concern for Paul's future: schooling, possible apprenticeship in some artist's studio, his precarious health, the unpaid doctors' bills.

Not all was bleak and hopeless, however. The summer of 1914 saw the publication of *Der Prinz von Theben* by Kurt Wolff's publishing house, Verlag der Weissen Bücher, Leipzig, with three color prints by Franz Marc, and the following year the same publishers brought out a new, greatly expanded edition of *Meine Wunder*.

Like many of her Expressionist peers, Else Lasker-Schüler contributed to anti-war periodicals. Typical of these was *Der Bildermann*, which took a strong pacifist position. Kokoschka, Barlach and Kirchner were among the artists who contributed bold works to its pages. *Das neue Pathos*, published in Berlin between 1913 and 1920, with many wartime interruptions, was primarily a literary journal. There were others. Some moved their offices out of Germany, to Switzerland or Prague. But for all the writers and artists who survived, the war had knocked their youthful idealism out of their heads and hearts.

In Zurich, she was publishing in the periodical *Mistral* (later, *Sirius*) and her poems were read at the Cabaret Voltaire, as early as 1916, at the very dawn of Dada, along with works by Tristan Tzara and Aristede Bruant. While she did not belong to the circle of dadaists, she was, in a sense, a dadaist before Dada existed. Hans Richter, the dadaist painter and pioneer filmmaker, counted her among the initiates. She was always good for an argument.

"When I arrived in Zürich in August 1916," he writes, "the artists and intellectuals used to meet in the Café de la Terrasse. Only a few months later, we moved to the Café Odéon.... The only one of us to continue holding court at the Terrasse was the poetess Else Lasker-Schüler; but even she sometimes honored us with her presence at the Odéon, to read her poems ... and to argue obstinately with us."[38]

Richter contributed a drawing—an Indian crown, all feathers—to her book, *Der Malik*,[39] in which she had this to say about going to war: "Abigail Jussuf [the Malik] was firmly determined: under no circumstances would he take part in this human slaughter."[40]

Not just Richter, but nearly all her artist friends contributed crown drawings for the coronation of the Malik: Franz Marc, the toy crown; Heinrich Campendonk, the huntsman's crown; Ludwig Kainer, the ceremonial crown; John Höxter, the Hebrew crown and wreath; Egon Adler, the high priest's crown.[41]

In 1916 more than 75 of her own graphic works were exhibited in Hagen at the Folkswang Museum. Those she sold went for from between 5 and 300 marks. Presumably, she did not sell enough to sustain her, because she continued to ask people if they knew of any likely buyers.[42]

In July 1917, her *Gesammelte Gedichte* (*Collected Poems*) came out, again from the Verlag der Weissen Bücher. It is hard to imagine that she was not deeply gratified by this event. She mentions the fact without comment in a postcard to the blind poet Adolf von Hatzfeld: "Mein buch heraus" ("My book is out").[43] It was a milestone.

While she had the satisfaction of seeing her books in print with a highly visible publishing house, and while she was still in demand as a performing artist, giving readings that were frequently more like cabaret acts, the fact remained that even with readings, magazine publications, the sale of a drawing here and there, she barely had enough to see her through. And not all of her readings went well. She was worn to a frazzle by all the travel, she still frequently had to contend with unfriendly, even jeering, audiences. In October 1917, she suffered a debacle at a reading in Cologne. From Cologne she had to go on to Darmstadt and then for fourteen days to Switzerland. "I am deadtired damn it!" she wrote again to Hatzfeld. "They can all go to hell. What they put me through."[44]

By 1917 the once sustaining and invigorating correspondence with Karl Kraus seems to have ground to a halt. "Dear Karl Kraus," she wrote in May 1917, "You never write to me.... I have wanted to (write to you) for a long time, but you are no longer interested in me." The letter goes on to tell of her worsening health and finances: "I am literally starving." Then she mentions all the good friends who *have* tried to help. And again: "Karl Kraus, I believe you have something against me. What? Did you really at one time like my poems?... My soul is torn apart, my body broken." Finally, in a postscript overcoming, and simultaneously proclaiming, her pride, she asks him if he knows anyone who might buy her pictures. "Alms I do not ask."[45]

Almost word for word, the abandonment complaint is repeated in a letter to Franz Jung. It too begins, "I don't understand why you don't write. I am so destitute...."[46]

And to the architect, Hanns Hirt, whom she met through their mutual friend, Fritz Huf, in 1914, and with whom she had struck up a friendship: "I never heard from you again after my last letter.... I had thought we would be friends and had rejoiced to meet a real *Mensch*. What came between us I do not know.... I am writing this letter because I no longer have time for friendship, I could not offer anyone new any act of friendship my friends are all in the War. I can't talk to Fritz Huf, since he never understands me or thinks he has to misunderstand me. I would like never to have been at all."[47]

As it turned out, this letter was the beginning of a rich friendship! And the turning point in her relationship to Huf, on whom she cannot heap enough abuse in her ensuing correspondence with Hirt. He uses people, she had been warned: "in his megalomania he seemed to think I was in love with him, something that never was and never will be...."[48]

One of the saddest letters to Hirt tells of the possibility of an impending operation. "I would rather go to War; War does not drag out the way illness does. I am afraid of illness.... I was no longer Water. I am Water therefore I am not woman. A star only falls in the lap of a body of water [a reference to her poem "Versöhnung"]. One can lay the night like a cloak about one, there are stars that one can drink out of jagged bowls.... I cannot go on writing, I am too sad."[49]

And one of the strangest, and possibly, most revealing, letters is the one immediately following, written shortly after, where it is still not clear whether she will have to be operated on or not. She is still feeling very weak and debilitated. It begins: "Dreadfully tedious and trying are those who flaunt their souls, waving them about like flags—it becomes a habit, like endless holidays. I can understand you very well. As a small child I frequently imposed cruelties on myself when I didn't want to feel anything...."[50]

It appears from the letter that Hirt has paid her a visit, but she is unsure whether he wants to see her again. Altogether she seems unsure of herself. There are a lot of words crossed out, and the tone of the letter is tentative and probing. Only when she assumes her role of prince does she seem on surer footing. Once, presumably as her Biblical namesake Joseph, she struck Potiphar's wife, who tried to seduce her. Once she met Hadrian. She even loves boys, and has toyed with the idea of being a *Strichjunge* (male prostitute) herself—"perhaps out of cynicism," "Not out of frivolousness, but to stick my tongue out at my difficult life."

"Only once," she writes, "did I form a *Gestalt* (configuration); we slept on a blanket as on sand in the desert. Back to back; sometimes I was his lizard, then I lay between glass walls or I was his coral reef or his seaweed and grew around his limbs and around his heart or I was his flesh-eating flower.[51] Afterwards there came an earthquake and I lost myself in him. Now I can no longer entertain such musings; slime clings to me.... No one loves me. That needn't trouble you, I no longer long for that.... In my heart my cynicism is no longer sad, but like a clown."[52]

There are times when she cannot sleep, when she has to go out, "get drunk, or wander about or do other things or unthings (*Undinge*). I have no one to whom I can say these things."[53]

Nearly all her letters in these war years are punctuated with the horror and dread of war itself. Writing again to Hanns Hirt, she says, "I can no longer understand the world. Jussuf prays for those at the front" ("Jussuf betet für die Krieger").[54] But nothing compares with the last extant letter to Hirt, which is undated: It ends: "Burn all my books as I have just burnt them all all all. I am so empty that death itself will find nothing left to feed on in me."[55] As with her last letter to Karl Kraus ("I hate you"), it did not mean that the friendship ended on that note. With Hanns Hirt, as with Karl Kraus, that appears not to have been the case.[56]

And all this time her inner life kept throwing up old demons to haunt her. To Gottfried Benn:

> My sweetbeloved Giselheer [two birds flying] I believe we will never see each other again, but I think of you always and paradise begins to bloom in me again, and a bush on which wings sprout. We want to fly far away, come to Switzerland, there are lazarets here too. I'll cross Lake Zurich in an hour with the gulls to visit you sometimes. I am so exhausted; last night I wept from sheer exhaustion, I have so much to do.... I am so sad, always so alone.... I wish you would look at the camelia trees with me in Tessin, and then on to Milan across the *Lago*. Or should we walk along the shore of the Lake for two hours. In Kolberg there are lady's-smock meadows. You want to? I have lots of money for this. But I look so ugly all the time otherwise I would write very differently to you [three stars] ... I am sad. You probably feel sorry for me, that shames me. How gladly would I fight for you to the death. Your Prince.[57]

This letter, written between January and March 1918 while the poet was in Zurich for the first time, is a keen reminder of how she could live on two levels simultaneously: while she tries to maintain the fiction of her dream world, and even stir the ashes of her old love, she is altogether aware of the realities of the moment, the war, her appearance, the longtime rift between the once-lovers. But as the war years close in on her, "Thebes" itself begins to fade. The potency of this long-cherished fantasy universe as a shield against reality, if it ever was that, has worn itself out. While she continues to sign herself "Jussuf," or "Your Prince," and to adorn her letters with calligraphic symbols and emblems, she is no longer able to sustain her never-never land. A new sobriety takes hold.

CHAPTER NINE

1918–1925: "I Unload!"

"Die Händler aus dem Tempel jagen!"
("Run the money-changers out of the temple!")
Else Lasker-Schüler: *Ich raume auf!*

On November 11, 1918, the armistice in the West was signed. Germans were forced to accept that they had lost the war. The period from the end of the war to the Nazi takeover of power in 1933, known as Weimar, is marked by controversy, paradox and diversity.

It began with a weak coalition government under social democratic leadership, followed by a series of provisional governments in which the splinter parties of the extreme right and left made ominous gains. Political confusion and periodic economic crises led to an instability and unrest from which the Nazis would be the ultimate beneficiaries.

During the first three months of 1918, Else Lasker-Schüler spent most of her time in Switzerland. When she was in Zurich, she stayed at the Hotel Elite, and it was probably from there that she wrote to Gottfried Benn ("My sweet-beloved Giselheer"), asking him to come and join her, knowing he would not.

She was either giving readings or trying to arrange for readings which frequently did not materialize, looking for ways to earn money, or just to get money. In fact, the first half of 1918 found her frequently in railroad stations, mapping out itineraries on trains, in hotel rooms, in Zurich, in Locarno, and again in Zurich.

123

If a woman happened to sit down next to Frau Lasker-Schüler on a train, she would rummage in her bag until she found a tiny ball of knitting and begin to knit furiously. She was sure this would induce conversation, and as long as it was not about literature she was happy. Anonymity was a respite from literature and "literati." As she wrote to Karl Kraus in 1921, "You can't imagine how the literary world revolts me."[1] Planning a benefit ball for a poor family in 1920, she chose the motto: "Literatur verboten" ("Literature prohibited").[2]

Very likely, for travel, she would be wearing a dark coat, frayed at the sleeves, and a nondescript suit with a blouse underneath. It too could be seen as a kind of costume, a camouflage, the kind of uniform that would in itself discourage the unwanted kind of exchanges in railroad cars.

In August she returned to Berlin, moving into the Hotel Koschel, Motzstrasse 78, an address she would keep till her emigration in April 1933. According to Helene von Nostitz, who went there one day in 1921 hoping to see the poet and took a good look at the hotel while she waited in the lobby, it was modest, provincial-looking. And, being so near to the Nollendorfplatz, seemed to fit right in with the turbulent bustle, with people of all walks of life constantly coming and going.

"The whole hopelessness of the big city engulfs me," von Nostitz wrote, "its lovelessness. Harsh-colored, vapid ads stare blankly through the windows; ads for gas and other lighting fixtures, or for india-rubber goods."[3] The Berlin Baedeker of 1923 lists the Hotel Köschel under "Hotels Garnis (breakfast supplied in all; some also with hot and cold cuisine)." It is listed as having 60 rooms. Else's room looked out on a courtyard, where the yowling cats unnerved her, not least out of concern for the birds whom they chased.

In January 1919, the Spartacus Union, whose leaders were Karl Liebknecht and Rosa Luxemburg, became the Communist Party. On January 15, Freikorps troops murdered Liebknecht and Luxemburg. In Switzerland, Else Lasker-Schüler came under suspicion of association with communist organizations, in part because of her connection to the Cassirer Verlag, which was publishing the works of Rosa Luxemburg. While Else had not been involved in any such activities, her sympathies were certainly with the courageous and idealistic Rosa Luxemburg. In 1931, when a big rally was held in Berlin for Liebknecht and Luxemburg, she wrote to her friend, Paul Goldscheider, simply, "I'm going."[4]

The connection to the Cassirer Verlag was to prove crucial in her life over the next few years. In 1910, Cassirer had married one of Reinhardt's most gifted actresses, Tilla Durieux, with whom Else was friends. It was the Cassirers who had treated her to a night on the town after her break-up with Walden, when she had gone dressed as the stranger from the East. In this same period, Else had written an essay about Tilla, describing her in her various roles. As a bawd in Scholem Asch's *Gott der Rache* (*God of Vengeance*), for example: "I see her sitting in the middle of the sofa, sprawling with the insolence of a just-freed slave, aware of her power to destroy as she sees fit...."[5] The Cassirers moved in very different social circles, more upper-crust, so to speak, and so, after their marriage, they and Lasker-Schüler saw less of one another.

In 1919, while here and there a stipend had come her way, Lasker had no new book out and no foreseeable, reliable source of income. Then two things happened that would suddenly change her fortune. Negotiations with Paul Cassirer began for a ten-volume edition of her works, and in the same year, 1919, she would see the long-awaited performance of her play *Die Wupper.*

But for the moment she was still hard pressed. One of her more desperate tactics in hard times was to put things in hock, hoping to be able to retrieve them later. And so, in 1919, she sold some of Franz Marc's cherished postcard drawings to the Nationalgalerie in Berlin for 8300 marks, mainly in order to be able to pay her son Paul's doctors' bills.[6]

Therefore, when Cassirer bought up the rights for all her works from the Kurt Wolff Verlag and began preparing a ten volume edition of her entire oeuvre, she was elated.

The whole period immediately after the war was one of frantic activity, of brief euphoria followed by long depressions and disillusionment. It was not a period of great poetic productivity.

And whenever she contemplated her lifelong *Leidensweg* (road to Golgotha), her sense of isolation returned to plague her. All she could see was an accretion of losses. She was quick to take offense, and slow to forgive. "I hate and despise mankind without exception,"[7] she wrote to Karl Kraus in 1921. It is frustrating not to have his replies to her letters, if only to see how he dealt with her sudden outbursts and over-reacting.

Beginning in 1922 and 1923, she started putting out feelers, and expressing the wish to extend her already considerable geographical web to include America and Jerusalem: "Ja wie ist Jerusalem?" ("Why not Jerusalem?"). "Everybody translates me," she wrote to Hugo Bergmann,[8] "and the money goes to the 'Dollarlande und Hebräerstaat' and I get nothing out of it."[9]

She wanted to find a way to give readings in New York and Chicago, perhaps to Jewish groups, and, although she did not have Zionist sympathies, yes, she wanted to go to Jerusalem.

And of course she wanted to take Paul with her. Toward these ends, she writes to her niece's widower in California, Louis Asher, about coming to America: "Direktore Reinhardt he would take me with himself to America. He lobt me allways verry much." And repeating a request from an earlier letter: "My son is painter (Zeichner) he would love to be two jears [sic] in America to pain [sic] for papers but later."[10] To plead Paul's case, she includes a letter of recommendation for Paul from Albert Einstein, who describes him as "a skilled graphic artist, the son of an important artist..."[11] and tells Asher how much Einstein likes Paul.[12]

If she was out with Paul, and they met someone on the way, Paul would ride his bicycle to the next street corner, and wait there for her to catch up, probably so as not to be embarrassed by what she would be saying about him. And if she was not urging Paul or herself on some patron or publisher, then she was trying to help one of her friends or protegés. This did not always endear her to people. Raised eyebrows and snide remarks were frequently what she reaped. Her extravagant claims for Paul and for her friends' talents only made people stop taking her seriously.

How well she knew that she could get on people's nerves. "When you see me, you will at once ascertain that I am not importunate..."[13] she wrote to Harry Graf Kessler, only infuriating him the more. How well she knew that they made fun of her silly crushes! And how little she was able or willing to do anything about it. Sometimes she even tried to "forewarn" people not to pay attention to the gossip that was forever buzzing about her, as she did in a letter to Erwin Loewenson: "Dear Mr. Lowison [sic], I would be most unhappy if you were to believe any of the evil gossip...").[14] But the facts were too often against her, and her efforts to deny them, counter-productive. This time it was Paolo Pedrazzini, "the doge," with whom she had fallen in love in Locarno and to whom she dedicated the 1923 Bibliophile Edition of *Theben* (*Thebes, Poems and Lithographs*).

In Switzerland once again she accosted Harry Graf Kessler, importuning him—in his office as military attaché on a secret peace mission—to do something for that same impoverished aristocrat, Adalbert von Maltzahn, who had made her the butt of Kurt Hiller's bad joke at the Café des Westens back in 1915. Kessler noted in his diary: "Bonn—Basel. letter from Else Lasker-Schüler, who wants to present a certain Maltzahn to me.... 'With his kind beautiful eyes he is certain to be useful in advancing the peace effort.' Damn fool of a poet."[15]

Another entry: "Yesterday, in Zurich 'die Lasker' rang up five times ... Else Lasker-Schüler, who runs around in the fool's cap-and-bells of 'Jussuf, Prince of Thebes,' and who thinks to promote peace through some stripling with beautiful eyes, nonetheless represents, in all her insignificance and folly, an organic part of the whole preposterous enormity."[16] And a year later, his pique over this dreadful personage finds new sparks on which to ignite when she tries again to importune him at a party at Cassirer's art gallery: "For four years I have been doing everything in my power to avoid this impossible person.... Now I couldn't avoid being introduced. I wished her good day and excused myself."[17]

None of these instances, however, prevent him from recognizing "the lightning flashes of genius" in *Die Wupper*,[18] which he had gone to see in its first performance at Reinhardt's Junges Deutschland Theater in Berlin.

One could draw up a list, beginning with Walter Benjamin, of people who couldn't stand to be around Lasker, because they found her either overbearing, silly or hysterical, but who freely acknowledged her genius as a poet. And so it would continue up until her death. To name just one other from this same period in her life, Bert Brecht, after hearing her read in Munich in June 1920, wrote in his diary: "good and bad poems, overwrought, unhealthy, but individual ones very beautiful. The woman is old and flabby, jaded and altogether unappealing."[19] One reason why she may have appeared old to Brecht was that she was 51 in 1920, not 44, as he assumed.

She was someone whose person and whose art easily lent themselves to parody. She knew this, and sometimes she reveled in it and could capitalize on it. Remember the little girl in *Konzert*, who fixed her eyes on you, knowing that made her look exotic?

In Franz Blei's 1922 "Bestiarium," there is a drawing of a scarab lying in the classic "submission" position, flat on its back, defenseless, but here, with a distraught face turned around to peer at the viewer. The drawing is titled "The lasker-schüler" and is described as follows: "This is the sole surviving scarab of the kind once found in the tombs of the royal mummy. [The reference is to her own tale that she was descended from some royal Egyptian or Biblical figure.] It escaped from an open mummy coffin, by swishing its blue-green shimmering wings. But now it is expiring all too quickly in today's desert sands, where the insect gives off its strangely melodic sigh."[20]

There was no end to the parodies of her poems, some maliciously attributed to the poet herself, as well as brazen imitations, not to mention invented as well as true stories about the artist's eccentricities. In some instances there was anti–Semitic intent, and the results, needless to say, were even less edifying.

One of the first winds of good fortune to come her way after the war was that *Die Wupper*, the play which had lain in a drawer for ten years aside from a reading which she herself had given at the Gnu (cabaret), was about to cross the boards. She had passed up one opportunity herself, when she spurned Max Reinhardt the first time around in 1910 or 1911. Reinhardt had asked to see *Die Wupper*, but much as she had admired the theater man in the past, she was so horrified by his Everyman, that she asked him to send her *Wupper* back to her.

It was after a performance of Hofmannsthal's *Jedermann* ("Everyman"), which he had staged at around the same time in Berlin. In one of her *Briefe nach Norwegen* (*Letters to Norway*), she had written to Walden:

> I went to see "Jedermann" or is it called "Allerlei" ["Hodge-podge"]? I think it's Allerlei for Jedermann or Jedermann for Aller-lei: Step right up, ladies and gents, for the giant Punch and Judy show ... an evangelical play for the benefit of baptised Jews ... very uplifting. All the baptised Jews were very uplifted, especially by the blond Germania angel in blue and double chin. To the right a human fleck, to the left a blotch of angel ... Jedermann here, Jeder-mann there—.

In the end she wonders, "Does Reinhardt need money? Or what's the matter? He would do better to get his gang to steal it for him. He shouldn't allow himself such indulgences. Outside the theater, the social democrats were going wild. It was election day.... With the evening fell my last hopes for a production of my play by Reinhardt—whom I have so often admired."[21]

Now, in 1919, the time and the setting—his special projects theater Das Junge Deutschland—turned out to be just right. For one thing, there had been a shift in artistic tastes. Whereas in the first decade of the century, Expressionism was *the* avant-garde movement in poetry and painting, by 1920 it had become old hat, i.e., establishment, and to the Expressionist poets themselves something of a bore. The war had destroyed whatever shreds of idealistic utopianism they had possessed, and new artistic movements, Dada and futurism, the new objectivity and constructivism, were taking its place. By fusing naturalist subject matter with highly subjective treatment, and by adapting some of the recent artis-tic trends to its own purposes, Expressionist drama could function in a timely, creative way. And in fact the twenties would see a whole crop of brilliant Expressionist plays on German stages. In addition, the gather-ing heat of workers' revolutions fed into the ferment in the theater.[22] Writers and artists were beginning to probe the unrest that lay beneath the surface of what would soon come to be known as "The Golden Twen-ties."

Lasker-Schüler's play *Die Wupper*, set in the Rhineland, around the river which flows through the industrial city from which it takes its name, was thus ideally suited for Reinhardt's Junges Deutschland, a forum for innovative productions, to stand alongside the usual Classics offerings of his Deutsches Theater.

The river, surrounded by belching chimneys, is the main artery of proletariat life, and provides the main metaphor for the play. "Meshugga is trump!" cries out a fat man from the stage. Milling around the river are hosts of half-insane visionaries, misfits, perverts, and displaced victims of the late industrial revolution, with names like "Lange Anna" ("Long Anna"), "Pendelfriedrich" ("Pendulumfriedrich"), and "Der gläserne Amadus" ("The Goggle-eyed Amadus").

Designated by its author as "A City Ballad," the play is a series of phantasmagorical scenes in which flawed but endearing characters live out or recount their strange, unfulfilled urban lives. Or, put differently, a dark-visioned surreal drama played out against a background of social conflict.

Cover drawing for *Der Malik: A Kaiser's Tale, with Illustrations by the Author*, for the new edition of her collected works in the Cassirer Verlag, Berlin 1919. (Schiller-Nationalmuseum / Deutsches Literaturarchiv, Marbach).

It was Reinhardt's number one man, Heinz Herald, who directed this first production. Friedrich Hollaender wrote the score. Ernst Stern designed the stage-sets. The production was a great success.

With their trapezoidal houses and cubist configurations, Ernst Stern's stage designs remind one of early Expressionist films, like *The Cabinet of*

Dr. Caligari. One can see the new stylistic influences at work both in film and on the stage.

A new aesthetic was coming into being in architecture and city planning as well. These years saw the birth of the Bauhaus. And in 1920 Else Lasker-Schüler read her *Hebrew Ballads* and other poems for the opening evening of the Bauhaus in Weimar. Among those present was Walter Gropius.

A year later her short prose piece "Der Wunderrabbiner von Barcelona" saw publication, again with Cassirer. (For a discussion of "Der Wunderrabbiner" in a somewhat different context, see Chapter Two.) The prose narration of "Der Wunderrabbiner" is framed by two poems. Set at the beginning, "Got Hör" ("God Hear") is the opening prayer.

"Gott Hör…"

Um meine Augen zieht die Nacht sich
Wie ein Ring zusammen.
Mein Puls verwandelete das Blut in Flammen
Und doch war alles grau und kalt um mich.

O Gott und bei lebendigem Tage
Träum ich vom Tod.
Im Wasser trink ich ihn und würge ihn im Brot.
Für meine Traurigkeit fehlt jedes Mass auf deiner Waage.

Gott hör, in deiner blauen Lieblingsfarbe
Sang ich das Lied von deines Himmels Dach.
Und wurde doch für deinen ewigen Hauch zu wach.
Mein Herz schämt sich vor dir fast seiner tauben Narbe.

Wo ende ich, o Gott, denn in die Sterne,
Auch in den Mond sah ich in alle deiner Früchte Tal.
Der rote Wein wird schon in seiner Beere schaal
Und überall die Bitternis in jedem Kerne.[23]

"God Hear…"

Night closes in around my eyes
And holds me in its tether.
My pulse put fire in my arteries,
Yet all around me was a cold gray weather.

O God and in the warmest shoals
I dream of death.
I guzzle it in water and gag on it in bread.
You cannot even weigh my sadness on your scales.

Fairgrounds. Stage set by Ernst Stern for Heinz Herald's production of *Die Wupper* **in Max Reinhardt's Das Junge Deutschland Theater, April 1919. Watercolor and mixed media, 54 × 72 cm (Theaterwissenschaftliches Archiv Köln).**

God hear, dressed in your favorite shade of blue,
I sang the song about your skylight dome.
But I was still too callow to go Home.
My heart's ashamed of being black and blue before you.

Where will I end, O God, for everywhere
I look, the stars, the moon, on both your plain and hill,
Already in its berry the red wine's fruit grows stale...
And everywhere the bitterness at every core.

After the terrible pogrom with which the story ends, and which is painted in dark Goyaesque tones and shocking images of death and mutilation[24] (not unlike Ernst Stern's angst-ridden stage sets for *Die Wupper*[25]) the piece ends with a quiet poem of hope, in which reconciliation between Jews and Christians through the love and wisdom of the miracle rabbi is foretold.

In July she wrote to Karl Kraus: "Just now I wrote the Wunderrabiner, which came over me like a revelation, I was totally shattered...."[26] But for all this excitement, theater success and publishing, Lasker's financial worries had not abated. Most worrisome was Paul, whose health remained precarious at best, and who was still financially dependent on her. She made repeated attempts to find an opening for him, whether as an illustrator at a periodical or as an apprentice in an artist's studio.

She inquired of Ernst Stern whether he might find work for him in one of the theater's ateliers.[27] But then Hans Richter, the Dadaist graphic artist and film director who had been an admirer of hers since he first met her at the Café de la Terrasse in Zurich in 1916, must have offered to apprentice him.

"My boy will start to work on Monday at Mr. Richter's atelier," she wrote again to Ernst Stern. "Mr. Richter has gone out of his way to be kind."[28] And if Stern could employ him in his atelier at the theater as well, she asked that Paul be paid a salary of "not under 300m. a month." But the boy's failing health caused all these plans to abort.

Not everyone liked Paul, but already as far back as 1913 and 1914, Franz Marc had taken a liking to him and found him gifted. Of course, in Marc's case, it was partly that Paul reminded him of himself as a young boy. While Paul was away in Vienna, he was accused by an "ogress,"[29] Frau Dr. Eugenie Schwarzwald, of making drawings from photographs and palming them off as "original," something he had never pretended they were. His mother was so incensed at the accusation that she shot back, "Oh, yes. I too copy my poems from others."[30] It must have been a terrible scene, Lasker-Schüler coming away totally demolished by this woman's allegedly sadistic assaults.

Not infrequently, drawings and caricatures of Paul's did appear in periodicals. Some of the early ones, done when he was just a boy of 15 or 16, show remarkable psychological insight.[31] We owe a number of very telling line drawings of his mother to him as well. He seemed to see her as stern and serious, intense and inscrutable, with the brim of her hat pulled down over her eyes. His only recorded verbal comment about his mother was to the effect that he wished he had had a more ordinary mother.

If only she could have exercised some restraint in trying to further his career. But her nerve-drilling insistence, the relentless importuning on her part, did him more harm than good. (As previously noted, this was true not just of her efforts on her son's behalf.) She certainly irritated Karl Kraus with her repeated requests to help Paul and turned on him when he refused to be manipulated, almost destroying one of the most valuable friendships of her entire life. "As you never once invited my boy to see you, for that I hate you and nothing in the world can change that," she wrote to him in March 1924, after Paul's stay in Vienna, ending her letter to him again with the words, "I hate you."[32]

On the other hand, she could be totally disarming, ingenuous and naive, in her requests. To Ernst Stern, with whom she was in close contact now because of *Die Wupper*, for which he had designed the sets, she dashed off a note, asking—as a very special favor—if he could lend the boy, out of the Theater's costume collection, a cowboy suit for an upcoming New Year's Ball. One can be sure he will have been happy to comply.[33]

Ernst Stern's admiration and understanding of the poet come across in a striking drawing he made of her, which appeared as the

Else Lasker-Schüler. Lithograph by Ernst Stern. Frontispiece in *Das Junge Deutschland*, volume 2, number 7, 1919 (Schiller National Museum/Deutsches Literaturarchiv, Marbach).

frontispiece in a then-current issue of *Das Junge Deutschland*. It is a lithograph marked by bold cross-hatchings. We are staring head-on at a vulnerable but determined woman, at odds both with herself and with the world around her. A riveting, unforgettable image. Clearly, she had won the admiration and friendship of people like Richter and Stern because of the kind of person she was: honest and uncompromising.

Even when she was in Berlin, she appears to have been spending less time at the café than in the past. "Café des Westens is *very* interesting, but I go just for an hour a day at the most, because I have so much to do."[34] However, she did take time out to meet with Gottfried Benn at the Café Nurnberg.

For years Else Lasker-Schüler had been struggling, with varying degrees of success, for better contract conditions with her publishers. In 1913, she had counted herself lucky to come under the protection of the famed Kurt Wolff Verlag in Leipzig. Wolff was a charmer, an aristocrat, an aesthete who could barely bring himself to mention the word money. As he said himself, it would be too tasteless to put a figure on her books. Instead, he decided to make her a "gift" of one hundred marks a month for the three books he would print. "I do it gladly, gladly, my little Else Lasker-Schüler."[35] The three were *The Collected Poems*, *Prince of Thebes*, and a volume of essays. Then, after refusing her urgent request for an advance on her *Hebrew Ballads*, Wolff did everything to place impediments in her way when she tried to switch publishers.

This she succeeded in doing, and with great éclat. In 1919, Paul Cassirer not only took on a complete edition (*Gesamtausgabe*) of her works, but in addition to the regular bound edition, he printed a deluxe edition of 100 copies, bound in leather with raw silk, each numbered and signed by the author. Cassirer also asked her to illustrate the "Wunderrabbiner" ("Miracle Rabbi").

He was instrumental as well in getting his friend and colleague, Alfred Flechtheim, an influential gallery owner and publisher, to commission Else to make color illustrations for the special deluxe edition of her *Theben*. To do this work, which required good lighting, the artist was given space in the gallery. Flechtheim came around to admire her work, smiling his suave, thick-lipped smile approvingly. When it came time for her to be paid, however, Herr Flechtheim inquired, delicately, "And how much electricity do you suppose you will have used, Frau Lasker-Schüler?"[36]

Cassirer himself would lose his halo and eventually come under her knife. "A shark," she later called him. After launching her with grand gestures all around, he abused, according to her, his power over her fate, asking her to take work home with her, and subjecting her to other indignities, the while stinting on her royalties. All of these "benefactors" would be dealt with summarily when the time came. And the time was not long in coming.

If her good fortune seemed unduly short-lived, it is only fair to say that there were larger, more impersonal forces at work. Inflation had already begun to make itself felt in Germany, and in 1923, when the government started printing currency without backing, the bottom fell out.

In September, the business manager of the Cassirer firm, Walter Feilchenfeldt, informed her that she was due to receive $20, of which $5 was to be in dollars, 9.45 billion in the worthless paper marks. She was ready to go on the warpath. "Ich räume auf!" ("I unload!") She called her famous tomahawk, and she lashed out at the whole cutthroat world of commercial publishing.

For all its personal venom, the pamphlet had a broader thesis, and must be seen against the backdrop of post-war social and political unrest. Remember that on January 15, 1919, Carl Liebknecht and Rosa Luxemburg had been brutally murdered by the *Freikorps* (free corps). After trying to

form a Soviet-style workers' government in Munich, Else's friend, the anarchist scholar Gustav Landauer, was beaten and killed by Reichswehr troops.
Ernst Toller, the pacifist poet and playwright, was imprisoned, along with
Erich Mühsam, who had been active with Landauer in organizing the *Rätere-
publik* (the workers' councils) in Munich. In her pamphlet, Lasker-Schüler
pays tribute to these martyrs, and says, "The poet is better equipped to build
a world than to form a state."[37]

It does not take much imagination to see how the general political climate and her anger over the fates of her artist friends fueled Else Lasker-
Schüler's specific fury. "Let us organize like workers,"[38] she admonishes her
literary confrères. Long before the fact, she envisaged a writers' union, or
better yet, cooperative publishing houses run by writers themselves. "Die
Händler aus dem Tempel jagen!" ("Run the money-changers out of the temple!")[39] was her call to arms. Certainly critics who saw her as unpolitical,
weltfremd (spacey), will have had to take another look. She had put herself
in the forefront of political agitation.

The year was 1924. "Ich räume auf" ("I Unload: My Case Against My
Publishers") came out under her own imprint. She went on the road reading it to audiences all over Germany. It is a 47-page, hour-and-a-half long
diatribe.

The woman across from you is sitting for her portrait. Perhaps she has
just gotten back from one of her rabble-rousing speeches, "Ich räume auf."
She happens also to be a dear and much revered friend. You became friends
back in your Berlin days, 1920 and 1921, when as a young man, you joined
the activist socialist group around Pfemfert's *Die Aktion*, and got to know
Herwarth Walden. You will have much to talk about—old friends, Germany
after the War. You, too, have been very active among artists, helping found
left-wing artist organizations. And she wants to hear about Poland, where
you were born. And Hasidism, your roots. You talk, and gradually she
relaxes, and you can paint her.

This is the way I imagine Jankel Adler's portrait of the poet coming
about. It is so intimate, you can almost hear their voices in the room. And
they are definitely engaged in serious talk. Unlike Kokoschka, who said,
when asked why he had never painted Lasker-Schüler, that he had never
really understood her, Adler seems altogether at home with this woman.

So it's worth paying attention. He sees her, for one thing, as a very solid
(cubist) chunk of woman. (In its geometric starkness the portrait reflects the
influence of Russian Constructivism.) None of this starry-eyed idealism or overwrought *Schwärmerei* of the early portraits of the poet. On the contrary, it is
a very sober and sobering view. As if the painter wanted to document the poet's

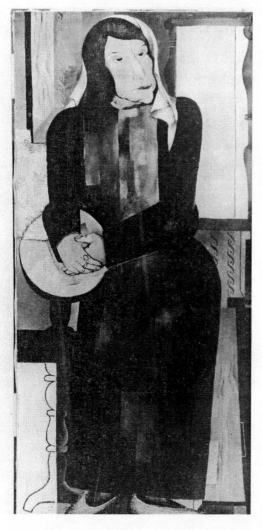

Else Lasker-Schüler 1924. Portrait in Oils by Jankel Adler (© 2001 Artists Rights Society [ARS], New York/VG Bild-Kunst, Bonn; courtesy Von der Heydt Museum Wuppertal).

mythic stature, while remaining absolutely true to the more earth-bound limits of her existence.

Thus he paints her feet in gold-embroidered slippers, but plants them firmly on the ground. Beneath the diaphanous fold of her upper garment, the outline of a breast and nipple can be discerned. A blue crescent moon, her personal emblem, is emblazoned on the signet ring she wears on her finger. Her eyes are heavy-lidded, like a wise old eagle; her cheeks are heavy-jowled. Her brows are knit, but her jaw is set. A formidable person, it tells us, one who has known suffering and sorrow. For this painter, whose life was writ in blood and suffering, she is an altogether *sympathique* figure.

Adler, whose work enjoyed great fame abroad, died in London. His entire family had been wiped out in the Holocaust. His portrait of Else Lasker-Schüler hangs today in the von der Heydt Museum in Wuppertal, alongside an Adler self-portrait. It is as though their dialogue had never ceased.

In 1925, Hindemith's two songs[40] to poems of Else were performed in Dusseldorf at a celebration of Rhineland poets. But the year did not end well. At Christmastime, she visited Paul in Munich, where he was studying with a Professor Ehmke. Paul was unable to shake off a "grippe" and very high fever. Dr. Ferdinand Sauerbruch was called in, and a diagnosis of tuberculosis was finally established.

∿ ∿ ∿ ∿ ∿

CHAPTER TEN

∿ ∿ ∿ ∿ ∿

1925–1933: Weimar

"Erst kommt das Fressen, dann kommt die Moral."
("First comes eats, then homilies.")
Bert Brecht: *Dreigroschen Finale*

It will come as no surprise that after her vituperations against the entire tribe of literary book publishers, Else Lasker-Schüler found no publisher for seven years. (It is also true that she had no manuscript to offer during this period.) This was not a situation she could well afford. True, there were numerous publications, essays and poems, appearing ubiquitously in newspapers and periodicals throughout the twenties. The *Berliner Tageblatt*, in particular, paid very well for "feuilletons" (short analytical sketches on a wide range style midway between reportage and personal).

These essays and short prose pieces dealt with a variety of subjects, from an ebullient review of the Russian cabaret *The Blue Bird*, to a tongue-in-cheek request for financial aid, in the name of her realm, Thebes, to the Minister of Finance, deploring the fact that her brochure, "Ich räume auf," had spelled the ruination of her Thebes. Many were nostalgic pieces about her childhood in Elberfeld, and one about the Baltic sea resort, Kolberg, "before one was threatened there by 'Swastiklers.'"[1] Together, these would eventually make up the book *Konzert*. In addition, we see her drawing furiously to meet increasing demand; the sale of her drawings had really taken off. But still, in the distance the reverberating volley of her pamphlet, echoing back and forth in the feuilletons across the land, had potential book publishers running for cover.

137

On January 7, 1926, Paul Cassirer committed suicide. She wondered whether she had played a role in his death. In running the book-mongers out of their temples, she had not spared Cassirer. She found it hard to forgive him. First the inordinate praise, tainted by overweening pride of possession: "This is the Prince of Thebes, the Else Lasker-Schüler, the flower of my House!" he would say, presenting her to his guests. "The greatest poetess of our time—of all time."[2] No superlative seemed good enough. How he had let her down! His defense: her books did not sell.

Theirs had been an unfortunate relationship, she admitted in a letter to a friend on his death, one that had begun with glowing promise, only to sour over time. If he had behaved more decently, she sighed, things might have worked out differently. She was acutely sensitive to his good qualities. They had, after all, been friends. (Tilla Durieux, Cassirer's wife, at one time even thought Else was in love with him.) And he had been generous in his support.

But she would not let her feelings intrude where they had no place. Sentimentality, she noted, is merely the obverse side of the coin of brutality. She would have none of that. And so, re-affirming her unbending aggressive stance toward her publishers, she stated, "Gandhi's strategy of passive resistance worked because there you were dealing with Englishmen, here, however, with beasts in every form."[3] These words could be applied more broadly than she perhaps was aware at the time. In any event, by mid-May 1926, she had won out against the firm of Cassirer, and the rights to her books reverted to her.

In one sense, a very real sense, one could say that all of this was irrelevant, that these events occurred literally "outside" her. What really occupied her and would continue to be her main concern and worry over the next two years was the steadily deteriorating health of her son Paul. Of course, this concern too was made more acute by insufficient funds.

By Christmas 1925, Paul was so ill with "the grippe" that he was referred to Dr. Ferdinand Sauerbruch, the famous surgeon, who made the definitive diagnosis: tuberculosis. It is at this time, shortly after a visit to friends on Christmas Eve, that she had a vision of King David, who she claimed came to her in her room at the hotel, and sat on a low stool beside her. "He wore a black cloak and a black turban. His eyes were ashen. He remained a long time seated next to me." Without speaking, he foretold that she would suffer *grenzenloses Leid*.[4] And that is how it would indeed come to be—boundless pain and grief over Paul. The seriousness with which she took her visions is evident in two prose works, *Das Hebräerland*[5] and *Auf der Galiläa*.[6] It would also become a sore point in her relationship with Gershom Scholem in later years. He simply refused to believe she had ever "seen" King David.[7]

By mid–May Paul had spent almost three months in a Munich hospital. Drs. Sauerbruch and Epstein still believed his condition was curable. He was to be moved to Sanatorium Agra in the vicinity of Lugano.

From now on the poet's life became a harried shuttling between Berlin and Switzerland, where she tried to arrange readings to cover the mounting expenses of Paul's illness, and to give her an excuse to visit him more often. She tried to busy herself during the day so that she wouldn't think about him all the time. That left her exhausted every evening. At night she prayed for Paul and "for all sick people and animals and all that is sick in the world."[8]

It is both touching and troubling to see how she tried to control Paul's entire environment in order to spare him any unnecessary pain or even embarrassment. Writing to her friend, Elvira Bachrach, whom she hoped would visit Paul, she says, "But please, please, let him know ahead: he is such a gentleman, will want to shave...."[9] By the same token, she writes to his doctors that in case his condition should worsen, "*please, please* do not let him know."[10] Before his hospitalization, she would deliver his love letters for him in person, something he was allegedly too shy to do himself.

At a time when her fame as a poet was at its peak, her place in German literature assured, she was actually writing less poetry than before. Prose and personal letters were her preferred modes of expression. These, and her tireless graphic work, done both for money and for the satisfaction it gave her, kept her busy. And not just busy, but working, it would seem, at a frenzied pace. Work, after all, was a way of holding back the furies, and silencing the voices of doom. There was not much she could do to save Paul. She tried to come forward with medical advice and suggestions about other doctors who might be brought in on his case. But by mid–1926, all she could do was cling to faint hopes proffered by his doctors that a cure might still be possible. In the end she could just look on as he wasted away. If she had felt helpless before, in the face of other deaths, nothing could be compared to the visceral suffering she would undergo now.

So she struck up epistolary correspondences with people she had never met. Paul Goldscheider was a poor Viennese medical student in 1927, just 25 years old. He was also, like her own son and her beloved deceased brother, named Paul. A warm, rich exchange developed between them. It was especially intense in the period from 1927 to 1929. They stayed in touch, if sporadically, until 1938,[11] when he sent her money for a trip to Palestine. At a time when he was setting out in the world, his friendship with Else Lasker-Schüler was for him, like for so many of her youthful admirers, an unforgettable experience.

When she answered his first letter, she had no idea who or what he was. Of course this made her all the more curious. Yet keeping his face *and* his profession a mystery made it somehow easier for her to write to him, at least initially. She was also wary, if not outright ambivalent, for just this reason. "Who are you, that you know this about me (that I am susceptible, in my vulnerable state, to flattery)? Just as if you were an intruder, breaking in on my life! Do you know acquaintances of mine in Vienna? In Vienna there is much that is wonderful, but also much '*küss die Hand*.'"[12] She can't make up her mind whether to draw him in or hold him off.

Since people thought she was seven years younger than she really was, she was sensitive about looking "old," and possibly therefore hesitant about meeting him or even sending a photograph. Goldscheider remembers her picking him up from the Anhalter railroad station (Anhalter Bahnhof). It was the spring of 1928. As with everyone who ever met her, her appearance made an indelible impression on him: "She wore a black fur cap cocked to one side; around her neck a string of colored glass beads. She looked ill, jaundiced." But, oh, the blazing eyes: "like glittering black diamonds."[13] With Goldscheider she went to see Bert Brecht's *Dreigroschenoper* (*Threepenny Opera*), presumably in the Pabst film version. When they came out she commented, "Plagiarism; but the plagiarism of a genius."[14, 15]

Asked, in 1969, whether he thought she was insane, Goldscheider, who had known her from 1927 to 1938, replied: "She was eccentric. She was obsessed, but in no way insane."[16]

Correspondence was not made any easier by the fact that she was repeatedly injuring her right arm, having operations on it, or keeping it in a splint. But up until her dying days, she relied mainly on pen and paper, preferring it to the typewriter. How could she have done her incomparable rebuses otherwise?

She was also spending time at the Romanische Café, drinking cocoa and munching anise cookies, frequently in the company of a group of East European Yiddish writers and artists, including Abraham Stenzel, a young Yiddish poet who became her ardent admirer, her good friend Jankel Adler, their mutual friend, the "golden" Aribert (Aribert Wascher) and, in all probability, Peretz Markisch, who would come to the café on an occasional visit from Warsaw. It is more than likely that in this animated circle Else Lasker-Schüler overcame some if not all of her West European, assimilated-Jewish, biases against the "jargon"-speaking Jews of Eastern Europe, as well as becoming more seriously acquainted with the writings of the Cabbala.

The café was the meeting place, much as the Café des Westens had been for the pre-war generation, for avant-garde artists and left-wing politics, and now, for a brief period at least, for this newly arrived contingent of Yiddish artists as well. If the Café des Westens had earned its nickname as Café Megalomania, the Romanische was known among its Yiddish regulars as *Kibutz-goles* (meeting-place of the exiled) or *Rachmones-Café* (place of refuge).[17] The decibel level would not have been any lower than at the old hang-out.

Nor are the tales about her antics any less wild. Her very first meeting with Stenzel was undoubtedly at the introduction of Jankel Adler at the café, though probably it took place a few years earlier. The story attached to it, however, sounds like an almost exact replay of the Hiller-Herzfelde episode. It goes like this: Else sends a note over to Adler, who is sitting with Stenzel at another table, saying she wants to meet Stenzel. There is a third man at the Adler-Stenzel table, however, and when the little slip of paper arrives, he waves it off with, "That's just a crackpot yid who drives everyone nuts" (*"Das ist bloss eine bekloppte jidene, die alle Leute meschugge macht"*).[18] In response, Adler makes a move as if to attack him.

Toward Stenzel she seemed to feel protective, even motherly, but she was wary, and offended, when she thought he was "using" her to advance his own literary career. This was a suspicion she harbored about many younger poets who revered or flattered her, but it is not an unusual one for people who have achieved fame.

Stenzel, whose description of her dates from that same period, 1927 to 1928, as Paul Goldscheider's, sees more layers of her being. To him her face looks different every moment. "She bites her lips that have deep furrows at the corners ... her face is both bitter from experience and childlike with curiosity."[19] Elsewhere he says she could, to dramatize a point, affect the look of a satyr.[20]

He also describes her hotel room in these years. It is not unlike the impressions gleaned by Herzfelde and Franz Jung during the war years:

> The small hotel room looked like a doll's house, transmogrified as if by some magic spell—the *scholem alejchem* angels hovered everywhere. Every corner was hung with wispy silk cloths: blue, red, green, golden-yellow—scarves of every color. On one side ... stood a little table, covered with another such cloth, on which there were all kinds of colored crayons and pens, and a little pile of flattened-out gold and silver papers that looked as if they had been collected from cigarette and bonbon wrappers.[21]

With Stenzel too she goes to the movies, one silent Chaplin film after another with just a quick cup of coffee in between.

When Paul's condition did indeed worsen, she brought him back to

Berlin. A Palestinian painter and sculptor, Jussuff Abbo, who had a studio not far from her hotel, let her use it (but not rent-free) so she could be with Paul day and night. In September 1927, she moved into the studio. With her was her one-time housemaid, Hedwig Grieger,[22] who as a young girl had come to work for her and Dr. Lasker. Together, the two women ministered to the failing young man's needs.

During all these months, she wrote long despairing letters to Paul Goldscheider, letters full of little details from her daily life, attempts to establish intimacy with someone she has never met. "Do you too like notebooks with rubber bands around them? And pocket knives? And marbles?"[23] And while she tells him over and over how heavy her heart is with sorrow, she cannot bring herself to name the cause. Only once, in November, one sentence. Not even a sentence: "To see my poorest boy in a fever the entire time for almost two years now."[24]

On December 14, Paul died. Like a shy animal, "he asked me to go behind the curtain, I had to swear to him I would—he was so weak he could barely talk."[25] One cannot avoid the cruel conjecture that Paul, too, at the crucial moment, found it necessary to banish her. The funeral was on December 18. Along with Gottfried Benn, Hedwig Grieger was most certainly there, as she would be on other occasions when the "Frau Doktor" could hardly have managed without her.

When she tries to write to Paul Goldscheider, "der blaue Jaguar" (as he has taken to calling her) finds herself barely capable of holding a pen. She is exhausted, drained, an empty vessel. Everyone, she says, had been very kind to her. Or nearly everyone. The sculptor, from whom she rented the studio, was not so nice. He was constantly at her, demanding money, never enough. He even sued. She apologizes for not having been more active in finding work for Goldscheider's brother, who was unemployed, and whom she had promised to help. This was December 1927.

The weather conspired with her melancholy: "Now it's raining again. Thunder and lightning." The best distraction would be travel. Maybe she'll come to Vienna for Easter with Maria Moissi (wife of Alexander Moissi, the actor). That would give her the opportunity to repair and renew her old friendship with Karl Kraus, whom she hasn't heard from in *years*, as well as visit Goldscheider. Out of sheer nervosity she flits from one travel plan to another. No, not Vienna after all. "Vienna is too dull, too many big yawning spaces devoid of human beings."[26]

Instead, Goldscheider should come to Berlin: "You will be my guest. I am allowed to have guests at the hotel twice a year. am the little kid at the hotel … I'll show you around … Aquarium. Zoo—5 minutes away. Everything my treat. Aquarium I *love* to go."[27] In the end Goldscheider comes to Berlin.

As for Kraus, that friendship would be repaired, though it would never again be as intense as it once was. Kraus had, however, already shown that he was above petty grudge-bearing, when after her "KK I hate you" letter of 1924, he dedicated his collection of epigrams to Else Lasker-Schüler, when it came out in 1927. And she, for her part, had been going to every one of his brilliant lectures in the last days of March in Berlin.

She did have a bone to pick with him or at least a slight chip on the shoulder. A letter dated "12.Oct.28" has a kind of motto before the salutation: "I *never* collect autographs—only love letters." At Kraus's last lecture, it seems that a certain Herr Sachs, acting as usher, had had the gall to ask her—right in the middle of the lecture—to move. She was sitting in the *Loge* (a private box). But "Herr Sachs had told me I *should* be seated in the *Loge*. So someone must have been playing a practical joke on me. I was then further insulted; I asked for your address, not because I wanted to visit you: I wanted to write to you. I have no time to pay house calls. I am busy preparing my trip to Amsterdam, Paris, Marseilles, London,—from everywhere abroad I have invitations to read...."[28] Earlier that year, in March, she had invited Kraus to "Come at once" to an exhibition of her graphics, a real portrait gallery of their friends, all "venerable monsters"— 75 drawings. "My nerves are being sold off the walls, take them, take them all back at once to Vienna." Everyone, she tells him, "including Benn," is here.[29]

By the end of the year she was able to report to Goldscheider that she had been on the move all year, and had unimaginable success—"like a ballerina". She earned a lot of money, but nearly all had flown out the window. This was the case with her all her life. Either she *had* no money or it disappeared under her fingers in no time. Finally, she tells him, there's a tycoon who is going to buy her pictures.

In fact, she told him, she is toying with the idea of building a little house for herself on the North Sea, on stilts, like a bathhouse with steps that go straight into the water! It would cost about three or four thousand marks, which is what she should receive, at the least, as an advance for her two new books, *Konzert* and *Arthur Aronymus*. And, of course, Goldscheider would have to come and visit her there.[30] But two months later, she wrote that despite her streak of earnings and commissions, "I am forever sad and dark, and no longer believe in 'das blaue Wunder.'"[31]

Then, in December 1930, she had an appointment to see the publisher, Ernst Rowohlt—"he at least is a *Mensch*"[32]—a meeting that would lead to the triumphant resolution of her publishing deadlock. But despite these triumphs, her heart was black, she had lost the ability to hope.

She had not, however, lost her sense of humor. Her letters sounded

Else Lasker-Schüler, Kleist Prize winner, 1932 (Stadtbibliothek Wuppertal, Else Lasker-Schüler Archiv).

perky still. To Goldscheider she wrote that the *Frankfurter Zeitung* had given her an advance of 200 marks for an essay, an additional 300 still to come. In German, "advance" is *Vorschuss*; literally, a shot ahead of time. She says this will be followed by a *Schreck-schuss* of 300 marks, a shot fired in shock, presumably when they get the article itself. The *Frankfurter Zeitung*, founded by her uncle, Leopold Sonnemann, was one of the most influential newspapers of Weimar Germany.

Overworked, she dreamed of spending three months in the summer at the seashore, playing in the sand. But right now she was getting ready to go to a memorial celebration for "the political poet, Rosa Luxembourg," and Karl Liebknecht, to be held in January in Berlin.[33]

The winter was a cold one, in more ways than one. In September's Reichstag elections, Hitler's party had a showing that took the Nazis themselves by surprise. Uncertainty about the future invaded every sphere of life. On Christmas Day, a state of emergency was declared throughout Germany.

Else Lasker-Schüler was so cold in her room that she couldn't finish a letter she started to the child of a friend. The teeth of all 72 tenants in her hotel, she says, are chattering from cold.

Instead of letting up, her pace seems only to have quickened. And what with "pilgrims" knocking at her door, people making requests of all kinds, other tenants wanting to do their laundry in her room because it had hot water, and work, work, work, there was no time even for the movies until her heart acted up on her again and she was forced to cut back.

But not for long. By May she was getting ready to leave on the first of June, this time with the mother of Maria Moissi, to go by night train to Vienna. She planned to visit the young Goldscheider in Vienna, but she didn't want him to pick her and Frau Moissi up from the station. Why? She seems to have rejected his recommendation of a modest pension, in favor of a real hotel. Slightly embarrassed, she confessed to "an aversion to *pensions*, and would rather be taken for a snob if it comes to that...").[34]

She also appears to have hoped to see Freud while in Vienna, as "he talked so kindly to me by telephone"[35, 36] in April. And in Vienna she was to give a reading at the Ottakringer Workers' Home, a reading arranged by Goldscheider, for which she would take no fee. The money should go "for chocolate for the workers' children."[37]

During this whole period of political and economic unrest, the figure of Gottfried Benn keeps emerging from the shadows—and then receding. Only to appear again. Mentioned perhaps in a letter, and then only in three words: "Benn is here." He was a presence. In the meantime (as of April 1932) he was a member of the Academy, his calendar filled with engagements to speak at medical congresses. But, like Else Lasker-Schüler, he had not been publishing poems. He seems not to have been writing any either. He was clearly disgusted with the whole literary scene, plus the inefficiency of the Weimar government, and in particular with the way authors, not to mention poets, were treated.

The tone and tenor of their relationship in these years is reflected in their meager but emotionally charged exchanges. First, a brief answer by Benn to a card in which she inquired after his well-being: "Lieber teurer Prinz, a thousand thanks for your card. No, there's nothing wrong with me, nothing's happened to me, everything's O.K., live my usual life. Your thinking of me is very kind and I thank you ["Sie," polite form, not "Du," intimate form] warmly. Ever your worshipful admirer / Benn."[38]

That same year saw the publication of Paul Hindemith's *Das Unaufhörliche*, with libretto by Gottfried Benn, and he sent her a copy with this dedication: "Else Lasker-Schüler, the great lyric genius / in friendship and admiration. Gottfried Benn 18/XI.31."[39] This shred of memorabilia was found among the few things in her room in Jerusalem after her death.

On the 17th, just one day earlier, Benn had written her a more personal, supremely telling note. It was on the 14th of December, four years earlier, that Paul had died and Benn stood at her side at the grave. He writes:

> Lieber Prinz, I think of you often in these days. Please do not imagine that because I do not write much, that I do not have you always in mind. Please be assured of the opposite. But even talking these days is difficult.
>
> Nevertheless, if you should ever, in the times ahead, need me, know that I am at your disposal day and night, my apartment is open to you and my food and drink is yours as well. But surely it won't be as bad as some people think, do not be uneasy.

Fare well! Again there is snow on the ground as on that day in Weissensee, four years ago tomorrow. [Paul's funeral was on the 18th.] Give greetings to the grave from your old faithful friend and comrade Benn.[40]

It is hard to read these lines even today and keep a dry eye. But, alas, Benn did not live up to his promise. In one of the more inexplicable defaults of intellect and character that marked the Nazi period, Benn, for a few years at least, became a turncoat.

On July 20, 1932, Von Papen dissolved the (SPD) Prussian government, after a series of Landtag elections in which the Nazis had been gaining strength. In August, the last issue of *Der Sturm* appeared, and Herwarth Walden embarked on a tragically misguided conversion to Marxism and emigrated to the Soviet Union."[41]

Also on July 20, a letter went off to Paul Goldscheider, expressing regret at not being able to get away for a visit to Vienna. "Work and street fighting outside—for a change!" She wrote that it would be nice if he and his wife, a physician, could move to Berlin, "But we'd better wait and see. No one knows how things are going to be. *Frightfully* uncertain."[42]

Then in November, the long overdue, almost too late recognition of her place in German literature: the Kleist Prize. Malicious anti–Semitic smears from the right-wing press went up all around like the stench of a bonfire. But nothing could take away from the satisfaction she must have felt, after all the years of having been passed over. Perhaps the telegram Benn sent her to mark the occasion meant as much to her as the Prize itself. Who can say?

berlin f 36 II/II (1932)

else lasker-schueler
motzstr 78
hotel der sachsenhof
der ke listpreis so oft geschaendet sowohl durch die verleiher wie durch die praemierten wurde wieder geadelt durch die verleihung an sie ein glueckwunsch der deutschen dichtung

gottfried benn
(The Kleist Prize, so often sullied as much by those who awarded it as by the recipients chosen was once again ennobled by being awarded to you congratulations to German poetry.)[43]

On November 30, after receiving the award, she gave a reading to a packed house at the Schubertsaal. We can be pretty sure that Gottfried Benn was in the audience. She read a few scenes from her play *Arthur*

Else Lasker-Schüler. The reading in the Schubertsaal, November 30, 1932 (Stadtarchiv Wuppertal).

Aronymus, whose subject, the growing acts of violence toward Jews in Westphalia around 1840, had taken on ominous prophetic tones.

The play is set in her father's village, Gaesecke, called here Hexengaeseke (witches-gaeseke). (In Chapter Two, St. Vitus, we heard the taunts chanted at Dora by children passing the Schüler's garden.) The family worries that, as in the Middle Ages, "our daughters will be burned at the stake."[44] But the play ends on a hopeful note. The family is about to sit down to the Passover meal. Along with the children, there are a host of guests, rich Jews and poor, as well as the bishop of Lavater of Westphalia and the local priest. Frau Schüler speaks: "Und mit einem bisschen Liebe gehts schon, dass Jude und Christ ihr Brot gemeinsam in Eintracht brechen, noch wenn es ungesäuert gereicht wird" ("With a little love it's possible that Jew and Christian break bread in harmony together, even when the bread that's offered is unleavened").[45]

The reading at the Schubertsaal was Else Lasker-Schüler's last in Germany. On January 30, 1933, Hitler became Chancellor.

꙳ ꙳ ꙳ ꙳ ꙳

CHAPTER ELEVEN

꙳ ꙳ ꙳ ꙳ ꙳

Exile: The Switzerland Years

"I absolutely do not care/
Where to be absolutely lonely"
        Marina Tsvetaeva: *Homesickness*

"Perhaps exile is the poet's natural condition."
        —Joseph Brodsky

The years of exile were punctuated by three trips to Palestine: the first in 1934, then in 1937, and finally in 1939.

1933–1934. Switzerland   The winter of 1933-1934, like the last one before she fled Germany, was a cold one. She suffered not just from the harsh climate; she found the people where she was staying in Zurich, at the Augustinerhof, cold and unfriendly. She likened it to an orphanage.

All through January and February Else Lasker-Schüler complained about the cold. "Everywhere too cold here—."[1] She wrote her letters from the post office, "where I go to get warm...."[2]

Nothing was going well for her. In November she was fined by the Zurich Office of Aliens for not registering upon arrival in the country, and for practicing her profession, *Dichterin* (poet) without authorization. She had just given a reading in Bern.

With no work permit, and as a most unwelcome alien, Else Lasker-

148

Schüler spent her days in the café, not, as formerly, holding court, but along with countless other refugee artists and writers, waiting. Work permits were hard to come by. Before one could even think about publishing, one had to get the approval of the Swiss Writers' Union. This Lasker had obtained, but she still had no work permit. Nor did many of her cohorts. This meant that in addition to bureaucratic rudeness, she often had to contend with bickering and bitterness among the émigrés themselves.

These early months of exile played havoc with her health, and her sense of displacement and impotence left her exhausted: "For ten months now (since April 1933, that is), I have felt like a child's top, spun round and round, and then left lying, all played out, in a corner."[3]

Back in Germany, unbeknownst to her, Gottfried Benn, in words reflecting the new political climate, wrote to Tilly Wedekind, the widow of the proto-Expressionist dramatist, Frank Wedekind, in January 1934, "warning" her about Lasker-Schüler: "Don't let Lasker-Schüler make you go soft or sentimental. She is very strange and very brilliant, but as a person very questionable and romantic. Add to that of course fanatically anti-German and lies like all such hysterical people."[4]

Romantic in her assessment of Hitler? Anti-German? Nothing could have been further from the truth. She was never anti–German. As Klaus Mann said, speaking for the émigré circle which included Else Lasker-Schüler, "Hitler is not Germany!"[5] The "true" Germany, they tried to tell the world, was *against* Hitler.

In December, Klaus Mann made this entry in his diary: "To the Augustinerhof to Lasker-Schüler. The very real ruin and brokenness of her spirit. Traces of *legitimate* artistic madness."[6] Because his comment is utterly without malice, it seems doubly ominous.

She was, of course, sensitive to criticism, and quick to take offense. After a reading on Radio Zurich, in February 1934, the poet complained to Jakob Job, the director of the radio station, that his critique of her reading was totally off the mark. "Surely," she said, "you couldn't have meant what you said, that *I* recite with pathos. Precisely what I deplore in others...." Moreover: "Never do I hear a kind word from the Swiss."[7] And in a fit of pique she offered to return her fee. Her sense of outrage (and wounded pride) must have been very great indeed for her to have offered, in her desperate financial straits, to return her fee. Nonetheless, she put up a real fight to be allowed to read her own poems another time, rather than have a professional actor—or worse, actress—deliver her lines and share her fee. She did have a suggestion however, that might serve both their ends: Why not have Max Welti, the feuilleton editor of the *Neue Zürcher Zeitung*, read a scene or two from her new play, *Arthur Aronymus?*

Zurich seemed to offer little that could lift her spirits. Not even the lake: "I look forward to nothing."[8] And, "Nothing gives me joy. Everything in me is broken, dried up."[9]

And yet, when the possibility of a trip to Palestine by way of Alexandria presented itself in January, she *did* look forward to it. She wrote to Emil Raas, her friend and advocate in Bern,[10] and to Klaus Mann about it, saying how excited she was.

To Klaus she went on to say, "I am heavy with grief and tread the paths with the holy ones over and over in my mind—that is, if they would take this heap of rag-and-bones with them"[11] Klaus answered her letter the next day and copied in his diary some of the lovely passages in the letter like the above.[12]

The trip to Palestine came about through an invitation from an admirer, a German woman married to a Greek, who Else imagined was a shipping magnate. Frau Pilavachi had written asking her to come for a visit, promising to arrange for readings in German émigré literary circles in Alexandria.

For years she had dreamed of writing a book about the Holy Land. With the money she hoped to earn from the lectures and readings in Alexandria, she would suddenly be able to realize the dream. And after nearly a year of abject penury and unendurable cold in Zurich, the warmth of Egypt seemed irresistible. She could not wait to go. To Emil Raas, she rhapsodized, "I want to tend the flocks in Palestine, and graze with them in the meadows where the grasses grow tall as people and one can hide among the rustling stalks."[13]

But she was also hedging her bets, hoping the whole time to be granted permanent asylum in Switzerland. The invitation came just when she was trying to build a new life for herself in exile.

The Pilavachis, who were not as rich as she had assumed, were paying her steamship fare on the Italian liner *Esperia*, but she still had to get from Zurich to Genoa before sailing on to Alexandria, so she wrote to a Dr. Carola Kaufmann, a woman in Basel whose name had been given to her as a possible patron.[14] Carola Kaufmann was happy to oblige.

On the 21st of March, Lasker-Schüler left Zurich for Genoa, and on the next day proceeded by ship to Alexandria.

Just three days before she was to leave, she had an urgent request to make of her childhood friend, Elvira Bachrach, in Ascona. It was Elvira whom she had commissioned to visit Paul while he was in the sanatorium in Agra. Now, Else asked if Elvira would please go to the little shop that sold fine linens on the road from Ascona, "next to or two houses before the Café Swizzera," and where Else had purchased some handkerchiefs during the summer, "with brown squares (indicated on the page by a square), or arabesques with green arabesques with red and yellow...." She would like to have six more, to be sent collect. "*But* it must be at once. Because I am leaving.... I fell in love with the little handkerchiefs." (At the time she didn't have money to pay for more.) In the margin, she wrote: "*Please* write out my address for the shop, they must mail it at once, otherwise too late."[15] We can presume that Elvira went out of her way to oblige.

The journey itself, with long overland travel third class, was an ordeal. She had to change trains three times in the night. In fact, the entire visit in Alexandria turned out to be a disaster.

"I stayed at the home of a liar, a fraud," she wrote to a friend. "For a year and a half she had wooed me and inveigled me with false promises.... She had done nothing to arrange the ten lectures. Nor was there a single room in the entire house in which I could work or paint."[16] One can imagine she arrived exhausted and conceivably out of sorts. But her complaints, colored by her emotional state, did not altogether reflect the realities. In this case she set the record straight herself. In a letter to Hugo Bergmann,[17] over a year later, in December 1935, she explained that it was because Rudolf Hess's parents lived in Alexandria and spread anti–Semitic poison in the literary circles, that the talks and readings had been cancelled.

But how is it that she never even acknowledged the generous gift of Carola Kaufmann, the benefactress who had helped pay for her journey out, and whom she then stood up in Zurich, without apology or explanation?[18]

Following the debacle in Alexandria, the visit to Palestine was calamitous for different reasons. Given her expectations, it was destined to be fraught with deep, conflicting emotions. Moreover, it came at a time in her life when her inveterate sense of exile had been made all too explicit, and her ability to cope with its day-to-day disruptions diminished.

Palestine presented her with glaring contradictions, discrepancies between dream and reality that she had to resolve if she was going to write her book. To her Swiss benefactor, the silk manufacturer Sylvain Guggenheim, she confessed when she got back: "I can no longer maintain my one-time belief in the greatness of the Jews. And I should say that I am not Hebrew for Judaism's sake, but for God's, who can test my heart and my pain."[19] By referring to herself as "Hebrew," rather than Jew, she is making a distinction that is hard to define, but crucial to understanding her sense of apartness. She talks as well of her "boundless bitterness," about the way she was treated in Palestine, and gives that as a reason why she can't bring herself to write her book.

In fact, she was unable to write until many months after she returned to Zurich. Art was wine, she said, it had to ferment.[20] She needed the filter-

Else Lasker-Schüler, 1936 or 1937.
Photograph by Leonard Steckel
from a newspaper clipping of
1952 (Schiller National Museum/
Deutsches Literaturarchiv, Marbach).

ing agents of time and distance to assist in the process. In truth, the process involved forced forgetting and suppressing as well as selective and enhanced remembering.

Das Hebräerland, like all her prose works, weaves fact and fantasy into one confluent tapestry. In order to do this she had to bend fact. But to bend fact was to distort history. In her book, accounts of actual events that she witnessed meld into ecstatic ravings about the Holy Land, and are intermingled with her own suggestions about how to improve relations between Arabs and Jews, along with lots of wishful thinking given out as fact. Everywhere she claims to see "real friendships among the Semitic half-brothers, between the Hebrew farmers and the wildest Arab nomadic tribes. Laden with fruits, from 'the good brothers,' the dark-bearded men return to their wives.... Arab children play with Hebrew children in the side streets off Jaffa Road.... Why not all people of all lands?"[21]

Still, the book contains passages of minutely observed details, like the description of water-pipes being laid from the sea to Jerusalem, or the behavior of Arab donkey-drivers: "their animals are like toys to them. They pat them from time to time gently on the back, comb the hair on their necks—only then to beat them once again to their hearts' content."[22]

And woven into the fabric of the book are anecdotes about real people, like her encounter with Gershom Scholem,[23] or this description of a dinner at the home of the Jewish novelist, Samuel Josef Agnon. She says it was a Sabbath meal, and there was another invited guest, a Talmudic scholar. After Agnon completed the ceremony with the wine, Else raised the silver goblet to her lips and finished off the wine, making a toast to her host and his beloved "Gewerett." The horrified Talmud scholar reprimands her, reminding her that this is a Holy Sabbath dinner, not a birthday party. Both Agnons rush to her defense, when she compounds her transgression by inappropriately reciting the solemn prayer, *Shema.* To the clear delight of her hosts, she tries to instruct the stern young man by means of a parable: "Once there was a shepherdess among the people of Israel, who, when she wasn't tending her flock, made poems to God...."[24] (See Appendix 10, page 197.)

Das Hebräerland also contains some tie-dyed skeins of purple prose. Describing the Hasidic rabbis wrapped in their prayer shawls, all eighty of them wending their way down the Jaffa Road to the Wailing Wall, she writes, "This gobelin, woven of eternal threads, the veins and silken hairs of the ancient tribes of Judah, was tattooed over time into the very skin of my temples."[25]

Like the graphics of Ernst Ludwig Kirchner, from which she drew inspiration, her drawings for *Das Hebräerland* are an attempt to capture the rhythmic flow and lithe movement of street life. The drawings also permit her pictorial whimsy to break through, as in the frontispiece drawing from *Das Hebräerland,* where, if one looks closely, one may note the monkey on the wrist of one of the young pioneers, and the wide-open mouths of the singing men. "Friday afternoons our Chalizim come streaming out of their Emek onto the streets, singing their happy songs; Palestine's pigeons, their very eyes those of the watchful birds."[26]

If one cannot rely on her objectivity with regard to Arab-Jewish relations, one has to say that her harshest words are reserved for Jews. She rails against the British-built King David Hotel, which must have been modeled on a New York luxury hotel, "and dares to usurp the Biblical name."[27]

She snipes mercilessly at the Yiddish-speaking Jews of Eastern Europe, gossiping on the beach at Tel Aviv. Her ear picks up the "voice of a striped bathing-suit, leaning over a polka-dot smock: 'A Jewish mountain Bedouin, Agathe, one of ours.'"[28]

Bohemian and cosmopolitan she may have been. But she was still very much a product of her upper middle-class, German-assimilated upbringing (her mother read Goethe as well as Heine to her children), and she had trouble acknowledging Yiddish, which, she said, "is in no way related to the ancient language of the Hebrews. It naturalizes with ease, and loses itself in alien ground."[29] This bias seems not in the least to have diminished her respect for the poetry of her friend Abraham Stenzel, nor did it keep her from publishing her own poems (in the 1920s) in the Yiddish journal *Der Onheyh,* in Berlin.

Hebrew, however, was, for her, the language of the Bible, and although she never learned to speak it herself, she laid claim to it as if it were her own "mother" tongue. To a well-meaning admirer at one of her readings, who offered to translate her cycle of *Hebrew Ballads* into Hebrew, she reacted with genuine astonishment: "But they already *are* in Hebrew."[30]

It was in April of that year, 1934, shortly after Lasker-Schüler had arrived in Palestine, that Gershom Scholem wrote to his friend Walter Benjamin (like Benjamin, Scholem had known her from their early days in Berlin): "Things here [in Jerusalem] are lively as ever. Else Lasker-Schüler—who would fit in just about anywhere in the world better than in the true Orient—is here at the moment, and as far as I can judge, is right on the brink of madness. All the same, she continues to be a truly fascinating and enigmatic figure. She claims to have had a thirty-minute conference with King David, for which she now expects me to provide cabalistic enlightenment. Unfortunately, I am not at all convinced she really saw him. As you can imagine, I have been much in disfavor since this exchange with her, and she refers to me now as "Herr Dispute."[31]

Writing to Benjamin again just a week later, he calls her "a ruin more haunted than inhabited by madness."[32] Scholem was probably right in his insight, however, that she did not fit in, in Jerusalem. In a way, she should never have expected to. She was neither a political nor a religious zealot. She did not even speak the language.

To judge from her letters, the eight weeks in Palestine were one long breathless trek through the country ("today by tram to Jericho"), giving talks and readings, visiting Biblical sites, Bethlehem and the Garden of Gethsemane, distributing candy among the children, marveling at Tel Aviv, "gold-digger city: Mexico and Sea."[33] And always worrying about how to deal with the Swiss authorities on her return.

1934–1937   Back in Switzerland in June, her difficulties seemed only to multiply, her bad luck to pursue her. In the fall, she was even bitten on the street by a dog. And although, despite her blocks and misgivings,[34] she does finish her Palestine book, *Hebräerland*, it will not find a publisher for another two years.

Some of the hardships she was suffering arose simply out of the fact of emigration. The constant barrage of warnings and threats from the Swiss authorities, along with her renewed attempts to get extensions, wore her ragged. Anyone who has had to deal, as a foreigner, with these offices, even in more favorable circumstances, must sympathize with her plight. Even the dank smell from the depressing buildings, the long public-school stairways, and endless corridors smelling of floor wax, is enough to make one lose heart. Her files with the Swiss Police for Foreigners (Office of Aliens) in Zurich go back to 1933.

In 1934 alone there are about ten different summonses and notifications, both from the city and canton of Zurich. On November 15 of that year we read: The petitioner [who, we may note, has, once again, given a false date of birth, 1891] has been professionally active without a permit for some time, and in fact failed to file notification of her arrival and a request for permission to stay...."[35] She was fined 37.10 Swiss francs.

It would appear that she was guilty both of being professionally active and of not being able to support herself, a real double-bind. Increasingly, over the next years, the authorities tried to find reasons to expel her, while she sought ever new reasons to stay. Most cogently, she argued her ill health, which would make any travel hazardous.

There are many indications that under the stress of emigration she was becoming ever more frangible. And demanding. It is not exactly as if she had always been possessed of great equanimity, and now suddenly had become fractious, but at some point what people called her eccentricities began to take on worrisome aspects, in particular, elements of paranoia. As a friend, it must have been painful to witness. Nor did she have an easy time with herself.

"I don't remember what it was exactly," she wrote to Emil Raas when she got back from her first Palestine trip, "but I do know that I probably wrote to you too often from here, in my pain and loneliness. Like someone will knock again and again on the window where someone with blue eyes that can smile kindly lives. But you always thought I wanted to beg a piece of your life, or even take it—make a slave of you...."[36] And years later, in the thick of their friendship, she told him, "No one who has ever had anything to do with me has not suffered for it."[37]

She had good and loyal friends in Switzerland, yet she seems to have been picking fights with everyone she knew. After another one of her poems appeared in Klaus Mann's *Sammlung*, and simultaneously in the *Neue Zürcher Zeitung*, she called him up to complain, raising foolish objections.[38] He found it irritating enough to note in his diary.

Klaus Mann continued to make quizzical observations about her in his diary: "—Ran into Lasker-Schüler. Her ruined little monkey-face with the penetrating eyes."[39] And again: "In the afternoon with Lasker-Schüler in the 'Terrasse.' Spooky the way she prattles away, and yet in between totally brilliant." He cites examples: "about Palestine, the rabbi of Alexandria, poor Julie Wassermann [a mutual friend, the first wife of Jakob Wassermann], and ghostly apparitions (a bloody arm with hand in the room)."[40]

In addition to the Mann siblings, and her other émigré friends in Zurich, she had made a number of Swiss friends. Among them were Max Rychner, the literary critic and publicist, Max Gubler, the painter, Hanns

Hirt, the architect. And then there was Emil Raas, who represented her in her legal affairs. Finally there were her many patrons, in particular, the silk manufacturer, Sylvain Guggenheim, who seems to have been a bottomless well of generosity and financial support during her Swiss years. This list does not even include all the people connected with the Zürcher Schauspielhaus whom she would get to know when her play *Arthur Aronymus und seine Väter* was premiered there in 1936. And still she felt isolated and embattled. And poor.

But even when she saw her situation as desperate, she was sensitive about "taking alms." She says she is afraid to visit Jews, for fear they might think she wants something from them.

So while having devoted friends should have helped, she was not always able to appreciate the fact, and nothing, really, could ameliorate her feeling that she was, and always would be, alone. By the same token, nothing could prevent her from misconstruing some harmless or well-intended remark or action, regardless of its source.

Then there were curious instances of ingratitude. Not just to Carola Kaufmann, whom she never bothered to thank for helping to finance her trip to Palestine, but to the Jewish Community of Zurich, which had been paying her rent at the Augustinerhof while she got settled in Zurich. She complained to Sylvain Guggenheim that they had cut off their support on her return from Palestine, and proceeded to launch into this tirade: "Ja, every child in Germany knows how I bestowed honor on our people there. I don't ask for thanks, but *Noblesse*. Often I walk through the streets here, afraid my parents in heaven might see me—so run down...."[41]

It was at about this time, shortly after she had gotten back from that first Palestine trip, that she wrote to Elvira Bachrach to say that the minute she got off the bus at Ascona she was told that she had many enemies there. Who, she'd like to know, has been spreading slander behind her back?

She had known Elvira since childhood in Elberfeld, yet she could accuse her of talking behind her back. As she had been ready to admit to Raas, she knew how her obsessive demands—like running errands to linen shops for her (Elvira Bachrach was 70 years old)—got on people's nerves and wore them down. But she could not help herself.

And then comes a very curious footnote to her biography in these years. In a letter to Sylvain Guggenheim in September 1934 that includes greetings for the upcoming holiday, *Versöhnungstag*, she writes, "Duce Mussolini had the Italian Consulate here give me a present from him. I hope to go to Rome sometime in the future. For now I want to go to Ascona."[42]

Later, in 1937, writing this time to Schalom Ben-Chorin[43] in Jerusalem, she makes a coy reference to her Mussolini connection: "Mussolini *entre nous* has twice made very lavish gifts to me. He wanted me to come to Rome, on my return trip. Just between us!!"[44]

As late as 1938, she believed that Mussolini would offer safe haven to the Jews. To Teo Otto, she once said, "I'm thinking, like, dictators, um, they always have these gigantic desks at the far end of these incredibly long rooms, and behind the desk there sits this fellow. And it's to him I'm going to go."[45]

She even boasted to Heinrich Mann that on her first trip to Palestine she had been received by Mussolini in Rome and that all her books were standing on his desk."[46] (This is conceivable; especially if she had sent them to him.) Heinrich Mann wrote back to her, "I would advise you ... keep this strange and lovely experience to yourself."[47]

Perhaps this was another of her fantasies. But wouldn't all this gushing over Mussolini make her forfeit any claim she might have to political prescience? How explain it?

Back in 1926, when Else Lasker-Schüler was publishing in the periodical *Querschnitt*, there was an obituary of Eleanore Duse—by Benito Mussolini.[48] And in 1927, there was a very serious appraisal of his own literary works by the British critic Francis Hackett."[49] It is altogether possible that Mussolini had taken notice of Else Lasker-Schüler's work and even written about her. Being susceptible to flattery is no crime. It has also been suggested that when she was on the Italian ship on her way to Palestine, she saw movie clips of the youthful Mussolini...

Of all the people she became associated with in Switzerland, probably none took her in so naturally as the theater crowd. They were perhaps more used to people "acting out." And some of them, at least, like Ernst Ginsberg, who had known her in Berlin, and Teo Otto, with whom she felt a special kinship because he came from the same Rhineland that she grew up in, accepted her eccentricities as part of her genius. Some, like Teo Otto, even delighted in her mad ways. Teo Otto spoke the same Low German dialect she would lapse into when she felt chummy with someone. If for Klaus Mann her erratic behavior was sometimes troubling (was his yardstick his father?), and even posed an intellectual dilemma for him, for Teo Otto it was not.

Otto, who had his main contacts with Lasker-Schüler during this period, when he was designing the sets for *Arthur Aronymus* at the Zürcher Schauspielhaus, had this to say about her appearance and purported madness:

> ... she looked like a lost bird of Paradise.... People made fun of her, called names after her in the street.... I have no idea how she put

her various outfits together. The blouses didn't go with the skirts, and she frequently wore fur in summer, while in winter she wore summer blouses and a funny-looking coat.... She struck certain people as spacy, as if she didn't have all her marbles. But if they thought that, they were very much mistaken. She was an enchanting irritant in this dreary world of book-keeping and numbers....[50]

And it was an actor, Ernst Ginsberg, who brought out the first Else Lasker-Schüler book, *Dichtungen und Dokumente* (*Works and Documents*), in 1951, after the poet's death. In a section devoted to personal reminiscences, he tells how she appeared on his doorstep in Zurich, shortly after his own emigration, very early one rainy morning in November 1933, altogether disheveled, agitated and seemingly oblivious of the hour and the weather. Could she read him a poem, she asked, one that she had just written that night. Pointing to a particular line, she asked him to tell her what he thought it could mean. The poem was "Die Verscheuchte" ("One Banished"). To his answer she replied "in the melodious tones of her Elberfelder dialect, '*Ja, Jung, so kann dat jemeint jewesen sein!*'" ("Yeah, boy, maybe that's what it meant").[51]

The obsessive urgency of her visit, her total absorption in the poem, stayed with him all his life. Over time, however, Ginsberg could not get around a serious concern. "Her personality bore not only the *Signum* of genius, but at times as well—love and veneration oblige one to say it—a tragic derangement...." He regarded her as the vessel of some preternatural inspiration, an intuition over which she had no power. And where this intuition failed her, he believed, her thoughts and language sank into a "mire of confusion."[52] Unfortunately, this assessment of her literary powers led to a severe bowdlerizing of her published works, in particular her last play, *IchundIch* (*IandI*), that took place under his supervision.

In 1936, the German émigré publication *Pariser Tageblatt* printed an excerpt from *Das Hebräerland* before the book was out. In addition, there were the always welcome sales of drawings and paintings at 250 marks each. Taken together, these earnings, along with a few lucrative readings plus one more "gift" ("This will be the last time I ask, really") from Sylvain Guggenheim, tided her over till her book came out.

All in all, things were now going well enough that in September she was able to move to more congenial surroundings: the Hotel Seehof, in Zurich. Her new room, she says, is like a ship's cabin, with two portholes, and the attic roof running diagonally down to the window. There is a big carpet on the floor, and the hotelier has even agreed to replace the bed with a chaise lonque, "as I can't stand beds." And "always my own blankets and pillows."[53]

All year long old friends keep turning up. In May, Lasker heard from Jankel Adler who had been in Warsaw since late 1935. He had gone first to Paris after leaving Germany in 1933. She had written him a card, inquiring after him. He replied:

> I thought I was dreaming, seeing your cherished handwriting[54] again, and had I not been ashamed to do so, I would have wept. I have been in Poland for nearly a year and a half ... much that is lovely here, but I still don't have enough distance ... deep bitterness hinders my ability to see objectively ... there are, for instance, the great masses of Jews who live in terrible misery, and the political situation is not exactly a happy one—in the last half year I have been working in film. Right now the first film in Yiddish, for which I have made the sets, is running in Warsaw. I saw our friend Aribert in Paris in 1934, he's still the old Ari.... And how do you live, my prince?[55]

Adler wanted her to come to Warsaw, give a few readings and get to know the real heart of Judaism (viz: Hasidism). He closes with a hug and warm greetings for his beloved "Jussuf."[56]

In June 1936, her *Landsmann*, Teo Otto, paid her a surprise visit. He was designing the sets for the upcoming production of *Arthur Aronymus*, which would finally open in December at the Zürcher Schauspielhaus. Otto had been the third of that trio (Ginsberg and the actor Kurt Horwitz were the other two) who attended that reading where they feared she would require them to call out, "What's coming from on high?"

Suddenly, there he was, standing in the *conditorei* (bakery/café) in Ascona where she had rented a room on the second floor, right above the bonbons and pastries. They must have had fun conversing in "elwerfelder Wupperdeutsch." (Teo Otto came from Remscheid.) And he brought a little gift from the ensemble, she tells Ginsberg in a word-tipsy manic letter from Ascona.[57]

The high spirits held through December, when the play opened. Ginsberg played the Nightwatchman, Altmann, whose drunken snores are the curtain-raiser. He has to blow his horn to wake the village, where the famous rabbi of Paderborn is visiting. Gently, softly, he blows into his horn, while the priest who is passing by listens. "*Eck blas jo schofa—Ihm zu ehren*" ("I'm blowing the shofar to honor *him*"), he says. When the astonished priest asks, "How do you come to know how to blow the shofar?" he replies, "*Eck versteh eben auf katholisch zu blasen und—anders*" ("I happen to know how to blow Catholic and—other").[58]

Ginsberg considered *Arthur Aronymus* the poet's greatest achievement. As a Jewish convert to Catholicism, he found its theme, Jewish-Christian reconciliation, especially moving.

On December 24 she thanked Ginsberg and the entire cast for their grandiose performances. Then on January 7: "I am in dreadful spirits, *ja* I am not up to life in any form.... I yearn for home for our garden.... What does the world want of me?"[59]

What had happened? For reasons that are still not altogether clear, after just two performances, the production was forced to close. Mixed reviews, poor attendance, personal clashes, pressure from the German embassy in Switzerland, are some of the explanations given.

For all involved in the production, but immeasurably for its author, the closing of *Aronymus* must have been a profound disappointment. The better part of January was spent trying to get the play back on the boards, but to no avail.

From its printing in 1932 by the theater division of the S. Fischer Verlag, the play had enjoyed a *succès d'estime*. Reading the manuscript in Locarno in April 1936, Franz Werfel, who had known the poet through the Kurt Wolff Verlag, and whose own relationship with her had just barely survived its own hairpin curves, wrote to her: "Your 'Arthur Aronymus' is an altogether wonderful work. Through your unique genius, you have succeeded in tackling what is today the touchiest subject, the most dangerous theme, in a drama of such human and religious depth that a reader, like myself, had to cry at least 27×."[60]

But how could anything, even the warmth and affirmation of friendships, make up (especially after the joyful collaborative work on the long-cherished project) for the disappointment and despair at the closing of *Aronymus*? From her earliest hopes to see the play performed—first in Düsseldorf, then Darmstadt, Berlin—all aborted—to this latest reversal, a cumulative frustration.

Add to this unsettling daily news items, arrests in Ascona. One could hear the mad dogs barking.

1937–1939   Else Lasker-Schüler continued to be hounded by the Office of Aliens, who kept granting her short-term visas and threatening to deport her if she didn't leave when the expiration date came round. She was trying to organize another trip to Palestine, in the hope of earning some money with readings and talks and the sale of pictures, and at the same time placating the Swiss authorities by leaving the country. By mid–June 1937 she was boarding an Italian steamship in Trieste—the guest of Lloyd-Triestino Steamship Company—on her way for the second time to Palestine, but with the unambiguous wish to return to Switzerland.

Her ticket, first class, was a present from the Italian-Swiss branch of

Lloyd's; she seems to have cajoled them into letting her be their guest, praising their shipping lines in verse, and telling them how she loved to paint Italian ships!

Meanwhile, the Swiss authorities, not trusting her to keep her word, were checking up to see whether she had actually left the country.

One of the first people she met on this trip to Palestine was the writer and journalist Schalom Ben-Chorin. For many years he had been an admirer of her work, but he had never met her. On the evening of her arrival, he paid her a visit at her hotel.[61] Needless to say, she was exhausted, and looked it. But over and above this, he found her "driven by nameless fear, a tormented soul. Like a caged beast she paced back and forth in the narrow incommodious room, fuming about its inadequacies. But when I suggested she move, she became even more furious. 'I beg you, say nothing to the managers, they have been so kind to me....'"[62]

Ben-Chorin was a biblical scholar who had made a special study of prophetic texts. He had published a book about Luria, the great master of the Cabbala. Unlike Scholem, Chorin was convinced of the genuine nature of her prophetic visions. One reason why he was so certain was that she couldn't have plagiarized them, because as she loved to "admit," she was so unread. But was she? When she wrote her Jakob poem, she insisted, she had not yet read the Cabbala. One wonders.

Her sense of frustration in Palestine had many causes. She could not visit those sections of Old Jerusalem that she would have liked, because the Old City was closed off for security reasons much of the time. She was repelled by the very modern busy-ness of the city. Most painful, perhaps, was that the central Zionist and cultural organizations of the city were not willing to provide rooms for her to give readings in. Instead, private individuals came forward. But it was an affront. To sum it all up, she said woefully, "I believe that out of Erez-Israel has come Erez Miesrael."[63, 64] But when she was back in Zurich, she had a strong yearning, "like the bird of passage [*Zugvogel*],"[65] to return.

Arriving back in Zurich on September 4, the whole process, beginning with the official request to stay, started all over again. To the utter chagrin of the authorities, they could find no grounds to expel her: "She was able to demonstrate a cash holding of 200 Fr.—I could not gather any negative reports. The hotelkeeper's wife assured me that Lasker is a harmless person and fulfills her financial obligations."[66]

Her book *Das Hebräerland* came out in March 1937, with eight original drawings by the author. Oprecht, her new publisher, agreed to pay her a monthly allowance of 100 francs over a period of six months, in lieu of an honorarium or royalties, as she was not supposed to be engaged in gainful employment in Switzerland (she still had no work permit). In addition to this sum, she was receiving 200 francs a month from the firm of Reiff and Guggenheim (silk manufacturers). Guggenheim was truly a friend. However, far from being an ameliorating factor in the eyes of the authorities, these sums merely served to reinforce their argument that she was totally dependent on the goodwill of a few highly-placed private individuals.

The Swiss authorities and police continued their unremitting attempts to be rid of Lasker once and for all. One of the many police reports contains this interesting addendum: "It is to be noted that the petitioner's (German) passport expires on 25 January 1939, and will in all likelihood not be renewed, it being the case that during the well-known book burnings in Berlin 9500 copies of her books were burned. She views as her particular enemy Herr Minister Goebels [sic]. One cannot avoid the distinct impression that this woman, who is only 49 [sic] years of age, manifests clearly visible signs of a persecution complex."[67]

In November of 1938, another report utilized complaints from her landlady to make a case against her: "Her room is in such a state of disorder as to defy description...." And again, "One gets the distinct impression that one is dealing here with a chronically mentally disturbed person."[68] Then, after some more hemming and hawing, the officer stated that while "she cannot be shown to be actively derelict in any regard, nevertheless, her landlady would be glad to be rid of her, because she is becoming increasingly unclean in her personal habits. It is pointless to serve her with eviction notices. She simply does not move...." And then comes the familiar infamous refrain: "Nothing more to her discredit could be ascertained."[69] As is obvious even from these short excerpts, these reports were jewels of Swiss bureaucratic gobbledegook.

On September 26, 1938, her German citizenship was officially revoked. In December all her works were placed on a blacklist of forbidden writings.

Else Lasker-Schüler spent much of her time and most of her money at the movies. Wild West movies were her favorites, but she enjoyed Clark Gable and Mary Pickford or the Ritz Brothers if it came to that. One of the troubles with Jerusalem was that, unlike Berlin or Zurich, there were too few moviehouses, and so she had to see the same movie over and over again. There were days when she went to the movies three times.

By year's end she was so worn down by the stress in her own life and the horrific events in Berlin that once again she could not wait to embark on a trip (her third) to Palestine.

CHAPTER TWELVE

Mein Blaues Klavier

"Making her way along the narrow streets of Jerusalem, the small gnome-like figure kept close to the housefronts, walking cautiously, as if along the edge of a ruler, prepared to ward off some imminent assault."[1] That was the way the poet was perceived by those who knew her during the last years of her life in Jerusalem.

Sigismund von Radecki

March 1939 Third voyage out. Another harrowing journey. Five other women in her ship cabin. Else had become ill already in Marseilles and for days after her arrival in Palestine, she was still sick. Worst of all, she was almost blind. Given the nature of her work, this was terrifying.

On arrival in Jerusalem, she again moved into the Hotel Vienna, where she had stayed before, and where Schalom Ben-Chorin had visited her on her arrival in 1937.

Again, as each time before, she hoped, after a brief stay, to return to Switzerland. The law required that she be out of the country for three months before being eligible for re-entry.

Aside from the necessity of meeting the Swiss regulations, her main purpose in coming back was to write a second book about Jerusalem, notes for which she had already begun to gather in 1937. Several journal entries and notes for chapters were already written out. Among these were notes for her last play, *IchundIch* (*IandI*). (See Appendix 11, pages 198–203.)

163

Just before she left Zurich, she delivered an emotional farewell address to her Swiss friends. It was March and German troops had occupied Prague. In September, Germany invaded Poland. The Second World War had begun. Determined as she was to come back, she knew how volatile the political situation was in Palestine. Already in November 1938 she had written to Sylvain Guggenheim, "If I come back, what with all the fighting,"[2] a direct reference to the Arab uprisings from 1936 on. From Jerusalem she made two attempts, in August and September, to obtain a visa to re-enter Switzerland and twice her request was refused. Apart from the impossibility of obtaining a visa, her health would have made another trip unfeasible.

Just how weary, broken and demoralized she had become during these last years is reflected in her letters. In many instances, the word "broken" itself recurs. And, writing to her old friend Jethro Bithell in 1940, she exclaims, "I am allways so sorry in this magnific country, but I am so allone in my heart."[3]

The only front on which one could say that Else Lasker-Schüler was winning her battle for existential survival was the economic front. From 1940 forward, she received a monthly stipend from Salman Schocken. Schocken, who had emigrated to Palestine in 1934 became the publisher of Kafka and of the Jewish novelist and later Nobel prize winner Samuel Josef Agnon. Thanks to Schocken's generous support, she was able to live quite comfortably.

Altogether her income was roughly that of a married, middle-ranking civil servant. But even so, her friends lamented that as she became more and more erratic in her ways, money disappeared between her fingers like water.

Lasker's letters to Schocken, in the period 1939 to 1940, are another instance of the way the poet let down her guard in letters, giving full vent to her depressions and inner turmoil. From love's heartbreak to writer's block, she flashes her relentless strobe light inward on herself: "I *can* not write at all. *How* can I go on?"[4] She begs him to help her in her financial plight.

In May 1940, writing again to Salman Schocken (who had been a successful businessman before he turned maverick publisher), she describes an incident in which she was out of control, and embarrassed at her own behavior: "I had a kind of accident yesterday" she begins, "and my eye bled...."

But that was not all. "Now I have to tell you something truly awful— I took back the two pictures from the museum [her own]—the reason I would rather tell you in person...." Evidently she felt that the pictures had not been duly appreciated by the director of the Bezalel, the National

Museum, in Jerusalem. "I mean, for the museum pantry, to make the jars of marmalade feel more at home, for that my watercolors are too good (?) Director Narkiss objected to this and that, couldn't seem to make up his mind, I sent for the pictures and I'm glad I did. We nearly came to blows." But then she adds, "Please don't say anything to him, he looks so miserable."[5]

One can only marvel at the sangfroid with which she is able to assess the disagreeable impression her behavior and appearance made on others. Not only are her letters full of apologies, but she signs herself, "Your loathsome eyesore" (*Dein Ekel*), which in three words seems to sum up the way she saw and sometimes felt about herself. And over and over again, she lamented, "I am at the end of my tether."

Enclosed in this same letter to Schocken was a copy of a touching letter she had written to Pope Pius XII. She still held out the hope that the pope would intervene on behalf of the Jews. The time of year, the ostensible occasion, is Easter:

> I beseech the Holy Father to explain that we in Jeschurun or in any land wheresoever, have never drunk the blood of a Christian or slaughtered a child at Easter. We, who are forbidden to eat an egg if there is even a drop of blood in it.... Jesus Christ was after all a son of David ... and he would have loved from his heart our spiritual fathers: Luria ... Maimonides.... "Protect my lambs," He said ... I kiss the hand of the Holy Father, into whose life the soul of Jesus Christ has descended—rises and sets and rises again, like the red glow of dawn and dusk.[6]

For this letter to the pope, especially for what some viewed as its maudlin close, she heaped much derision on herself. The ingrown émigré circle was nothing if not critical.

As for her appearance, what was there new to say? It had always been eccentric. Now she might be wearing, along with her coral-red earrings and other geegaws, a thick fur cap, even on the hottest summer days. If she had arranged to meet someone at a café, she might come wearing a black velvet cape and black-and-white checkered knee-breeches of shimmering taffeta. And she always carried an umbrella. Old age appears to have bent her, not just metaphorically speaking. Judging by drawings of her during these last years, she looked like the crooked old woman in the nursery rhyme. Or did she? Sigrid Bauschinger contends, "Here again it is most likely a case of the legend prevailing over the reality."[7] But if this unkind image of her owes more to myth than reality, she did not hesitate to seize upon it. One of her alter-egos in her last play is a scarecrow!

M.S. 44

Above and opposite page: **Two drawings, done in 1944, by Miron Sima* (1902–1999), of Else Lasker-Schüler as an old woman (collection Mishkan Leomanut, Museum of Art, Ein Harod, Israel). *Born in a Jewish Settlement in Czarist Russia, Miron Sima witnessed pogroms already as a boy of 17. In 1923 he went to Dresden where he became a student and friend of Otto Dix. In 1933 he emigrated to Palestine, and in 1934 he met Lasker-Schüler on her first trip to Jerusalem. Over the years up until her death, he made sketches of her, sometimes catching her unawares, out walking or in a cafe. "Locked up within her own loneliness," he wrote, "she carried her confinement with her like a nun's convent."**

Jehuda Amichai,[8] who was just a child in the thirties, remembers seeing her, muttering to herself on the street. Boys mocked her and threw stones at her.

If people stared at her on the street, she assumed they were spies (*Spitzel*). Given what she had been through, it was understandable. Unfortunately, it tainted her judgment. When Manfred Sturmann (who became the administrator of her literary estate) first tried to approach her, she eyed him with mistrust and antipathy. The Grosshuts, who ran a second-hand books store in Haifa, and who became her close friends, told similar stories of having to break down her initial mistrust. She knew that people thought she was paranoid, so she went out of her way to state, "Truly, I am not mistrustful...," explaining that for years she had had to suppress and conceal her anxiety.[9]

She had an explanation for everything. Sometimes she would fall asleep at concerts and talks, but in her canny byzantine way, she would explain that she was altogether cognizant of what was going on, only as if in a dream.

But now, no matter what she did, whether she was pulling out a soiled man's handkerchief to wipe her nose, or behaving in ways that others designated as "gross," she harvested sniggers, or at best pity. Increasingly, she was her own worst enemy.

In 1941, with amazing energy, resourcefulness and dedication, she formed a reading circle, which she called Der Kraal. The Kraal was her last real venture in Palestine, the answer to her despairing question, "What am I to *do* here?" It was a very ambitious undertaking. In addition to literary readings, there were talks on philosophy and religion. The meetings required considerable organization. She planned the topics with the speakers, arranged for the time and venue of the meetings, wrote out the invitations in colored ink, and delivered them on foot to some thirty-odd

guests, all hand-picked, of course. Most of the meetings were held at the Centre de Culture Française in the Ben Jehuda Strasse, and began at 8:30 P.M. It was an interesting, elite group—rabbis, university professors, poets and philosophers—who came together at her bidding.

Regardless of who the speaker was, or whether she herself was giving a reading, these were most emphatically *her* evenings. She could be gracious and she could be rude. On a whim, or out of pique at some trivial trespass, she might disinvite a speaker whom she had asked to read or lecture. Nor did her failing health prevent her from being as contentious as ever.

But if she did act on momentary pique, she would almost invariably be seized with regret. Sometimes she was able to repair the damage, sometimes not.

Heinz Politzer, a friend of her friends, the Grosshuts, was well-known as a Kafka scholar, and was co-editor with Max Brod of the collected works of Kafka. From 1960 on taught at the University of California, Berkeley. But he was someone with whom, she claimed, there was just "bad chemistry," and there was nothing she could do about it. So she reneged on her word to have him speak at the Kraal. But then, a few days later she reported to the Grosshuts, "everything bathed in butter" between them. Politzer was one who went along with her out of compassion, loyalty, and sincere admiration. Werner Kraft was a poet and critic who grew up in Hannover and emigrated to Palestine. In 1931 he had sent Else Lasker-Schüler some poems, to which she responded noncommittally. She also rode a roller-coaster of friendship with him. Both men helped propagate her work after her death, and both contributed to a better understanding of her late poems, although Werner Kraft failed fully to appreciate her monumental last play, *IchundIch*, from which she read excerpts for the first time in July 1941.

To Martin Buber, whom she had known since 1901, when he published some of her poems in a periodical he edited (*Ost und West*), and with whom she'd had, from the start, a touch-and-go, hate-love, I-Thou "dialogue," she apologized for having been rude and interrupting him during his talk in the synagogue. But, to repeat, it was hardly the first time they had clashed. Back in Berlin she had insisted, on one occasion, that the poet Stefan George was a Jew, and became furious when Buber contested the fact. (She had been mistaken.) But he always forgave her. After all, she was "a true poet." Moreover, his I-Thou funny bone must have tingled when she sparred with him.

Here is an excerpt from the letter she wrote him in December 1942 after his talk:

> I was so—(I don't know how to explain it) fuzzy last evening, I probably didn't make clear how much I wanted to thank you for your story-telling. I mean, I was—like in a kaleidoscope—the kind you give children to look through. Ja sometimes, because I am ill and overtired, I couldn't keep my eyes open. But that was altogether fitting for the "Wanderung" that you, Mr. Bible-story-teller (Adon Bibelerzähler), were describing. As if I had lain down under a fig tree or cedar to rest; woke up and continued on my wanderings, without having ever lost you.... You are at bottom a gothic Jewish story-teller. Dr. Sonnenschein[10] was absolutely thrilled. He loved Saulus Paulus, and called out, pointing to me, "But *she* doesn't like Paul!" As you of course know, Adon (Sir), Paul was a Roman carpet weaver. And his speeches are like weaving ... so strangely twisted, ending in fringes and tassels. Hard to follow in all their shades and stitches. When the heathen broke away from him he said: "Can't you love me just a little bit?" Their belief was less complicated. Jesus of Nazareth was more "vegetal" (natural). He didn't coerce people and if we only knew more about his simple doctrine, there would still be JewChristians [*Judenchristen*][11] today and that would

provide a bridge between Jews and Christians. Jesus a poet; Paul more talent for scholarly disquisition.... Adon professor, I am not a Zionist, not a Jew, not a Christian; I am however a human being, a deeply sad human being. I was a simple soldier of God; I can however no longer fit into any uniform. I flow with the days, one into the other. Perhaps God the Eternal believes in me, I do not know how I in my humanness can believe in Him? And still perhaps lie in His Invisible Hand. We all weeping. Your Prinz Jussuf (E L-Sch).[12]

But shortly after apologizing about the synagogue incident, her temper flared up at Buber again, and their relationship ended abruptly—once and for all, a little over a year before her death.

When her ever-generous friends, the Grosshuts, gave her a coat for winter warmth, she needed to know whose it was before accepting it. After all, she reminds them (and herself), she is "Jussuf!" (and not just "euer Ekel!") In the end she returns it out of misplaced pride. How many friends would put up with this kind of behavior? Never mind strangers.

Apart from the Kraal, the other activity that kept her going, and occasioned intermittent spurts of euphoria, was her work on her last play, *IchundIch.*[13]

In a letter to her friend Margarete Kestenberg, in December 1940, Else Lasker-Schüler wrote, "Have a wonderful new play."[14] Her only concern was that her manuscript, written by hand—the hand that had been giving her trouble over the years, and had gotten worse with age—would be undecipherable.

Already in September 1940, her euphoria over the new work had broken through in a letter to Salman Schocken: "... I find my former high spirits returning."[15] Expanding a bit about the play, she says, "I wrote it first of all—out of intense unrequited love to me; out of eternal misery; despair; dreadfully earnest and wonderful fun. One can and then one can't go on."[16]

And in June 1943, she reported to the Grosshuts in reply to a query about why she had no typescript (she sounds almost petulant) that she *did* type up her play two years ago "here in Jerusalem under excruciating circumstances—Siberian cold: "*I* can read it, and if it is to be published, I'll copy it out again...."[17, 18] In fact, owing not least to the inflammatory nature of its subject matter—it ends with Hitler and all the Nazis sinking into a laval stew—it never did see publication in her lifetime.

Apart from its artistic merits, the play provides a panoptic view of the poet's inner world, with its infinite contradictions and dichotomies: angelic/demonic; male/female, to name only two of the most obvious.

Ernst Simon, undated photograph (courtesy Uriel Simon, Jerusalem).

Nearly everyone who writes about Lasker-Schüler's last years seems perturbed and embarrassed by her late love. The letters to Ernst Simon, teacher, humanist, religious scholar and editor of the correspondence of Martin Buber, who, as they never tire to point out, was thirty years her junior, and "a family man," were until recently under seal in the Else Lasker-Schüler archives in Jerusalem. In any case, his to her (also until recently under seal), are models of tact and decorum. When she pleaded with him to tell her he loved her—"Lie to me"—he refused, saying he held her in far too great esteem to do that.

Her poems to him, which make up an entire cycle in her last volume, *Mein Blaues Klavier* (*My Blue Piano*), are a uniquely poignant corpus of charged erotic poetry.

Simon, whom she dubbed "Apollo," celebrating his features "carved in marble" in verse, was first known to her as the German translator of the Hebrew poems of Bialik, whom she loved. In 1928, as a young man, Ernst Simon emigrated to Palestine. From 1935 on he taught, first at the Jerusalemer Lehrer Seminar, and then later in the department of education at Hebrew University. (In 1948 he was a guest professor at Jewish Theological Seminary in New York.) Simon was actively engaged in fostering Jewish-Arabic understanding, and in trying to establish a bi-national state. The Jewish theologian Franz Rosenzweig considered him the most talented member of his generation.

In September 1941 Else Lasker-Schüler attended Yom Kippur services at the synagogue Emit we Emuna. Simon gave the sermon. After hearing him speak, she wrote him two letters and sent him a poem. On September 22 he replied: "I am happy that my sermon had something to say to you. But how could you think that I disparage what you call 'play.' How well I know that for the poet there is nothing more serious than his 'play.'

The masters of the Haggadah, about whom I talked so much yesterday, played—in fact with God...."[19, 20]

She quickly enlisted him as a speaker at the Kraal. Apart from his fine features, and "lofty" bearing, Ernst Simon, like Gottfried Benn, possessed a beautiful speaking voice. It was a strong factor in his erotic appeal for Else Lasker-Schüler.

In addition to celebrating this love in poems, she agonized over it in letters, some of which Simon read, in consternation, to their mutual friend, Werner Kraft: "How can I answer this??"

He was actually quite capable of standing up to her, and of withstanding her need to control. On one occasion where she berates him for missing a Kraal meeting, on some excuse she finds insufficient, he replies, "It may be that for you these things are unimportant, but ... to me they are important, and I ask nothing more than the basic human right to be free to attend to matters that are important to me."[21]

As Werner Kraft notes in his diary on September 29, 1941, "She is 'in love' with S. with all that goes with it: cunning (trickery), devilry, noble renunciation, wild craving...." He continues: "Her hatred of T.S. (Ernst's wife, Toni) boundless.... There is something evil and senseless in all this." He agrees that Simon is quite right to rebuff her advances because "It is impossible to give a demon just a finger...."[22] One senses, in Kraft's reactions, the dismay and even terror that her friends experienced, standing by helplessly, observing what they saw as her mental, as well as physical, deterioration. His own words failing, Werner Kraft cites Shakespeare, "Oh, what a noble mind is here o'erthrown."[23]

Sometimes Werner Kraft did find words: "The confusion, the way she went on, was hard to take, the more so as you felt at the same time it was all calculated and put on.... She uses everyone as means, particularly those whom she claims to love.... She wants only to devour her beloved."[24]

Contrarily, both men found the poems astonishing, audacious. Werner Kraft even jotted down some lines from a letter she had written to Simon, he found them so striking: "Once, my head lay in your hand. God, who is no philistine [*Spiessbürger*], did not object."[25]

Sometimes the poems sound as if they were written from the vantage point of the beyond. She looks back, not in anger, but in deep regret at what never was. Images of stone, of marble and granite abound:

"So lange ist es her..."

Ich träume so fern dieser Erde
Als ob ich gestorben wär
Und nicht mehr verkörpert werde.

Im Marmor deiner Gebärde
Erinnert mein Leben sich näher.
Doch ich weiss die Wege nicht mehr.

Nun hüllt die glitzernde Sphäre
In Demantkleide mich schwer.
Ich aber greife ins Leere.[26]

"It is so long ago..."

I dream so far from this earth
As if I were already dead
And will be em-bodied no more.

In your marble gesture
My life comes back to me, nearer,
But I know the paths no more.

The glittering globe wraps around me
A heavy diamond cloak.
I reaching out grasp the void.

The incongruity of her youthful passion with her old face and body was a source of real torment to her. There are no photographs of Else Lasker-Schüler from this period in her life. She refused to allow any to be taken. She knew how she looked. Drawings of her in Jerusalem, by Miron Sima and Schalom ben-Chorin, may seem like cruel caricatures, but from all we can gather, they are not. Werner Kraft, who met her late in her life, could not believe she had ever been attractive. Martin Buber's wife, who had known her in Berlin, had to convince him of her extraordinary beauty.

Age had always been difficult for her to face as a woman. She yearned for the comfort of physical love and knew (as she had known already when she wrote to Benn from Zurich) that that road was closed to her. Still she could not help feeling all the contingent emotions of love: jealousy, rage, humiliation. The poems, in their mantra-like invocations, "Ernest, Ernest," are wrenching in their immediacy. There is no attempt to disguise their urgency: "Es ist so kalt und spät, Ernest/Ernest" ("It is so cold and late, Ernest/Ernest").[27] And again:

Ernest, ich halte deine Hände fest!...
Innigverwachsenes Geäst
Deine und meine beiden.
—Es sang ein Vogel heut im Nest
Im Mandelbaume in den Weiden
Ein weiches Lied von uns und meinen Leiden.
Ernest...

Sag einmal nur: Ich "liebe, liebe, liebe, liebe" dich
Dass meine Seele länger nicht vor Scham erröte—
Wenn auch von deiner Lippe Pfad
Das blaue "Glückskleeblat" verwehte.
Beseeligt blühte auf dem Hauch des Lethe
Die Trauerrose meines Leibes Beete.[28]

Ernest, I hold your two hands tight in mine!...
Branches welded close entwined
Inward yours and mine
—Today a bird sang in its nest
In a meadow almond tree
A gentle song about us and my sorrows.
Ernest...

Say just once: I "love, love, love, love, love" you
So that my soul no longer needs to blush for shame—
And if from your lip's path the blue
Fourleafclover blew away,
Blissful bloomed the sorrowrose,
On the breath of Lethe,
Of my body's flower-bed.

In the end she is resigned, sad. But ultimately it is a sadness she almost can no longer feel. Yes, "It was so long ago," as if she "were already dead." She reaches out to love, but "grasps emptiness."

It is true, hyperbole is her natural habitat, like when she complains to Werner Kraft about "Apollo-Ernest" failing to come to a Kraal evening, decrying it as "all but: Criminal." But when she learns that her young idol is going on a trip and she feels *no* sadness, and thus realizes that she is indeed dead inside, one feels *this* is not exaggerated, this is truly sad. Falling in love was her way of keeping herself alive, of keeping her antennae out for experiences that would feed her spirit, feed her poetry. When she could no longer stoke this flame, she wanted only to die. In June 1944, she says as much, again in a letter to Werner Kraft, a sad, bitter letter that ends, "Everything, yes, everything is over in me, even [my feeling for] E. Alas. Love, friendship are hands. Mine, my own, broken."[29]

As with all her love poems, the biographical moment serves as a catalyst. However, one would be missing the point if one failed to note that the overarching spiritual guiding force is her faith in love as the source of all art and worthwhile human endeavor.

Else Lasker-Schüler's last poetry volume, *Mein Blaues Klavier*, which included all of the above cited poems, and whose publication, happily, she did live to see (June 1943, Jerusalem), is dedicated to "my never-to-be-forgotten friends in the cities of Germany—and to those who like myself were driven out, and are now scattered throughout the world...." The blue piano of the title poem refers to a toy, a doll's piano, that she had as a child.

But it not only speaks of her childhood. The blue bespeaks her life-long affinity for the color blue, in all its accrued weight, including her Blue Rider loss, Franz Marc. Much has been written about this poem, which has been called the quintessential poem of exile. One reason it holds such an esteemed place in exile literature is, as Sigrid Bauschinger points out, because "it is as though despite all the hateful events in the homeland, her love for this land is undiminished, and the yearning for it only the more intense."[30] There is deep sorrow in Else Lasker-Schüler's last poems; there is no hate.

It is hard to do justice to "Mein Blaues Klavier" in translation. Certainly the physical sense of brokenness, which applies equally to the poet as to the piano, does not come across as intensely in English. Partly it is the truncated quality of the original, which can not be reproduced without a loss of meaning in English.

"Mein Blaues Klavier"

Ich habe zu Hause ein blaues Klavier
Und kenne doch keine Note.

Es steht im Dunkel der Kellertür,
Seitdem die Welt verrohte.

Es spielten Sternenhände vier—
Die Mondfrau sang im Boote.
—Nun tanzen die Ratten im Geklirr.

Zerbrochen ist die Klaviatür...
Ich beweine die blaue Tote.

Ach liebe Engel öffnet mir
—Ich ass vom bitteren Brote—
Mir lebend schon die Himmelstür,
Auch wider dem Verbote.[31]

"My Blue Piano"

I have at home a blue piano
And can't play a single note.

It stands in the dark by the cellar door,
Since the day the world turned brute.

The stars once played four-hand duets
—The moon-child sang in the boat—
Now rats are dancing in its throat.

The keyboard is all fallen apart—
I weep for the pale blue dead.

Ah dear angels, open up
—I ate of the bitter bread—
The gate of heaven yet while I live,
Yes even against the rules.

The broken piano keys are suggested in the halting rhythms and irregular stanza lengths. The German language itself has become a broken thing, abused and misappropriated by Nazi-speak. (The actual poem dates from the Zuricher exile period.) The poem shifts erratically back and forth between childhood, adulthood and old age, with its yearning for release through death. Or to quote another line from this period: "Nur Ewigkeit ist kein Exil" ("Only eternity is not exile").[32]

"Mutter"

Es singt ein weisser Stern sein Totenlied
wie Sterbegeläut in der Julinacht,
und die Wolkenhand auf dem Dach,
die streifende, feuchte Schattenhand
sucht nach der Mutter.

Ich fühle mein nacktes Leben,
fröstelnd stiess es sich ab von Mutterland;
so nackt war nie mein Leben,
nie so in die Zeit gegeben,
als sei ich längst abgeblüht.

Hinter der Tage erlöschenem Schein,
zwischen zwei Nächten,
den zwei sich belauernden Mächten,
friere ich mutterseelenallein.[33]

"Mother"

A white star sings its mournful dirge
like funeral-bells in a night in July,
and the cloudhand on the roof,
the shifting damp shadowhand,
reaches for its mother.

I feel my naked life,
shivering shoved itself off from motherland;
my life was never so naked,
so rendered up to time,
as if I had wilted long ago.

Behind the day's extinguished light
between two nights,
the two lowering powers of darkness,
I freeze motherless all alone.

More and more the physical world around her shrinks, closes in on her. She was often too ill even to go to the café. On one occasion, she did not know how long she had been unconscious and experienced a severe memory lapse and disorientation. To get to her room in the Hamaalot-strasse, she had to climb 19 stone steps. She counted them each time going up. There were days when she could hardly make it.

In her declining health, the day-to-day aggravations and her distorted perceptions of events made her life all but unbearable. Her neighbors, as well as the landlady, treat her, she says, "like scum." One can sense how deeply injured she was by the very wealth of detail that she expends on petty incidents:

> I had cleaned up everything by seven o'clock: floor, chairs, etc., etc.
> Then I threw out the slopwater—and cleaned the basin with soap.
> After I had done this, the woman from the room next door, whom
> I actually had taken a liking to, came and started to yell at me as if
> she were balling out a cleaning woman: 'Ja, Mirra[34] is absolutely
> right when she gets angry and scolds you because there are still
> stains from the rag in the basin!!' Imagine my horror. And after I
> had scrubbed and scoured the sink in the bathroom myself. I sim-
> ply went back into my room.... I'm just not able to deal with such
> people![35]

If the other tenants in her house complained about her, this only fed into her fantasy that she was being persecuted, and that Palestine was a trap that she had fallen into. "It's too hard for me here among these peo-ple. Even David would have packed up and left."[36] On other occasions she referred to Israel as "Erez Misrael," sometimes, "Miesrael."[37] (Pun on "mis-ery" and "rotten," respectively.)

As she confided to Salman Schocken in 1939, "I am so deeply disap-pointed. Even if one has a good talk with someone (here), it is fleeting, nothing binds. Gone is gone, away away. There is no warmth here, no house feels any connection with another."[38] Or again, as when she wrote to Jethro Bithell in 1940: "I am allways so sorry in this magnific country, but I am so allone in my heart...."[39]

During the last two years of her life, she seemed to be ever more overwhelmed by the minutiae of daily living. She is in pain, she cannot manage, but her pride prevents her from accepting help. In June 1943 her last book of poems had come out. It was the last publication she would live to see. But she would have to struggle through two more winters in Jerusalem, with a bad heart and shattered dreams, before she would be liberated from exile.

In Zurich she had not expected to be embraced warmly, and so she never felt let down. But in Jerusalem she was stung by the cold. Of course, in both countries she had truly good and generous friends who cared about her. At times she could appreciate this. At others, she could not.

As she herself admitted, it had never been easy being her friend. Toward the end, it became even harder. She would get upset, tell people to go to hell, and in the next breath be overcome with remorse. In the last months of her life, her brief dispatches to the Grosshuts are staccato markings of such mood swings. What doesn't change is the ground bass: she is exhausted. She is ill. She is "desperate in my loneliness!" She begs for some sign of intimacy. "Please, say 'du'! to me."[40]

Werner Kraft was one of the faithful, and he kept careful notes on the time he spent with the poet over the years. On the 15th of November, 1943, he records:

> I come to her, at 11:30 in the morning. Dirt in her room. She has to do everything herself. She rages against her landlady, against the Jews, against everything. Makes herself an egg. Wants to eat it standing up. I say she should take a chair, I couldn't sit if she was standing. Gets annoyed with me, but does it. She has made cocoa, takes the pot, and drops it on the floor. She yells at me because she's always afraid I'm going to say something to her. I want to leave. She runs after me. "If you leave now, you'll never see me again...." Why do I write this all down? because I'm so aware of her situation that it sends shudders through me.... There is no helping her, but if I had poison, and she wanted to have it, I think I would give it to her. A few more wonderful poems, sure. But the price that she has to pay is too high. Maybe I should have helped her clean up the room, mop the floor, etc., despite her objections. I felt too weak to take up the fight with her.[41]

She must have wept after he went. To be so out of control and so exposed. But up until nearly the end, she could still charm people. Rachel Katinka was a woman who lived for a time in the same rooming house. After a long absence, she went back to visit Else Lasker-Schüler:

I had met her first in the long dim corridor of our house.... I spent long winter evenings in her room.... There was the small table, and on it the little cooker on which she prepared her meager meals. Next to it the typewriter, on which she wrote her poems—over and over. A glass with flowers in it was also on the table; watercolors, and toys of every description. Along the wall, a box with toys—the dolls which she had made herself and which she loved.... Her day began with the pigeons that had their cove beneath her window. She had given each pigeon a name, and she fed them with biscuit crumbs and chocolate ... "you glutton, don't eat so much, I can't afford any more, that's all I have...." Apologizing, she asked for a glass of boiling water, said "thank you." and disappeared again.... She worked hard during the day. At night she could not work, because her vision was poor. At night, as Jerusalem was under black-out, hers was the only window from which light shone. And if wardens came round and reprimanded her, she asked them in....

The last time I visited her, I found her ailing. Burning with fever, she lay in the reclining chair—her bed.... The room looked abandoned, the flowers withered, the dishes had not been washed.... It was noon already and she hadn't eaten anything. She was embittered and she said: "This Jerusalem for whose sake I got into fights already as a child, and was run out of school, this city that I have sung—is no home to me.... I want to take you with me to the Tessin."

She took off her ring and gave it to me. It was a tin ring with a colored piece of glass in it. I knew what this ring meant to her and said: "On your finger it is a precious jewel, on mine it will be a piece of glass—pity.' She laughed and kissed me...."[42] [For the most detailed and objective inventory of her room, see Appendix 12, pages 203–204.]

One day early in 1945 (winters had always proved her nemesis), a physician who had known her in Berlin, Dr. Adolf Wagner, saw her on the street, leaning for support against a tree. He wrote to Karl Wolfskehl, "She was blue in the face, starving and undernourished. I tried to assist her but she refused even to lean on my arm."[43] He did manage to get her to a little café where she gradually recovered her strength. But it was not long thereafter, on January 16, 1945, that she suffered her final heart attack.

In May 1945, in that same letter to Karl Wolfskehl, in which he described her miserable state at the end, Dr. Adolf Wagner also tells Wolfskehl about the play: "About four years ago, she wrote—in an ice cold room—a play, IchundIch. It deals with the downfall of Hitler, whose end she foresaw. It was loosely modelled on Faust. She presented it here, and it made a very strong impression ... *IchundIch* is, in the first instance, an apocalyptic reckoning with Hitlerism (a pity she didn't live to see the end she foretold for Hitler)."[44] That it would not be able to be published for years she also foresaw: "My book [the second Palestine book] will not be published for years," she had told Schocken in 1940, because of the play it contains."[45] In this prediction too she was correct.

On the 16th of January she was admitted to the old Hadassah Hospital on the Scopus. For six days "she suffered

Else Lasker-Schüler on her death-bed. Drawing by Grete Krakauer-Wolf, January 19, 1945 (the Jewish National & University Library, Jerusalem; Else Lasker-Schüler Archiv).

miserably. The heart refused to give up. Despite powerful morphine injections, the attacks recurred every ten minutes. At around five in the morning of January 22, her breathing became easier. The last morphine injection gave her the longed-for relief. At 7:25 A.M. she literally blew out her life, very gently, without struggle and in great peace."[46]

Two English-language newspapers carried obituaries. One appeared on the day of the funeral and gave details for those who might want to attend. It went on to describe Else Lasker-Schüler as "one of the most celebrated modern German poets."[47] The other read:

> *Poetess Buried on Mount of Olives.* Friends and admirers, including writers and journalists, were the chief mourners at the funeral of Else Lasker-Schüler, the German-Jewish poetess, who was laid to rest in the Mount of Olives Cemetery yesterday morning.
>
> In front of the Hadassah Hospital on Mt. Scopus, Rabbi Dr. Wilhelm,[48] of the Emeth Veemunah Synagogue, where Mrs. Lasker-Schüler had been a worshipper, recited the Prayer for the Dead and one of the dead woman's last poems: "I know that I must die."
>
> There were no eulogies. The Kaddish was said at the grave-side by the Hebrew poet, S.J. Agnon.[49]

This is the poem that her friend, the Rabbi Kurt Wilhelm, read at her funeral:

Ich weiss, dass ich bald sterben muss
Es leuchten doch alle Bäume
Nach langersehntem Julikuss—

Fahl werden meine Träume—
Nie dichtete ich einen trüberen Schluss
In den Büchern meiner Reime.

Eine Blume brichst du mir zum Gruss—
Ich liebte sie schon im Keime.
Doch ich weiss, dass ich bald sterben muss.

Mein Odem schwebt über Gottes Fluss—
Ich setze leise meinen Fuss
Auf dem Pfad zum ewigen Heime.[50]

I know that soon I have to die
But all the trees are still aglow
With July's long-awaited kiss—

Pale my dreams, and fading fast
I never rhymed so sad a close
In all the books of all my poems.

You break a flower off to greet me—
I loved it even as a seedling.
But still I know that soon I have to die.

My breath hangs low over God's blue waters
I set my foot down lightly on
The path to my eternal home.

Her tombstone,[51] made from rose-tinged Galilean granite, was designed by her architect friend, Leopold Krakauer.[52] It was altogether plain, with just her name in Hebrew letters cut into the stone.

Chronology

1869 Born in Wuppertal, February 11.

1871 Founding of the German Reich. Bismarck named chancellor.

1880 ELS diagnosed with St. Vitus's Dance.

1882 Death of her youngest, and favorite, brother, Paul.

1890 Mother's death.

1894 Marriage to Dr. Berthold Lasker, brother of Emanuel, world chess champion.

1897 Father's death.

1899 Birth of ELS's only child, Paul. Father unknown. Beginning of association with Peter Hille's circle "Die Kommenden." First poems accepted in the periodical *Die Gesellschaft*, Berlin.

1902 Publication of her first volume of poems, *Styx*, Axel Juncker Verlag, Berlin.

1903 Divorce from Berthold Lasker. Marriage, later that year, to Georg Levin, known today by the name she gave him, Herwarth Walden.

1904 Herwarth Walden founds the "Verein für Kunst."

1905 *Der Siebente Tag*, ELS's second volume of poems, is published by the Verlag des Vereins für Kunst.

1906 *Das Peter Hille Buch* is published by Axel Juncker, Berlin.

1907 *Die Nächte von Tino von Bagdad*, Axel Juncker, Berlin.

1910 Beginning of friendship with Karl Kraus. Breakup ofriage to Walden. First issue of Walden's periodical, *Der Sturm* appears. *Meine Wunder*, a book of poems, Dreililien Verlag, Karlsruhe.

1911 Franz Marc, Kandinsky, August Macke and others form association of painters known as Der Blaue Reiter (The Blue Rider), representing a historic breakthrough in Modern Art.

1912 Favorite sister Anna dies. Divorce from Walden becomes official. Meets Franz Marc. Beginning of postcard and letter exchange between them. Publication of Gottfried Benn's first book of poems, *Morgue*. First meeting with Benn. *Mein Herz*, an epistolary novel, F.S.H. Bachmair Verlag, Munich. Karl Schmidt-Rottluff paints portait of Else Lasker-Schüler "Die Lesende."

1913 Trip to Russia to visit Jakob Holzmann (Senna Hoy), where he is being held in a psychiatric prison. Publication of *Hebräische Balladen* (*Hebrew Ballads*), a book of poems, among her best known, A.R. Meyer, Berlin. Publication of *Gesichte*, a book of essays, Kurt Wolff Verlag, Leipzig.

1914 Beginning of World War I. Meets Georg Trakl. Walter Benjamin begins to frequent Café des Westens, describes being drawn into her circle. Suicide of Trakl at military hospital in Cracow. Publication of *Der Prinz von Theben* (a prose narrative), Verlag der Weissen Bücher. August Macke killed at Perthes-les-Hurlus, Champagne.

1916 Exhibition of drawings by ELS in Hagen. Meets Christian Rohlfs. Portrait by him, "Die Dichterin" ("The poet," ELS) Franz Marc killed at Verdun.

1917 First Dada event, Zurich. George Grosz in military psychiatric hospital, then discharged from army. Oskar Kokoschka wounded in battle; called up again; and shell-shocked: end of active service. Wieland Herzfelde and George Grosz found Malik Verlag, name taken from novel by ELS (not published till 1919). *Gesammelte Gedichte* appears, Verlag der Weissen Bücher, Leipzig.

1918 First Dada event, Berlin, at the I.B. Neumann gallery.

1919 Versailles Treaty officially ends World War I. Karl Liebknecht and Rosa Luxemburg are murdered. *Die Wupper*, Lasker-Schüler's play published in 1909, gets its first performance in Max Reinhardt's Deutsches Theater, under the direction of Heinz Herald. *Der Malik*, a fantastic tale set in the pseudo–Orient of her own devising, is published by Paul Cassirer as part of a ten-volume edition of her works.

1920 *Menschheitsdämmerung*, the first comprehensive anthology of Expressionist verse, includes poems by one woman poet, ELS. At the first Bauhaus evening in Weimar, ELS reads from her work; among those present is Walter Gropius.

1921 "Der Wunderrabbiner von Barcelona," a tale set in Spain and ending in a pogrom, published by Paul Cassirer, Berlin.

1923 Deluxe edition of *Theben*, graphic works and poems, published by Alfred Flechtheim's Querschnitt Verlag, Frankfurt am Main.

1924 Jankel Adler paints portrait of ELS, now at Von der Heydt-Museum, Wuppertal.

1925 "Ich räume auf!" ("I unload!"), a polemic against her publishers, printed in a private press, Lago Verlag, Zurich. Mass unemployment in Germany.

1926 Suicide of Paul Cassirer.

1927 Death of her son, Paul.

1928 Friendship and correspondence with new acquaintances Abraham Stenzel and Paul Goldscheider.

1929 "Black Friday": World economic crisis.

1931 Gottfried Benn sends ELS his text to Hindemith's oratorio *Das Unaufhör-liche*, with its dedication to "Else Lasker-Schüler, the greatest lyric genius, in friendship and admiration." In Berlin's National Gallery, exhibition of drawings and book illustrations by ELS.

1932 Awarded Kleist Prize. *Konzert* and *Arthur Aronymus und seine Väter* (the story version) published by Rowohlt Verlag.

1933 Hitler becomes chancellor. ELS flees to Switzerland. Ernst Ginsberg emigrates to Switzerland by way of Vienna.

1934 Klaus Mann prints three poems by ELS in his periodical *Sammlung*, Amsterdam. First trip to Palestine, by way of Alexandria. In Palestine, becomes acquainted with Gershom Scholem and S.J. Agnon. Beginning of long, running battle with Swiss authorities over permits and visas.

1935 Beginning of friendship and correspondence with Salman Schocken.

1936 Premiere of *Arthur Aronymus und seine Väter* in Zurich.

1937 Publication of *Das Hebräerland* by Oprecht in Zurich. Second trip to Palestine.

1938 German citizenship revoked.

1939 Germany invades Poland: World War II begins. ELS makes third and final trip to Palestine, where she will remain until her death. Exhibition of her graphic works at the Matthiesen Gallery, New Bond St., London.

1940 Salman Schocken begins monthly stipends to ELS in Jerusalem.

1941 ELS reads *IchundIch* in Berger Club, Jerusalem. Meets Ernst Simon, her last great love. Herwarth Walden dies in a Soviet prison.

1942 Founds the literary and philosophical club Der Kraal.

1943 The collection of poems *Mein Blaues Klavier* is printed by the Jerusalem Press, Jerusalem.

1945 January 22: death from heart attack suffered six days earlier. January 23: funeral and burial at the cemetery at Mount of Olives.

Appendices: Related Documents

1. From Letters to Felice, Franz Kafka (Schocken, 1967)

From 12 to 13 February 1913

"...And finally in yesterday's letter Lasker-Schüler was mentioned, and today you ask about her. I cannot bear her poems; their emptiness makes me feel nothing but boredom, and their contrived verbosity nothing but antipathy. Her prose I find just as tiresome and for the same reason; it is the work of an indiscriminate brain twitching in the head of an overwrought city-dweller. But I may be quite wrong; many people love her, including Werfel, who talks of her with genuine enthusiasm. Yes, she is in a bad way; I believe her second husband has left her; they are collecting for her here, too; I had to give five kronen, without feeling the slightest sympathy for her. I don't quite know why, but I always imagine her simply as a drunk, dragging herself through the coffeehouses at night. As you will see from Pick's* letter, he is giving a lecture about her, and for her benefit.

You know, dearest, I must be careful not to talk about strangers in my letters to you, in particular about people I find disagreeable. As though to revenge themselves for my criticism, having calmly allowed themselves to be described, they suddenly (since they can no longer be removed) start spreading themselves all over the place and try to hide you from my view, dearest, with their loathsome or uninteresting appearance. Away with you, Lasker-Schüler! ..."

*Otto Pick, Prague writer and friend of Franz Kafka.

2. Else Lasker-Schüler letter to Klaus and Erika Mann

20 Sept. 33
Dear revered
poet and Erika revered
with boyish eyes.

I beg you to understand me right, and not misconstrue this letter. I always say and write the way I feel. As a token of my deepest affection, allow me to send you these two marbles, delightful glass-pushers (in the glassiest sense). Thus life pushes me along. It is hard for me to say this—we cannot meet any more. I *can* not go against my sense of honor.

However, I would like to offer you some advice: open a cabaret that is "unpolitical." A political cabaret would not only put yourselves at risk of expulsion, it could harm your two poets: Heinrich Mann and your father, who is always so charming to me. Believe me! Despite the fact that I am viewed as unpolitical in my dealings with the two countries (perhaps not altogether honorable on my part).—Why don't you speak with Dr. Korrodi—*Neue Zurcher Zeitung*, he'll certainly help you by coming and writing himself. He and his mother are kind gentle people. I've known him since the beginning of the War (1914). He always tried to protect me. [inserted: apologies for corrections] Sorry, my arm in a sling.

And the largest Jewish paper here is the one I consider important: Editor: Oskar Grun. *Very* dear, very fine editor. Should I speak to him? Not *the other* Jewish papers.

The beginning of my letter is very painful to me. The reasons lie in the past, few years back—in any event they were such as to transform my life, making the greatest difficulties for me, and since taking revenge, taking the logical consequences, is never an option for me in the private sphere, it is therefore more a matter of honor. I beseech you to believe me! Please, dear poet, tear up my first letter, too; I, who only went to school very briefly 101 years ago, sometimes go over to the schoolyard and play, or walk among the lindens—

I hope that some people don't get the idea because of my poem in the—"Sammlung"—that I took advantage—of the opportunity?

[in the margin:] *Just* like I always wish I had been a child in Cairo—that's why the little poem: Cairo (I wasn't lying!)

Very sad all this. Prince Jussuf banished.

I'll be glad to write you with regard to potential audience, since I know everyone here and get around. [From *Briefe von Else Lasker-Schüler*, I (*Letters from Else Lasker-Schüler*, vol. I), ed. Margarete Kupper. München: Kosel-Verlag, 1969, p. 228.]

3. "Orientalism in Fashion"

From head to toe, a woman fashionably dressed in Orientalist taste (during its height in 1910), sported a turban, perhaps with a jeweled aigrette; a wrap-front tunic, cut either as the bodice of a dress or as a kind of loose-fitting jacket; flowing pants gathered in at the cuffs, a skirt fashioned similarly, or the combination thereof called a jupe-culotte. On her feet were shoes with upturned toes. Colors reminiscent of the most glorious plumage sparkled with metallic thread or fabric. From her wrist hung a beaded bag ornamented with tassels, perhaps made in the design of a magic carpet; inside were such necessities as a cigarette case or vanity items, crafted in precious metals, enameled, and set with stones of clashing colors. Her earrings were long and dangling, and her preferred jewels were pearls—ropes and ropes of them. Sautoirs of beads often reached the knees, culminating in tassels. Over her shoulders she threw a wrap, perhaps a burnous or a caftan, falling in supple folds, its cowl weighted with yet another tassel. Dressed thus en élégante, she went to dinner, or to dance the tango or perhaps to see the latest opera or ballet come alive.

This was a look that perfectly suited fashion at a crossroads. The Victorian age had left the sexes cemented in rigid roles that were easily discernible in their dress—men in the drab yet freeing uniform of business, and women in an almost literal gilded cage of whalebone and steel, brocade and lace. For most of the nineteenth century, Orientalism had provided fashion with occasional decorative flourishes and a favorite form of fancy dress. Its most far-reaching influence proved to be an "anti-fashion" look, based on a Turkish model, that was adopted by women seeking to advance women's rights. Perhaps the earliest example in this country is that of Frances Wright—author, abolitionist, and utopian—who was known as early as the 1830s for wearing Turkish trousers. Thus, there was a precedent for equating such a look with reform when, in 1851, a small group of suffragists, including Elizabeth Cady Stanton and Amelia Bloomer, adopted a uniform consisting of voluminous pantaloons worn under a knee-length dress with a fitted bodice and full skirt. Bloomer's newspaper The Lily published illustrations of this type of ensemble along with letters from satisfied wearers, doctors, and other interested parties. "Bloomers," as the trousers came to be known, eventually became so controversial that their original wearers began to feel that they diverted attention from the matters that most concerned them, and so they stopped wearing them. However, the practical bloomer remained in use for physical labor, and, increasingly, for sports.

Traditionally, high fashion, as epitomized by the Paris haute couture, was a matter of society's sartorial requirements realized with exquisite workmanship. In 1910, however, many new factors came into play. In June, the Ballets Russses performed Scheherezade at the Paris Opera, with sets and costumes by Léon Bakst. Its effect on the world of design was immediate. Those who attended the production or saw Bakst's watercolor sketches reproduced in such luxurious journals as Art et Decoration were dazzled by the daring color combinations and swirling profusion of patterns.... Couture was not the only metier to embrace novelties in color: jewelers such as Cartier were inspired by the East as interpreted by Bakst and began combining not just sapphires and emeralds but amethysts, coral, lapis, opal, and turquoise, in addition to enamels. After the decades-long reign of diamonds set in platinum in designs as fine as lace, this was a radical departure....

Its sensuality aside, part of the allure of Orientalized attire was its blurring of gender boundaries. Men in fancy dress draped themselves in pearl necklaces; women in harem pants revealed that they had two legs. The world couldn't help being stunned by the idea of pants on women when, six months after Scheherezade opened, women in trousers made the news.... At the end of 1910 came the first bulletin from Paris that Poiret was about to bring out bifurcated skirts. One person interviewed, a dressmaker, said, "The idea of this new skirt is not to popularize trousers for women, but to add a little touch of Orientalism to their dress...."

The early twentieth-century women who adopted this look wore it as a definition of who they were, attempting to place themselves outside society. While the height of fashion, it was also definitely daring, and those who took it up tended to be women of unusual accomplishment. [Holly Edwards, in Catalog of the exhibition "Noble Dreams/ Wicked Pleasures," pp. 227–232. Princeton University Press in association with The Sterling and Francine Clark Art Institute, 2000.]

4. Texts from The Nights of Tino: *"Ached Bey"*

Ached Bey is the caliph, and I am Tino, and I am passing the time in my uncle's palace. From a tiny porthole I can observe him when he lies on his roof and watches night fall. His beard rests over Bagdad and with every star that rises in the sky a wrinkle disappears from his much-wrinkled brow. Weary travelers of the desert ride by the palace on their dromedaries—*cha machalaa*!! ... in sleepy caravan tones. My uncle, the caliph, waves to them with his big hand, while I crawl through secret passageways over weathered stone floors past long-forgotten idols—I'd like to claw him with their fierce talons, except that the scent of the black Naomi-rose wafts toward me from his roof and intoxicates me. Naomi ... everyone at his court knows about the Jewess of his youth.—My uncle, the caliph, raises his large hand; the black fanbearers and Sudanese negroes obey, only the old palace servant approaches his ear gingerly (I am without a veil), but my uncle, the caliph, pushes him away with his big hand. We smoke opium from pipes covered with velvet and drink blue liquids out of diamond mugs. And I bend over the hieroglyphs of his big hand. Next morning my slaves have to help me into boys' attire, and I wear his sword with the emerald inlaid handle in my belt, and we ride on giant gray beasts up to the outer court—to the place where the traitors of the country are beheaded.... My uncle, the caliph, rests on a cushion between two marble columns, the cushion is red like a birthmark, and he raises and lowers his big hand, sending people to their bloody death. Beheaded sons of noble Mohammedan dynasties lean up against infidels, only the head of the young stranger still sits defiantly on his neck. Three times they sent for him and three times they brought him back—the grumbling executioners—through the bars of night. My uncle's big hand flutters in my lap, but I am unable to read the hieroglyphs in the pocking of his pulse. Finally, he lowers his big hand. Through the cracks in the stone gate the stranger's blood drips over the rough broad stones of the outer court in up to the feet of the caliph. Never have I heard a more eternal flow. It sings like Jehovah's priests on holy days, like Moses' mountaintop on Sinai.

My uncle, the caliph, lies dead in the palace, on his big hand.

In the mosques the dervishes pray and whirl in their shimmering mourning habits—dark stars that circle round his soul. And in the morning the wailing women come and weep, and before the palace there stand black, mummified women and they tender sacred objects, cats with shiny gold fur (for the caliph's grave). The sleepy eyes of the animals are the color of the Naomirose. And Jews march toward Bagdad, youths with heavy-lidded eyes, and maidens, wild black doves, and they throw stones at the stranger's grave—march cursing through the streets, making fists before the palace of my uncle, the caliph. He abides with Allah, but the Jews I see everywhere wandering. ... [H]is step is like the stone under him, but his lips are open, rosy poet lips, like the lips of the tyrant when he lay on the roof and dreamed of Naomi, the Jewess of his youth.

All my black beads are sunken like caves—from my headband hang the dark heads of my forefathers. My lips are dead, but from my eyes columns of fire rise up, following the traces of all the stars, of his singing blood—I dance, dance an unending dance that stretches like a dark cloud over Bagdad, I dance over the waves of the sea, I kick up the sands of the desert, and in front of the palace the people harken and the Jewish youths and maidens are struck dumb.... [From *Kritische Ausgabe* (*Critical Edition*), eds. Norbert Oellers, Heinz Rölleke, and Itta Shedletzky. Suhrkamp: Jüdischer Verlag, 1996–2000, ongoing. KA 3.1., p. 72ff.]

"The Fakir of Thebes"

"Innahu gad marah alleija alkahane fi sijab...." Priests in white robes crossed the road that leads to Thebes; I bowed before their holinesses, and beseeched them to take me with them. The pious men smiled kindly, only the fakir—he had been buried a number of times and had accumulated within himself earth's forces—wrinkled his brow when I made my request. He abhorred women; to exterminate them ranked as one of his pious works. However, he took note of the ring on my finger with its rare Caelum stone.... It came from the treasure of one of his vanquished enemies from Latium. The stone changed colors with the time of day. In the morning it appeared dream-like silveryed, at noon heavy with the bittersweet of lilac, and then it enveloped the twilight and darkened with the night in countless stars. The fakir stared unremittingly at my ring and mumbled incomprehensible words. I was frightened. When we reached Thebes and the women noticed the fakir among the other priests, they began to tremble and shake as in childbirth. Many of them let fall their jugs and rushed back into their dwellings. For whichever of the women the fakir touched with his fleshless hand would bleed for forty days. And it was like a plague when he appeared; in no time a quarter of the healthiest women of the city were bleeding to death. I, who walked alongside the bloodthirsty holy man, keeping in company of the priests, was spared—he continued to stare at my ring, at its stone, it shone bright as the sky over Thebes. I, however, was much distressed over the fate of the city, and as none of its denizens dared so much as to come near the fakir, I prostrated myself before him, clasped his cold foot, and beseeched him to stop sacrificing my sisters to his pious works. He cast a greedy look at my ring, at the marvelous stone in which I carried the heavens about. This was what he demanded in return for his mercy. I shook my head fiercely, and on that selfsame day every woman in the city bled. And it was like a gruesome sea flooding Thebes, from the luxurious green of the forests—all those drops of human blood!!! And not one house was left standing that was not reddened from the blood of its women, and did not shriek to high heaven. The Caelum on my finger warned me, a red night! And I fell down before the fakir, kissed his cold foot, and pleaded with him that he should touch me too with his fleshless hand. He let it drop slowly onto my shoulder. I did not even feel its breath of decay, it died as it sank. He, on the other hand, turned away from me, I being unworthy even of his pious work... [KA 3.1., p. 77f].

"I Dance in the Mosque"

"You must visit me three days after the rainy season. Then the Nile has receded and giant flowers bloom in my garden, and I too climb out of the ground and breathe.

A mummy as old as the stars is what I am, and I dance in the Age of the Open Field. Awesome my eye and my arm raised in prophecy, and the dance draws a narrow flame across my forehead and it grows pale and reddens again—from my lower lip to my chin.* And the many colored glass beads around my neck tinkle ... oh, *machmede macheii*.** ... Here, still shining, is the glow of my foot, my shoulders quiver ever so slightly—*machmede macheii*, my whole body sways the entire time with my hips, my body is a burnished star, Dervi, dervish, my body is a star. *Machmede, macheii*, my lips no longer ache ... my raptured blood drips sweet, ever deeper in trance, my finger rises mysteriously, like the stem of the Allah-flower. Machmede macheii, fanning my face, back and forth—and quick as an asp, my dance stretches and entwines itself in the stone coils of my ear. *Machmede macheii, machmede machmede...*" [KA3.1, p. 69].

To an amazing degree the modern dance movement, as exemplified by Ruth St. Denis and Mary Wigman, finds its literary counterpart in passages like this from *Die Nächte der Tino von Bagdad.*... Other literary examples from the same period are Oscar Wilde's "Salomé," and Mallarmé's "Herodiade."

*In coaching a dancer for Ruth St. Denis's solo, "The Incense," Martha Graham told her: "Your arms become the smoke, which is your prayer."

**Graham tells how Ruth St. Denis, rehearsing "The Incense," in 1906, "would talk to us in gibberish and we would talk gibberish to her. In other words, we were creating our own vocabulary." Martha Graham. Blood Memory, p. 65.

---

5. Letter from Maria Marc to the Mackes, with a postscript from Franz

Sindelsdorf 21.1.13

Dear Lisbeth, dear August,

I wish we could just sit down together and chat. There is so much to tell. Writing is a bore. But you have to hear at least some of it. Berlin was full of surprises for us. We were eager to meet the *Sturm* literary circle—well, it wasn't much fun, our expectations had been much too high. As the days wore on, we became ever more depressed, we thought what we were seeing was the way the metropolis corrupts—almost everybody seemed corrupted or depraved. Jealousy, envy and lies everywhere. No one trusts anyone—even the air is impure. Of course what made it interesting was that we were negotiating two enemy camps—on one side, Else Lasker-Schüler, Walden's divorced wife; on the other, Walden himself with his current wife, a complete goose. Lasker, with whom we had corresponded before we came to Berlin, is a remarkable personality and we took to her at once. (Walden had led us to believe their divorce had been friendly.) When you meet her, you begin to understand her poetry. She doesn't fit in with the people she lives among, but she too is depraved, debauched. At the moment she is suffering acutely. As a result of the divorce, which didn't go nearly as smoothly as Walden led us to believe, she is in severe financial straits. Her nerves are in a state of shock, and so we took her back with us to Sindelsdorf, hoping that would do her some good. But she couldn't take the loneliness and stillness of nature: for years now she has been shuttling between her own four walls and the cafés; so the sudden change, instead of calming her, had a disquieting effect on her frayed nerves. We brought her back to Munich, where she has friends and will undergo treatment that may prove more useful. We, however, are back in Sindelsdorf, and feel the urgent need for quiet—quiet. Can you understand that?

Before I tell you about Berlin and the other circle, I have to tell you what happened in Munich. August really missed something. How I wished he could have been there to enjoy this. We thought it would be nice to put our sick friend in touch with like-minded people, so we took her to Kandinsky-Münter. A rather cool tone hung in the air. Lasker bristles at Kandinsky's painting. "Professor," not Artist, is how she refers to him. And the glass painting, the holy pictures he has hanging all over the house, got on her nerves, and as Kandinsky doesn't know much about her, Else Lasker-Schüler, he got the impression that she was just another *Weltschmerzlerin* from the Café des Westens in Berlin. But they concealed these mutual impressions beneath a cool but civil tone. As always, Münter flitted about like a moth. Three days later I met her again at Franz's exhibition at Thannhäuser's; we had a very friendly chat. Münter busied herself with looking at the pictures, and she and I sat quietly together for about an hour, altogether harmoniously, while we waited for the others. Since the blow-up, Münter has been very nice. Neither of us can overcome the feeling of inner differences; but socially we've all found a *modus vivendi*, so that we can share those things which interest us and bind us together. Münter really makes an effort, and so do we, and we're all the better off for it.

So—we were sitting at Thannhauser's—Münter and I—when Lasker came in. After a most cordial greeting, and walking around together, Lasker says, "This painting is the one that moved me the most." Münter asks, "Which one, the tiger or the monkey?" Lasker: "The tiger." Münter: "What do you find so moving about it?" Lasker: "It looks so menacing." Then we go our separate ways again, perfectly harmless, looking at other paintings, etc. Suddenly Lasker walks up to Münter with a determined gait and starts in: "My dear woman, how do you come to insult me like that? I am through and through an artist," and she goes on in this vein, berating Münter. Upset by all this, I try to come between them and smooth things out, but Lasker-Schüler doesn't let up about the greatness and beauty of the pictures—but always with a rage directed at Münter, and all of a sudden she winds up, "I am an artist, I am very strong, a very strong person, and I won't put up with such treatment from a *nobody*." What do you think of that? August? You would have died laughing. I didn't feel like laughing though. I nearly died of embarrassment. It was like something out of a bad dream, or the theatre. But in real life I never experienced anything like it. It was as if your letter to Kandinsky that time took on material shape. And I'm standing there, seeing more blue, more green than in any of Franz's paintings. Lasker-Schüler has a real sixth sense, Münter's soul lay open before her from the start; she has truly *uncanny* insights into people. But—there had been *no* provocation, simply no reason to throw it up in Münter's face. I was so shaken, Münter had to calm me down. After a time the three men returned—totally oblivious—to the three battling women, etc., etc. Now laugh yourselves sick. That's really some story. Everything else pales alongside, e.g., Franz's swing back to Thannhauser and even Schmidt as the lesser evil. It would be nice to be able to gossip about the Berlin crowd—Walden and wife—the goings-on in this circle, but it's boring to write about, you have to tell it in person. Cassirer has reappeared on the scene, and spares no effort in recruiting the Blaue Reiter for his fall show. Franz remained cool to the core, you and he will have a lot to exchange on that subject. Did Cassirer ever get in touch with you again? Then there's an urgent warning against

Neumann, he's a foul swindler of a customer. August shouldn't let himself be taken in by him.

Once more Else Lasker-Schüler, she in *desperate* need of funds, has a 13 year-old son—and is herself at the moment so sick she can't work. Her friends, Karl Kraus, Dehmel, Princess Wied, Adolf Loos, Lagerlöf and others, have sent out a petition on her behalf. The Blue Rider circle doesn't have any money—moreover Else Lasker-Schüler wouldn't take anything from penurious artists. For that reason there'll be an auction at *Schmidt's*. Would you want to contribute a few things? Paintings or drawings—Berliners are participating too, Schmidt's giving something from his stock too. If you do want to give something, send it *soonest* to Schmidt. "For the auction for Else Lasker-Schüler."

How have *you* been, my dear Lisbeth? I think of you a lot, wishing you well, from the bottom of my heart. Please let us know when it arrives. There's still nothing in sight for me, which is why I'm trying to do a lot of other things.* I'll be taking piano lessons from Frau Klee—I'm looking forward to that very much. We were at Klees' recently, and she played the wonderful Cesar Franck sonatas very impressively. If I take lessons once a month from Frau Klee, I hope to advance, myself. I also want to take gymnastics in Munich; Franz drives me mad with his incessant nagging about my being fat.

It is beautiful here now, the village is so quiet and deep in snow; we take walks and recover from life in the city—Berlin and Munich.

How are your mother and grandmother? Please give them our best, your brother too. And write!

Warm greetings to all three of you from us both—in loving friendship,

> Yours,
> Maria

To Maria Marc's chatty letter, Franz added a brief postscript. "If August is putting on weight again and becoming too complacent in his ways, you might prescribe a fortnight of Else Lasker-Schüler for him—that should do it. But, all joking aside, she is a prodigious person." (August Macke and Franz Marc. *Briefwechsel*, DuMont Buchverlag, 1964, pp. 146ff.)

*Lisbeth was expecting a child. The Marcs could not, apparently, have children.

---

6. *"To Franz Marc"*

The Blue Rider has fallen, a great Biblical figure, on whose shoulder hung the scent of Eden. He threw a blue shadow across the landscape. He could hear the animals speak; he illumined their uncomprehended souls. He kept reminding me when he went away to war: it is not enough to be kind to human beings, but what you do for horses, who suffer indescribable things on the battlefield, you do for me.

He has come to the red shore, large angels bear his giant frame to God, who holds his blue soul, a gleaming banner, in his hand. I think of a story from the Talmud that a priest once told to me: how God stood with the people before the temple after its destruction and wept with them. Because wherever the Blue Rider went, he bestowed Heaven. So many birds fly through the night, they can still play wind and breath. But we below know nothing of these things, all we can do is massacre one another or pass each other by indifferently. In our sober midst, an unimaginable bloody mill is rising up, menacing, and all of us, all peoples will be ground to dust by it. We march the whole time over ground that waits for us. The Blue Rider has arrived at the end; he was still too young to die.

Never have I seen a painter paint with more tenderness and God-inspired earnestness. "Lemon oxen," "Fire buffalo," he named his creatures, and a star shone on his brow. But even the beasts of the wilderness became plantlike in his tropical hand. He magicked lady tigers into anemones, he threw a cloak of gilly flowers around leopards; he spoke of the pure kill, when in his painting the panther drags the antelope from the rocks. He felt like the young patriarch of Biblical times, a wondrous Jacob, the prince of Cana. With furor he fought his way through the thicket; his beautiful face shone reflected in the water, and often, when it was tired, he carried his wondrous heart home like a sleeping child, wrapped in hides.

'Greetings to your dear wife, Blue Rider, to your stable boy, your donkey in its stall, your bocks and does in the meadow, and not to forget, beloved half-brother, Russel, your faithful dog"

That was all before the War.
Franz Marc, the Blue Rider from Ried,
Mounted his war-steed.
Rode over Benediktbeuern down to lower Bavaria.
Alongside him his watchful, trusty Nubian
Carries his arms.
But around his neck he wears an image stamped in silver
And the stone amulet from his beloved wife.
Through the streets of Munich he raises his Biblical head
In the bright frame of the heavens.
Solace is in his almond eyes
Thunder, his heart.
Behind and to all sides, the many many warriors.

Berliner Tageblatt 9 March 1916 [*Kritische Ausgabe, Gedichte* (*Critical Edition, Poems*), #248; *Kritische Ausgabe, Prosa* (*Critical Edition, Prose*), p. 413f].

---

7. Excerpt from a ten-page letter to Karl Kraus describing the conditions under which Senna Hoy (Jakob Holzmann) died in Russia

16.5.14

At first Senna Hoy was in Warsaw in the Citadelle, before that he was in the Town Hall. I went at that time about seven years ago to Harden, who said he was the most courageous young man he knew, but that he could do nothing for him. A lie! I still hoped he might free himself, and so I wavered. Then he came to Moscow, and then there were always other things that I wanted to try to do; none of the friends wanted to help me.... Everything I attempted went wrong. Then I met Marianne von Werefkin, her father had been vice-regent to Tsar Alexander. She promised me that she would do everything she could. She wrote at once to her cousin in Petersburg, Assistant to Minister Dschunkowski, and he promised to help. Petition for clemency was submitted again but there was no reply. The brother travelled to Russia, spoke with Dschunkowski himself, who made a few emendations (and) sent the petition on to the tsar. With no result. Then we went over together; Senna Hoy's brother and myself. Dschunkowski wasn't there, he was taking the baths at Meran but his sister received me and sent me to the Office of War Ministry; there we were promised that if another request for clemency was submitted, it would go straight to the War Ministry, altogether bypassing the German Embassy.... Imagine, the Germans fantasized that S.H. wanted to murder the German Kaiser and that was why they opposed his release. Everyone there was friendly, I had Richthofen's letter of recommendation, but Russia could not the German Embassy was against it. That's what the Russians *said*, Werefkin told me in confidence.... Then S.H. wrote that he was so ill he was going to die.... He did not want to die yet, he thought of all there was still for him to do. From prison he was writing letters soliciting for the starving people banished to Siberia. He never asked for money, his mother sent him as much as she could every month to the insane asylum, she is poor. I never sent him anything Karl Kraus* that is beastly of me....

Your poor, grateful Prince of Thebes.

He lay at the end in the Prisoner's Ward of the Asylum Meschtscherskoje 4 hours from Moscow. I had all but lost my senses when I went in. We had to go his brothers and I through 8 towers high up between walls. In front of the gate before each tower stood 8 armed soldiers or guards. Next to his cell (he lay with 102 fever pneumonia horribly bedded down) insane prisoners ranted and raved.... [From *Briefe an Karl Kraus* (*Letters to Karl Kraus*), ed. Astrid Gelhoff-Claes. Köln, Berlin: Kiepenheuer & Witsch, 1959.]

She had no money to send him. It was hardly a year previously that Karl Kraus had placed an advertisement in Die Fackel, calling for contributions to assist her in her existential need.

---

8. George Trakl
"Abendland," 4. Fassung,
Dedicated to Else Lasker-Schüler

1

Mond, als träte ein Totes
Aus blauer Höhle,
Und es fallen der Blüten
Viele über den Felsenpfad.
Silbern weint ein Krankes
Am Abendweiher.
Auf schwarzem Kahn
Hinüberstarben Liebende.

Oder es läuten die Schritte
Elis' durch den Hain
Den hyazinthenen
Wieder verhallend unter Eichen.
O des Knaben Gestalt
Geformt aus kristallenen Tränen,

Nächtigen Schatten.
Zackige Blitze erhellen die Schläfe
Die immerkühle,
Wenn am grünenden Hügel
Frühlingsgewitter ertönt.

2

So leise sind die grüen Wälder
Unsrer Heimat,
Die kristallne Woge
Hinsterbend an verfallner Mauer
Und wir haben im Schlaf geweint;
Wandern mit zögernden Schritten
An der dornigen Hecke hin
Singende im Abendsommer,
In heiliger Ruh
Des fern verstrahlenden Weinbergs;
Schatten nun im kühlen Schoss
Der Nacht, trauernde Adler.
So leise schliesst ein mondener Strahl
Die purpurnen Male der Schwermut.

3

Ihr grossen Städte
Steinern aufgebaut
In der Ebene!
So sprachlos folgt
Der Heimatlose
Mit dunkler Stirne dem Wind,
Kahlen Baümen am Hügel.
Ihr weithin dämmernden Ströme!
Gewaltig ängstet
Schaurige Abendröte
Im Sturmgewölk.
Ihr sterbenden Völker!
Bleiche Woge
Zerschellend am Strande der Nacht,
Fallende Sterne.

"Occident," Fourth Version,*
Dedicated to Else Lasker-Schüler

1

Moon, as if a dead thing
Stepped out of a blue cave,
And many blossoms fall
Across the rocky path.

Silver a sick thing weeps
By the evening pond,
In a black boat
Lovers crossed over to death.

Or the footsteps of Elis
Ring through the grove
The hyancinthine
To fade again under oaks.
O the shape of that boy
Formed out of crystal tears,
Nocturnal shadows.
Jagged lightning illumines his temples
The ever-cool,
When on the verdant hill
Springtime thunder resounds.

2

So quiet are the green woods
Of our homeland,
The crystal wave
That dies against a perished wall
And we have wept in our sleep;
Wander with hesitant steps
Along the thorny hedge
Singers in the evening summer
In holy peace
Of the vineyards distantly gleaming;
Shadows now in the cool lap
Of night, eagles that mourn.
So quietly does a moonbeam close
The purple wounds of sadness.

3

You mighty cities
stone on stone raised up
in the plain!
So quietly
With darkened forehead
the outcast follows the wind,
bare trees on the hillside.
You rivers distantly fading!
Gruesome sunset red
is breeding fear
in the thunderclouds.
You dying peoples!
Pallid billow
that breaks on the beaches of Night,
stars that are falling.

Translated by Michael Hamburger. From Tim Cross, The Lost Voices of World War I. *University of Iowa Press, 1988.*

9. "George Grosz"

Manchmal spielen bunte Tränen
In seinen äschernen Augen.

Aber immer begegnen ihm Totenwagen,
Die verscheuchen seine Libellen.

Er ist abergläubig—
—Ward unter einem bösen Stern geboren—

Seine Schrift regnet,
Seine Zeichnung: Trüber Buchstabe.

Wie lange im Fluss gelegen
Blähen seine Menschen sich auf,

Mysteriöse Verlorene mit Quabbenmäulern
Und verfaulten Seelen.

Fünf träumende Totenfahrer
Sind seine silbernen Finger

Aber nirgendwo ein Licht im verirrten Märchen
Und doch ist er ein Kind,

Der Held aus dem Lederstrumpf;
Mit dem Indianerstamm auf Duzfuss.

Sonst hasst er alle Menschen,
Sie bringen ihm Unglück.

Aber George Grosz liebt sein Missgeschick
Wie einen anhänglichen Feind.

Und seine Traurigkeit ist dyonisisch,
Schwarzer Champagner seine Klage.

Kein Mensch weiss, wo er herkam;
Ich weiss, wo er landet.

Er ist ein Meer mit verhängtem Mond,
Sein Got ist nur scheintot. [KA.1.1 #250, p. 187f.]

"George Grosz"

Sometimes tears of many colors
Play in his ash-gray eyes.

But he's always running into hearses
That scare off his dragonflies.

He is superstitious—
—Came into the world under an evil star—

His handwriting's a downpour,
His drawing: dark alphabet.

Like corpses that float on the water
His people are all bloated up,

Mysterious loners with blubbery mouths
And putrefied souls.

His silvery fingers are
Five dreaming pallbearers

But no where a light in the lost fairytale
And yet he is a child,

The hero from leatherstocking*;
He's chums with the Indians.

As for all the others, he hates them,
They bring him misfortune.

But George Grosz loves his bad luck
Like a faithful foe.

And his sadness is Dionysian,
Black champagne his lament.

No one knows where he came from;
I know where he'll touch down.

He's a sea when the moon's shrouded,
His God is just playing 'possum.

*The hero of James Fenimore Cooper's Leatherstocking Tales, Natty (Nathaniel) Bumppo, was called Leatherstocking. Grosz frequently showed up at the Romanische Café dressed as a cowboy, with boots and spurs.

---

10. *"Parable of the Shepherdess"*

Once there was a shepherdess among the people of Israel, who, when she wasn't tending her flock, made poems to God. One morning she was very thirsty and she leaned far over the edge of the fountain to drink. Thereupon, out of the countless drops of water one drop, in which the whole of creation was reflected, rose over the fountainhead—the *Creator Himself*. And the shepherdess went to fetch a vessel in which to preserve the priceless treasure, but she found not a single one that was worthy of the beauty of the small polished droplet—not in the temple niches, nor in the palace gardens. Then she spun a goblet out of the transparent red threads of her pure heart, crystal in tone and of noble darkness in its offering, and she laid the pulsing Eternity, preserved in the tiny droplet, between the fine-spun walls of the heart she had sacrificed to God. The *Shema*, the holy hieroglyph from the plan of creation, outlasts the world. [From "Das Hebräerland," *Else Lasker-Schüler: Gesammelte Werke* (*Collected Works*), ed. Friedhelm Kemp. Kösel-Verlag, 1959, 1962, p. 835f. A5. p. 48f.]

11. IchundIch

"There is no man who differs more from another than he does from himself at another time."—Luigi Pirandello

IchundIch and Faust

IchundIch is an elaborate arabesque on the Faustian theme of two souls raging in one breast (or, as Goethe puts it, "zwei Seelen wohnen, ach, in meiner Brust"). The idea is a very Germanic one, begotten in the Teutonic north, where a certain Georg Faust enjoyed dubious repute, roaming from university to university during the Reformation. His insatiable thirst for power led him to make a pact with the devil, and writers, from Marlowe's day to this, have not tired of taking up his case: in Germany, most notably, of course, Goethe. And it was after Else Lasker-Schüler's death, and the end of World War II, that Thomas Mann published his monumental Faust novel *Dr. Faustus*.

Beyond Faust

One aspect of the Faust theme that drew Else Lasker-Schüler to it was the quest of the self for its other half. It is this quest for wholeness that marks the yearning expressed in an early love poem, and quoted in the play. "Ich finde mich nicht wieder/ In dieser Todverlassenheit!/ Mir ist: ich lieg' von mir weltenweit/ Zwischen grauer Nacht der Urangst...." (I can no longer find myself,/ In this godforsaken place!/ I feel: I'm worlds away from me/ Within gray walls of night's primeval dread....) The poem ends, "Möcht' einen Herzallerliebsten haben!/ Und mich in seinem Fleisch vergraben." ("I'd like to have a sweetheart/ And bury myself in his flesh.") [KA I, #62, p. 49.]

Ultimately the wish is identical with the wish to be united with God and is not unlike the I-Thou concept of her longtime friend, Martin Buber. IchundIch, written as one word, permits of the reading "ich und dich," a close if not altogether grammatical reading of Buber's "ich und du." (I and Thou). In the Prologue to IchundIch, which is spoken by the poet as if on her way to the theater for a "rehearsal" of her play, her words are addressed to a companion. Who is this companion ("Dearest friend")? Her alter-ego, a literary forebear, a Biblical mentor, or God Himself? All of the above? We are left to conjecture. Altogether, IchundIch plays ball with "identity" in ways that would have been disconcerting to theatre-goers not yet exposed to Beckett.

Then there is the seemingly fragmented nature of the text, plus a blatant disregard for smooth transitions. In fact, the play is a complex weave of highly diverse strands, all of which are carried through to the end. But instead of a single straight line of action, Lasker-Schüler uses a panopticon perspective, creating a microcosm-macrosphere.

IchundIch is imagined as a kind of total theater, a dream-theater (*Herzenstheater* is what she called it), whose audience is firstly the poet herself. It is envisaged as well as an illusionist stage of world history, with characters drawn from Biblical times up to the present (much like "Faust II"). To do this, it employs virtually every conceivable theatrical device, including film projections.

In his *Prolegomena zum modernen Drama*,* Rudolf Hilty names as specifically modern effects: alienation, disillusioning, playing beyond the ramp, theater within theater, the conflating of time and place (mixing periods and worlds), shifting or multi-perspectives; intrusion of parody. All are ways of representing existential real-

---

In Jeanne d'Arc bei Schiller und Anouilh, Zurich 1960.

ity and, with the exception of the first, *IchundIch* makes use of them all. One might add to this list, with regard to *IchundIch*, the mixing of high and low diction, including dialect, in a serious work of art. No wonder the play was deemed unplayable during her lifetime.

The play as key to understanding the poet and as artistic credo. *IchundIch* provides a key to understanding the many contradictions that plague ELS's biographers, along with her ability to embrace opposites. In conflating the male-female, old-young, demonic-angelical aspects of her characters, and accepting the antitheses as given, she gathers together all her own dichotomies and gives them their just, poetic due. There is only one character in the entire play who is pure evil, and that is not Mephisto, not Satan. It is Adolf Hitler. Not least, *IchundIch* contains her definitive statement about art, that truth lies in poetry, not in "fact."

Structure and Content

The play's structure builds parodically on Geothe's *Faust.* (It even contains parodic references to the well-known 19th century parody of Goethe's *Faust* by Friedrich Theodor Vischer.) But, just as parody is the highest compliment one can pay an author, so in the end everything here is made whole. Lasker's Goethe parody extends to plot as well as wordplay, in a collage-like treatment that contains just enough recognizability to set off alarm bells in the listener's brain. So, for example, when she says, "A witches' Sabbath has just sprayed me in the face," right after describing the hideous billboards she encounters on her way to the theater in her contemporary Jerusalem, she clearly wishes to call up Goethe's Walpurgisnacht scene. But the poetic inspiration that she draws from the billboards is altogether her own. "Billboard dreams light up to left and right;/ Their beams fly back and forth/ like spoonerisms in the night."

For the theater's location she chooses a sunken site near the Davidsturm, or tower of the citadel at the old wall of Jerusalem, known to the old inhabitants of the city as "Hell's Ground," because it had been the place where the people had forsaken their true religion and burned incense to Baal and other gods. It was therefore reviled by God and slated for destruction. In the Bible, in the Book of Jeremiah, it is called "the valley of slaughter."

The play has five acts, a prologue and epilogue. The Prologue is spoken by the poet from behind the curtain to the accompaniment of orchestral music, with sudden incursions of hurdy-gurdy sounds. Arrived at the theater, she addresses the audience. She gives us a synopsis of the plot, in *Knittelverse* (doggerel) like those used by Goethe in Ur-Faust and Faust Part I, as well as by Brecht in his *Moritatenlieder*. She speaks of the "Mordgeschichte/ Die ich an mir in finsterer Nacht vollbracht."

> Hear, good audience, the chilling tale—
> How I did murder me in darkest vale!
> And since I always tell the truth when I write verse
> Let all your doubts at once disperse.

The prologue goes on for quite a bit, always in rhymed doggerel, at the end of which she says:

> Most honored audience, you yawn out of *one* mouth.
> Why 'grace' the overture with all this poesie?
> Take it straight from me then, this report.
> Satan's devil of devils surrenders—last resort!!
> *Satanas aller Teufel Teufel hat—kapituliert!!*
> [line 37, p. 188] [The poet attempts in vain to continue]

EDITOR-IN-CHIEF SWET*: Were this a fact/ I would have printed it!!
THE POET: attempts again to continue her report—
SWET: The report is a canard!
FROM THE AUDIENCE: For the birds!
THE POET: You've twice interrupted my sentence, Mr. Swet.
A WOMAN IN THE AUDIENCE: That what's her name!
THE POET: In my lifetime I spoke—if only from the sidelines—the "truth"—
    naked—more naked than naked. Both in prose and in verse.!!!
A PROFESSORIAL TYPE: Verse ... I must say.
VOICES FROM THE AUDIENCE: Holland lost! Belgium perdu, France, Denmark, Nor-
    way ...
SWET: [calming the audience]: Haaretz would have printed the fact!!
THE POET: Mr. Swet, you are mistaken about what I haven't even said yet:
    Satan's devil of all devils has capitulated. Yes, sir!! However,—that is to
    God the Lord, in—the fourth act.
KING DAVID (one of the three Biblical kings seated in the boxes): [gets up impas-
    sive] Praise be to You, almighty—King of the world. Barukh ata adonai
    melekh haolam ... [KA 2, p. 188f].

Because—already in the prologue—she gives away the end, stating as fact the downfall and capitulation of Hitler, she is shouted down and mocked. All written into the
script! Yes, the whole chorus of derision: the press, the audience ... everyone, of course,
knows better. After all, it is 1940: "Holland lost! Belgium a goner. France, Denmark,
Norway...." Hitler, in short, will clearly win the war.

The curtain falls, but rises again immediately, as the "actual" play begins.

We see an odd assembly of characters. In what was once the king's loge (box) judging by its plush opulence, are seated, immobile, and looking like the painted figures in
a panopticon, three Biblical kings: Saul, David and Solomon. In the director's loge is
Max Reinhardt, who has come, we are told, from Hollywood to direct the play. Across
from him sit the Three Ritz Brothers, who will perform typically asinine antics, but
occasionally, through their seemingly inane repetitions, point up ironies or ambigui-
ties in the text—and then, the actors in the true drama: Mephisto, Faust, Frau Marta
Schwertlein (the Marthe Schwerdtlein of Goethe's Faust Part I) the Nazis, and their
leader, Baal, and finally, the author herself.

Act One opens with a spirited dialogue between Faust and Mephisto, full of insider
jokes about Goethe's bourgeois foibles. But just when we are getting interested in their
exchange, Director Reinhardt interrupts one of the actors to correct his delivery. Then
Mephisto continues taking Faust to task, not just for his bourgeois cop-outs but for his
soupy idealism. And so when Faust tells Mephisto he wants to perish with his coun-
trymen even though he's horrified by what they're doing to his country, Mephisto,
clearly at the end of his tether, says: "Oh, this world of man's contriving. If God weren't
God, he'd lose his mind." And Reinhardt takes the moment to remind the cast that
Faust and Mephisto are really twins. Marte Schwertlein keeps coming in, interrupting
to tell them dinner is ready. "The delicate angelwings will be burnt...."

Act Two brings on Göring, Goebbels, Hess—the whole sick crew, and features a
grand diner and entertainment at Hell's Palace, complete with a ballet of the flames. A
film projection on the wall will show the Reichstag in flames.

"It is my custom, gentlemen," says Mephisto, "that every guest, whether invited or

*At this time Swet was Jerusalem correspondent for Haaretz; later, he was Haaretz political corre-
spondent in the United States.

not, at my court—discuss his business with me over a glass of wine. I assume, gentle-men, it's a matter of tariffs.

GOEBBELS TO GÖRING (in a whisper): What tariffs is he talking about?
GÖRING: Shut up dogpaw.
MEPHISTO: ... I assume it's a question of delivering petroleum fresh from its source, gentlemen.
THE FOUR GUESTS: Heil Hitler! For Germania and for Rome, Your Excellency.
FAUST (correcting them): Highness.

Act Three opens in Hell's park; Faust and Mephisto are playing chess on a terrace, overlooking. Marte Schwertlein is at her spinning-wheel below. And nearby is a fountain with amoretti who pour water from jugs into the basin. In the middle of the fountain, *Psyche.* Among shrubbery to the right of the fountain a huge stoneblock: the idol, Baal.

Goebbels and Marta Schwertlein carry on an "absurd" amorous dialogue. Goebbels asks her who that awful monster is in the bushes. And the little monsters supporting the club-footed one?

FRAU MARTE: Hoho ho! ... He comes from an ancient noble breed ... and Dr. Faust says he possesses: a worldly cast of mind. (She strokes Goebbels' club-foot).
(Goebbels says he'd rather see Germany's God brought here to take the place of Baal.)
FRAU MARTE: You mean Jesus Christ?
GOEBBELS: As if Madamchen was born yesterday—the ole Jew no longer figures!
FRAU MARTE: astonished
GOEBBELS: The Führer sent him posthaste with his New Testament by 'Armer-sünderklingelbahn,' (poorsinnersloopline) and then in an 'Aeppelkahn' (applecart) on a pleasant water journey home to Bethlehem where he, the Jewish pastor, was born—... [Act 3, KA 2, p. 203].

Act Four has Mephisto reciting one of Goethe's best known poems, "Über allen Gipfel ist Ruh." But Mephisto sabotages the poem, by infiltrating slight but savage emendations (p. 209). This poem, recited again by Mephisto, will give way to a weep-ing, penitent Faust intoning Lasker's poem, "Chaos."—"I can no longer find myself/ In this strange eternal realm/ As if I lay whole worlds apart from me ..." (Act 4. KA 2, p. 223f). Mephisto mumbles some childish abracadabra, and with Faust in tow, they rise up, in superhuman stature, out of the surrounding mire. Mephisto turns to Faust: "Dear my brother, lean against me closer still, that you and I each other fill." Mephisto hands Faust the dagger. "Now run the dagger through my heart ... And that way kill the Moloch part!!!" Thus Faust and Mephisto become one.

There follows a dénouement with Hitler and his men being swallowed up in Hell's lava swamp, a most fit ending since, as we learned in the banquet scene, they have come to Hell to drill for oil, in Hitler's megalomaniac belief that no resource should remain untilled. As Hitler dies, the scene culminates in these lines: "Er hinterlässt nicht Asche, nicht das kleinste Häufchen Schutt!/ Es folgt ein unerlöster Tod dem Antichrist and Antijud!" (No ashes will remain of him, no remnant dust;/ But unremitting death awaits the anti–Jew, the anti–Christ!)

Mephisto however will have new life "and once again through the unfolding of my I-and-I, I'll come re-born and Easter-lily fresh to me."

Act Five plays in the garden of the author's Jerusalem ophthalmologist, after all the Nazis, big and small devils, have been drowned in laval mush. She is sitting on a bench very tired, very frail, near death, in conversation with her other (mortal) self, a scarecrow. They are joined, not altogether to her pleasure, by the reporter from Haaretz again, Mr. Swet. During this scene the poet dies, but we hear from her again, in an epilogue from the beyond—and behind the curtain, after it falls. "The play is over—I have no more to say.... But I hear a question coming from the nearby planet earth: It is Gretchen's question from Faust: 'Do you believe in God?' The poet, from behind the curtain, singing. 'I am so happy, I am so happy, God is here.'"

Performance and Publication History

Not until Henrich Böll read the manuscript of *IchundIch* in the 1960s and in his excitement over the discovery urged publication, did the complete drama see print. The play gradually caught the attention of German theaters, which began performing it, to general critical acclaim and the awed admiration of young avant-garde writers like Peter Handke.

Why had it taken so long?

The first editor of Else's works after her death was Werner Kraft. When it came to deciding whether to include her last play, Kraft had qualms. In his indecisiveness, he consulted Ernst Ginsberg and Martin Buber.

Ginsberg, like Kraft, was concerned about preserving the poet's image. He saw Else Lasker-Shüler as an inspirational poet, someone who, in her own words, very often didn't know where her poems came from. For him this was tantamount to saying they came from God. Ginsberg, who had converted to Catholicism, and who had played the night-watchman in *Arthur Aronymus*, regarded that play as the pinnacle of Lasker-Schüler's creative output containing, as it did, her most impassioned plea for Jewish-Christian reconciliation. Nothing she would write thereafter could ever approach this play in his mind. As to *IchundIch*, he wrote to Kraft: "I would beseech you from my heart—in the interest of Lasker's lasting place and untarnished image—to refrain from publishing this play. Yes, I must confess, I was shattered when I read it and could not keep back the tears.... Because this drama is the very mirror of the most lamentable ruins, a ravaged mind. One can really feel the spiritual night descending over the poet, and only here or there a shooting star."

And Buber? He too deemed the play weak, incoherent and in short, pitiful, uncontrovertible evidence of the poet's sadly waning powers.

So what did Kraft do? He opted for a middle way. He "abbreviated" the text, printing selected excerpts, citing as rationale "the obvious deterioration of her verbal powers." (He seems to have been altogether oblivious of the extraordinary control and skill in handling long lines with rhyme that she demonstrates and that so clearly refute the notion of her waning creative powers.) Totally lacking in his critique was any sense of the revolutionary, theater-historical importance of the drama.

Not that the play did not contain passages that needed polishing or re-working. The scattered but facile rhymes for rhyme's sake that she made fun of herself in her letters, and the puerile jokes she could not resist cry out for revision. But no one saw this better than she. Her manuscript is thick with notations for projected changes, so there can be no question of her being a doddering old wreck who didn't know what she was about. Perhaps the main difficulty was in reading her typescript! This too she knew. She would gladly have typed it up again if she had been stronger and if there had been any prospect of publication. Given the incendiary nature of its political statement, she knew that there was little chance of this happening, certainly not in Germany. The most she could hope for were private readings of excerpts under her aegis in Palestine.

The first complete performances of *IchundIch* took place in Dusseldorf at the Düsseldorfer Schauspielhaus on the 10th of November 1979, and a month later in Wuppertal.

In 1970 the unabridged text had appeared in the *Jahrbuch der Deutschen Schillergesellschaft* (ELA Marbach. #14:24-99), with notes and an illuminating analysis by Margarete Kupper of the unabridged book version which appeared ten years later, in 1980.

In 1989, Judith Malina directed a performance of the play in a translation by Beate Hein Bennett (*I & I*), at her Living Theater, on East Third Street, in New York. The production was reviewed by D.J. Bruckner in the *New York Times*. He wrote, "...this last exotic work of a most exotic poet is a compelling and disorienting experience. With its exalted vision, its distracting mixture of farce, tragedy and music hall skit, it is like a great ruin that baffles one's every effort to comprehend it. There is a lot to be said for a fine ruin." (*New York Times*. Arts/Reviews. Sunday, September 24, 1989) [see also Heinz Thiel. "'IchundIch'—ein versperrtes Werk?" in Schmid, *Lasker-Schüler: Ein Buch Zum 100*, 1969, pp. 123–159].)

Betty Falkenberg

12. Description of Else Lasker-Schüler's room, 24 February 1942

Nehemia Cymbalist (Zuri)

The room.

Two windows that have a view of the City. They are closed and covered with an oilcloth. In one corner a table with plates, cutlery, various miscellaneous grocery items, toothbrush and washrag, next to the table a chamber-pot, a nest of baskets (2), a box with a cover over it, and on top of this a pile of hats. Next to this and alongside it, two suitcases, one brown, one black, one over the other, and on top of these, a bunch of dresses. Alongside, in a corner, a wardrobe closet, hung with coats, and on top of the closet, a camel made of straw and strings; between the closet and the suitcases, a pair of boots, a pair of black shoes. And next to the closet, a folding-chair; on its arm a black coat. In the corner near the door a stand, on which a board with all her books, and next to that a small plate with various spools of thread, and another with an assortment of shells and corks, along with strings of beads made of shells. On the second board a cardboard box with assorted colored strings and papers. Leaned up against the stand her drawings with all those Egyptian-arabic figures ("indian-isch" in her words), next to the door there's a greenish vase with one iris (she says it's an orchid, a lily— that she placed there in memory of her deceased brother), alongside it a bluish vase with an almond-blossom branch, she says she found it "wounded" on the street and brought it back to her room. Alongside the vases a small bottle with an artificial flower with green leaves and white and yellow filaments. Then, a kind of fantasy horse made out of shiny tin. On the floor next to the stand (or bookcase?) more piles of boxes. On the window sills of the "curtained" windows are three little tin bottles with the word "alcohol" and a colored woven basket with various vegetables. Right under it, under the window, a similar basket with orange peels, cauliflower stalks, radish peelings ... opposite the window a simple folding table, over which a colored oilcloth, with red and yellow poppies. Between the table and the east-facing window, at an angle, her bed; a kind of military folding bed or a bed that folds together like a hand harmonica. The bed has no cover over it, which is how one can see how it folds together. Strung up on a string between the east window hinge and the table are damp washcloths and rags. There is a chair on the west wall, opposite the window, beneath which is a half-rug. She says: Is it so that one leaves a chair standing empty for the Messiah?—Yes! One leaves a chair for the prophet Elijah, Elias, and also this chair—cup here is in memory of my dead mother! And over everything the ceiling covered with spider webs wherever you look.—From *Else Lasker-Schüler's Jerusalem*, p. 121; JNUL, Else Lasker-Schüler Archive.

Notes

In the course of the writing of this work, five volumes of the *Kritische Ausgabe* (*Critical Edition*, abbreviated as KA) have appeared. Hence some chapter notes give KA as source. Others, as in GW for *Gesammelte Werke* (*Collected Works*), reflect the status at the time of writing. A complete update should be undertaken upon completion of the *Critical Edition*.

Abbreviations

BKK: Else Lasker-Schüler, *Briefe an [Letters to] Karl Kraus*. Ed. Astrid Gelhoff-Claes. Köln, Berlin: Kiepenheuer & Witsch, 1959.

Br I and II: *Briefe von Else Lasker-Schüler [Letters from Else Lasker-Schüler]*. Ed. Margarete Kupper. München: Kösel-Verlag, 1969.

BSch: Else Lasker-Schüler: *Was Soll ich Hier? Exilbriefe an Salman Schocken*. Ed. Sigrid Bauschinger and Helmut G. Hermann. Heidelberg: Lambert Schneider, 1986.

DD: *Else Lasker-Schüler Dichtungen und Dokumente*. Ed. Ernst Ginsberg. Kösel-Verlag, 1951.

DLA Marb: Schiller Nationalmuseum/Deutsches Literaturarchiv, Marbach.

FAZ: *Frankfurter Allgemeine Zeitung*.

GW I and II: Else Lasker-Schüler. *Gesammelte Werke [Collected Works]*. Ed. Friedhelm Kemp. Kösel-Verlag 1959, 1962.

JNUL: The Jewish National & University Library, Jerusalem.

KA: *Kritische Ausgabe [Critical Edition]*. Eds. Norbert Oellers, Heinz Rölleke and Itta Shedletzky. Jüdischer Verlag/Suhrkamp, 1996–2002 and ongoing.

KA 1.1 *Gedichte [Poems]*, 1.2 *Anmerkungen [Commentary]*; KA 2 *Dramen [Plays]*; KA 3.1 *Prosa 1903-1920 [Prose]*, 3.2 *Anmerkungen*; KA 4.1 *Prosa 1921–1945*, 4.2 *Anmerkungen*.

LBI: Leo Baeck Institute.

Mar: *Marbacher Magazin 7/1995*. "Else Lasker-Schüler." Ed. Erika Klüsener and Friedrich Pfäfflin. Deutsche Schillergesellscchaft, Marbach 1995.

Marq: *Else Lasker-Schüler/Franz Marc. Privater Briefwechsel [Private Correspondence]*. Ed. Ulrike Marquardt and Heinz Rölleke. Artemis & Winkler, 1998.

NYRB: New York Review of Books.
SB: Sigrid Bauschinger. *Else Lasker-Schüler: Ihr Werk und ihre Zeit* [*Else Lasker-Schüler: Her Works and Her Times*]. Lothar Stiehm Verlag, 1980.
Schu, sometimes Schuster: *Franz Marc—Else Lasker-Schüler. Karten und Briefe*. Ed. Peter-Klaus Schuster. Prestel, 1987.
StA wup: Stadtarchiv Wuppertal.
StA Zu: Stadtarchiv Zurich.
StB Wup: Stadtbibliothek Wuppertal, Else Lasker-Schüler Archiv.

Introduction

1. Expressionism as a movement had no single political agenda; just "anti-bourgeois." (Best to see it as part of an international avant-garde revolt.) Neither did it have a single style. Rather, it was a varied response to the modern mechanical world. The groups that gave Expressionism its identifying signature were German: in art, Die Brücke, Der Blaue Reiter; in literature, Der Sturm, Die Aktion.

2. Kandinsky. *On the Spiritual in Art*. 2nd ed. Munich, 1912.

3. Schoenberg and Lasker-Schüler were on friendly terms, and when he emigrated to Hollywood in 1933, she asked if he would consider writing music for a film version of her play, *Arthur Aronymus und seine Väter* (*Arthur Aronymus and His Fathers*). Schoenberg hedged: "If what is presented is within the limits of my means of expression, it will be a pleasure and I will fall upon the composition." But he also warned her of the bad taste and vulgarity of Hollywood productions.

4. While there is no evidence of a personal connection, or collaboration, between them, Hindemith composed three early songs for soprano and large orchestra Opus 9, 1917, to poems by Lasker-Schüler and Ernst Wilhelm Lotz. While these works are unpublished, Hindemith wanted them included in the complete edition of his works. In 1920, he again chose poems by Lasker-Schüler for two of his Eight Songs for Soprano and Piano, Opus 18: "Traum" ("Dream"), and "Du machst mich traurig—hör" ("You make me sad—listen"). The second was published in the December 1920 issue of *Melos*. The songs were first performed in Berlin in 1922, and then in Dusseldorf in 1925 at a celebration of Rhineland poets. It is highly likely that Frau Lasker-Schüler was in attendance at one or the other of the performances.

5. "Der Sturm pfeift über ein junges Haupt"—"Kismet," KA 1.1 #7. Also: "Dein Sturmlied" ("Brause Dein Sturmlied Du!") KA 1.1 #58.

Chapter One

1. *Arthur Aronymus* is the chronicle of her father's childhood in an observant Jewish family in Westphalia. Its theme is Christian-Jewish reconciliation, one of her lifelong dreams.

2. In 1913 she gave a memorable reading in the great baroque Church of St. Nicholas in the Mala Strana, intoning her Oriental prose pieces in an invented "Arabian," and creating something of a stir after the performance by standing in a niche intended for the statue of a saint. See Marie Holzer in *Aktion*, v. 3, no. 21 (1913) column 525ff.

3. *Völkische Beobachter*, v. 45. No. 323. 2 Supplement, p. 5, quoted in Mar, p. 226ff.

4. Gordon A. Craig. *Germany 1866–1945*. Oxford: Oxford University Press, 1980, p. 568.

5. See Christopher Zuschlag: "An Educational Exhibition." In "Degenerate Art," LACMA Catalogue 1991, p. 83ff.

6. Br II 427, p. 129f.

7. Br II 444, p. 144f.

8. Br II 446, p. 146f.

9. Else's oldest sister, Martha, had moved with her husband, Wormser, a business-

man, and their children, Alice and Margret, to Chicago. Louis Asher, who had been married to Alice, remarried after her death. His second wife was named Ines.

10. In 1918 Else Lasker-Schüler spent many months in Switzerland, staying in Zurich and Locarno.

11. Br II 487, p. 186ff.

12. Postcard to Hulda Pankok. Return address: Augustinerhof, Hospiz, St. Peterstrasse, Zurich. Postmark: Zurich, 20.4 [April].33. Hulda Pankok Archives. Courtesy Sigrid Bauschinger. Also quoted in Escherig, *Verweigerung der Einreise und Aufenthaltsbewilligung*, in "Meine Träume Fallen in die Welt." Ed. Sarah Hirsch. Peter Hammer Verlag, 1995, p. 136 (quoted without source).

13. ELS to Marcel Brion, courtesy Sigrid Bauschinger. (Also quoted by Manfred Escherig in *Meine Träume Fallen in die Welt*, p. 136. Without source.)

14. Br II 459, p. 156ff.

15. Personal corresondence to Rechtsanwalt Schönberg, L.B.I. Archives, N.Y. Collection Bodenheimer AL26 (lent by permission Sigrid Bauschinger).

16. Notizbuch: Meine Koffer etc. Sachsenhof. JNUL 2:149, cited by Escherig, in *Meine Träume*, p. 134f.

17. Br II 443, p. 143.

18. "Brief an Korrodi," GW II, p. 210ff; KA3.1, p. 425ff.

The "Brief an Korrodi" ("Letter to Korrodi") was incorporated in the volume of prose pieces entitled *Gesichte* (*Faces*, or *Visages*), second edition, Cassirer Verlag, 1920. Korrodi wrote of it: "Else Lasker-Schüler read the letter to me at one of her readings at the Zurich Jury Hall which I attended. Thus it is half real and half imaginary." See DD, note to p. 529.

The letter, like many of her "letters" to other recipients, was conceived both as a real letter and as a literary piece later to be incorporated into larger works or essay collections.

19. Querido Verlag was one of the most important émigré publishing houses.

20. "Die Verscheuchte," KA 1.1. 386, p. 290f.

21. Sigismund von Radecki. DD, p. 581f.

22. *The Sign of the Cross* is a lurid spectacle about Rome in the time of Nero, with Christians being fed to the lions, Rome set ablaze while chariots trample the screaming populace in the streets, naked slave-girls dancing, and Poppea bathing in asses' milk. When Rome begins to rise up against the emperor, he blames the Christians for the fire and rounds them up to die horrible deaths in the arena. The film had uncanny parallels to what was happening in Germany.

23. Klaus Mann. *Tagebücher*, p. 169.

24. *Ibid.*, p. 169 [sic].

25. Not only had Klaus founded what was viewed as a brazenly tendentious periodical, Erika was about to re-open in Zurich her wildly irreverent, wildly popular, Munich cabaret "Die Pfeffermühle" ("The Pepper Mill"). Together with Klaus, she composed hilarious chansons and skits that took direct aim at the Nazis. The cabaret became the object of attacks from stink bombs, and was eventually forced to close.

26. Her collection of toy marbles was, like her collection of buttons, started by her mother for her in her childhood, and the currency of her invented kingdom, "Thebes." A gift of marbles was tantamount to induction into her mythic world.

27. Br I 191, p. 228f.

28. *Ibid.* 192, p. 230ff.

29. Klaus Mann. *Der Wendepunkt*. 1952, p. 335.

Chapter Two

1. In 1955, K.J. Höltgen went through the register of births in Elberfeld for the relevant period and discovered the entry. Höltgen: "Untersuchungen zur Lyrik Else Lasker-Schülers." Bonn 1955 (Diss.) See also Leon I. Yudkin, *Else Lasker-Schüler: A Study in German Jewish Literature*, p. 3.

2. See Mar, p. 30 (stB, Munchen).
3. *Ibid.*, p. 47 (Berlin: Verlagsanstalt "Harmonie" o.J.101ff).
4. *Menschheitsdämmerung.* Ed. Kurt Pinthus. 1919, p. 350.
5. "ELS contra B." KA3.1, p. 271. Why Robinson? See Louis James, "one of Europe's central texts ... possibly because of the problematic main character." Also, Lieve Spaas, "the individual's refusal and inability to accept his assigned role in society...." Both in *Robinson Crusoe: Myths and Metamorphoses.* Ed. Lieve Spaas and Brian Simpson. Macmillan 1996, p. 1 and p. 99, respectively.
6. *Elberfelder Zeitung.* 11 Feb. 1869; in *Romerike Berge*, p. 2.
7. StAWup. In *Romerike Berge*, p. 3, plus note, p. 10. See also Eleonore Sterling, "Judenhass—Die Anfänge des politischen anti-Semitismus in Deutschland 1815–1850." Frankfurt am Main. Europäische Verlagsanstalt 1969, quoted in Mar, p. 20.
8. See *Allgemeine Wochenzeitung der Juden in Deutschland* (Dusseldorf 18 Juni 1965). Bernhard Brilling lists under the ancestors of Else the Rappaports, who can be traced back to the 15th century, and who are related through marriage to the famous Rabbi of Prague who died in 1609. See also SB, note 1, pp. 21–22.
9. See Gershom Scholem in *Encyclopedia Judaica*, vol. vii, col 501–507. See also "Golem! Danger, Deliverance and Art," Emily Bilski. Catalogue of the Jewish Museum, New York 1988.
10. See *Romerike Berge*, p. 3 plus note, p. 101 StAWup.
11. "Elberfeld im 300jährigen Jubiläumsschmuck" KA 3.1, p. 152.
12. "St. Laurentius." (*Konzert*) KA 4.1, p. 157.
13. "Kinderzeit" KA 3.1, p. 419f.
14. In 1819 there were attacks on Jews in many German cities. "Hep! Hep!" was the rallying cry of the rioters. See Robert M. Selzer, *Jewish People, Jewish Thought*, p. 528.
15. "St. Laurentius." KA 4.1, p. 157.
16. Else gave her the dress, which she wore at the next St. Laurentius Feast, where the Catholic children dressed in white as angels for the Procession.
17. "Der Letzte Schultag." (*Konzert*) TWII 696; KA 4.1, p. 145 ("Nur für Kinder über fünf Jahre").
18. "Wie ich zum Zeichnen kam." (*Konzert*) KA 4.1, p. 137.
19. Walter Benjamin. "Aussicht ins Kinderbuch" in "Angelus Novus." Ausg Schr 2, p. 151ff.
20. "Der Letzte Schultag." KA 4.1., p. 147.
21. See DD. p. 232f note
22. "Hagar und Ismael" KA 1.1, 280, p. 208.
23. "Elberfeld im 300jahrigen..." KA 3.1, p. 152.
24. *Cyclopedia of the Diseases of Children*, v.4, Lippincott, 1890, pp. 840–856.
25. "Der letzte Schultag" (*Konzert*) KA 4.1, p. 148.
26. "Schülerin Else" in *Romerike Berge*, 45 Jrg. 1, 1995, p. 15.
27. Letter to Franz Marc 17; *Der Malik*, KA 3.1, p. 446f.
28. "Wunderrabbiner" KA 4.1, p. 11.
29. "Elberfeld im Wuppertal" KA 4.1, p. 97.
30. *Ibid.*, p. 96.
31. "St. Laurentius." (*Konzert*) KA 4.1, p. 155ff.
32. In her 1910 essay "Handschrift," which first appeared in *Der Sturm*, she says her father's handwriting was like something out of *Struwelpeter*, the popular 19th century children's book whose moralistic stories, with their grisly illustrations of naughty children and the punishments meted out to them, were supposed to be humorous, but were deeply underlaid with sadistic import.
33. *Arthur Aronymus* (sc.7) KA 2, pp. 120–125.

Chapter Three

1. "Die Eisenbahn" (*Konzert*) GWII, p. 602; KA 4.1, p. 122f.
2. "Das Meer" (*Konzert*) GWII, p. 758; KA 4.1, p. 196.

3. Br II 297, p. 9f.

4. Bettina von Arnim. (1785–1859). Wife of German Romantic poet, Achim von Arnim, and sister of Clemens Brentano. Famous for her literary salons.

5. Leopold Sonnemann. Founder of the *Frankfurter Zeitung*. See Amos Elon, *The Pity of It All: A History of Jews in Germany, 1743–1933*, pp. 196ff.

6. Simson Goldberg. See Manfred Escherig in "Meine Träume Fallen in die Welt," pp. 79ff.

7. "Verwelkte Myrten" KA 1.1, 3, p. 10.

8. ELS in "Führende Frauen Europas," Neue Folge; KA 4.1, p. 188 ("Etwas von mir").

9. "Hebräerland" GWII, p. 867; KA 5, p. 73.

10. Ottomar Starke. "Was Mein Leben Anbelangt," p. 53.

11. Peter Hille. *Briefe an ELS*, p. 31.

12. "Die Kommenden," see *Auftakt zur Literatur des 20. Jahrhunderts, Buch aus dem Nachlass von Ludwig Jacobowski*. Ed. Fred B. Stern, 2 vols. 1974. v.1, p. 529.

13. Today it has taken on a new and tragic resonance from the last line of Paul Celan's famous World War II "Todesfuge: dein aschenes Haar Sulamith" ("Death Fugue: Your Ashen Hair Shulamite").

14. "Sulamith" KA 1.1, 221, p. 165.

15. *Das Peter Hille Buch* KA 3.1, p. 30.

16. *Ibid.*

17. *Ibid.*, p. 61.

18. Julius Bab. "Die Berliner Bohème," p. 78.

19. Peter Hille. "Else Lasker-Schüler" in DD, p. 565, 1902.

Chapter Four

1. *Peter Hille Buch* KA 3.1, p. 45.

2. Samuel Lublinski. "Die Bilanz des Moderne" Berlin, 1904, p. 166f; also quoted in Mar, p. 46.

3. Br I 3, p. 11.

4. Br II 310, p. 20.

5. Br I 1, p. 9.

6. Br I 32, p. 39.

7. Writing to her new English friend, Jethro Bithell, in 1909, she says: "Altogether, I find women's clothing ugly; when I'm in London ... I'll dress up as an Oriental. I'll send you a picture of myself as an Arabian prince." Br I, 32 from 6 November 1909.

8. Appendix 3: "Orientalism in Fashion." Catalogue Essay in "Noble Dreams/ Wicked Pleasures," Sterling and Francine Clark Art Institute, 2000.

9. Marina Tsvetaeva (1892–1941). Russian poet, best known for her *Poems to Blok*.

10. "Weltende" in *Menschheitsdämmerung*, p. 39. Jakob von Hoddis. Born 1887. Founded the Neue Gesellschaft with Erwin Loewenson, Kurt Hiller and others. In April 1942, he was interred near Koblenz, and as "Number 8," removed to be destroyed, "where, when and how, nobody knows." (Kurt Pinthus, in Biographical Note, *Menschheitsdämmerung*)

11. "Weltende" KA1.1, 135, p. 103. After her divorce from Walden in 1912, ELS published "Weltende" with the dedication to him removed, and in its place the words: "To Wilhelm von Kevlaar in memory of the many years...," a reference to a poem by Heine, "Die Wallfahrt nach Kevlaar" ("The Pilgrimage to Kevlaar").

12. *Mein Volk.* KA 1.1, 209, p. 157.

13. "Mein Volk," written in 1905, was later incorporated into the *Hebräische Balladen* (1913). It is sometimes read as the plight of the Jew in the diaspora.

14. KA 3.1, p. 69ff. *Die Nächte von Tino* came out in 1907. In 1906, Ruth St. Denis, who had not yet been to India at this time, created her famous solo dance "The Incense." Coaching a dancer for this role, Martha Graham told her, "Your arms become the smoke, which

is your prayer." As for Lasker-Schüler, not only had she not been to the Near East, she had not even utilized the resources of Berlin's Egyptian Museum, which housed one of the finest collections of its kind, but drew on impressions gathered at the Egyptian pavilion at Luna Park, where she was a frequent visitor. Similarly, Ruth St. Denis had been taken to see the pageant ballet *Egypt through the Centuries* at the Palisades Amusement Park in 1893. The hold of Eastern exoticism on artists' imaginations is a 19th century Romantic holdover in Western culture. In the Middle East it has an analogue in the cult of the Far East, which in turn looks back to the Middle Ages.

15. BKK, p. 13f. (24 August 1909) Such necromantic fantasies were not unusual. In "the Mummy's Secret," NYRB (17 June 1997, p. 57ff), James Fenton describes an exhibition at the Egyptian Hall in London in 1888, a strictly commercial venture (similar to Luna Park in Berlin). It featured murky lights, half-open coffin-lids, and very suggestive mummy portraits. In such a climate (international!) Lasker-Schüler's insistence that she was a reincarnation of an ancient (Biblical) king might not have sounded so outré—to anyone, that is, but Karl Kraus!

16. Br I 25, p. 29.

17. In a letter to Herwarth Walden (9 January 1906) Alfred Döblin wrote: "I find [Ached Bey] ineffably beautiful; it is suffused with a lyric mellowness beyond compare." He hopes he will get a chance to hear her read it! (Döblin: *Briefe*, Walter Verlag 1970, p. 37.)

18. Katherina Otto (Kete Parsenow) memoirs quoted in BKK, p. 124f (note).

19. Bilanz, *Lublinski*, p. 168, quoted in Mar, p. 46.

20. Maria Eichhorn was dubbed Dolorosa, and Marie Madeleine, Maria Magdalena, by Rudolf Steiner's second wife, because of the heavy-breathing hothouse verse they inflicted on their audience. They were, however, immensely popular at the time (see SB, p. 60.)

21. Alfred Döblin. *Autobiographische Schriften*, Ed. Edgar Passler, 1980.

22. BKK 27 March 10, p. 24f.

23. Br I 26, p. 30f.

24. In the poem "Weltende" too there was an allusion to a poem by Heine. It is worth noting that Heine is one of the poets who, alongside Goethe and Schiller, would have been read in the home of an assimilated, cultured Jewish family. One can be sure that this poet occupied a place of honor in her mother's bookshelves.

25. Jethro Bithell. *Contemporary German Poetry*. Walter Scott Publishing Co., London 1909. p. xxv. Many years later, in his book *Modern German Literature, 1880–1950*, Bithell had this to say about her: "She is her own strange self in her poems. She has no ethics of any sort, and for that reason cannot be an expressionist proper; ... What does emerge is that she is an Oriental princess—... who has the tales of Scheherezade to tell.... Her *Hebräische Balladen* have some Hebrew melodies, but for the most part are pathologically modern."

26. Br I 28, p. 32.

27. Br I 31, p. 37f.

28. Br I 29, p. 33.

29. Br I 32, p. 39ff.

Chapter Five

1. Oskar Kokoschka: *My Life*, p. 59.

2. *Essays. Oskar Kokoschka.* KA 3.1, p. 147.

3. *Ibid.*

4. *Op. cit.*

5. *Ibid.*

6. For more on the influence of Kokoschka on ELS's graphic works, see *Peter-Klaus Schuster: Franz Marc-Else Lasker-Schüler. Karten und Briefe*, pp. 132–134.

7. BKK, p. 24f.

8. See SB p. 93, note 18.

9. "Lasker-Schüler Contra B." KA 3.1, p. 269ff.

10. "Ein alter Tibetteppich" KA 1.1, 172, p. 130.

11. See Gershom Scholem, *Walter Benjamin: The Story of a Friendship*, p. 65: "When I mentioned three texts ... about lamentations—the biblical lament of David for Jonathan and the two poems on the same subject by Rilke and Else Lasker-Schüler—he replied that Rilke's poem was simply a bad one...." See also Benjamin, *Briefe* I. #60, p. 169 an Gershom Scholem. Bern, 13 January 1918. "Das Gedicht 'David und Jonathan' von der Lasker-Schüler liebe ich sehr ... Das entsprechende Gedicht von Rilke ist—abgesehen von allem andern—schlecht."

12. KA 1.1, 216, p. 161.

13. Br II 316, p. 25ff.

14. In the copy she used for readings, she had pencilled in "Caravan Ballad" under the title. The poem, central to the cycle, *Hebrew Ballads*, was written in 1920.

15. Teo Otto in *FAZ* 10 February 1969, reprinted as "Ein bergische Kräher Berichtet" in *Else Lasker-Schüler. Ein Buch zum 100 Geburtstag*. Ed. Michael Schmid, p. 45.

16. Tilla Durieux. "Eine Tür steht offen" 108f.

17. For more on this aspect of Orientalism, see "A Man from the East," by Tom Reiss in *The New Yorker*, Oct. 4, 1999, p. 68ff.

18. For more about the spread of Orientalism in Western culture, see also "Noble Dreams/Wicked Pleasures. Orientalism in America 1870–1930." Exhibition Catalogue 2000. Princeton U. Press and Clark Art Institute, Williamstown, MA.

19. Erich Mühsam. 1878–1934. Anarchist activist and writer. In 1933 he was caught in a Nazi round-up after the Reichstag fire. Repeated arrests. Held in a succession of concentration camps: Sonnenburg, Brandenburg, Oranienburg. In July 1934 he was brutally murdered at Oranienburg.

20. Emmy Ball-Hennings (1885–1948) Cabaret singer and poet. One of the more colorful figures of the avant-garde. Born Protestant but converted to Catholicism in 1912, she lived an extreme version of the Bohemian life, working at every conceivable occupation, including prostitution. From 1913 until her death, she wrote and published poems and novels. In 1916 she met and married the Dadaist Hugo Ball and emigrated with him to Switzerland. It was Ball who coined the nonsense word "Dada," to connote the *absurd* verbal-visual imagery practiced by artists of this ilk (Tristan Tzara, Hans Arp, Picabia, inter alia).

21. ELS let to KK ca. 13 May 1911. Quoted from photocopy of original, DLA Marb, courtesy Sigrid Bauschinger.

22. For Mühsam's account of this incident, see Mühsam, *Tagebücher*, pp. 34–40.

23. KA 4.1, p. 69 ("Ich räume auf" GWII, p. 534f).

24. "Dr. Benn" KA 3.1, p. 277.

25. Nell Walden. *Herwarth Walden—In Memoriam*, p. 37.

26. Sigismund v. Radecki. In DD, p. 579.

27. Nell Walden. *Herwarth Walden—In Memoriam*, p. 37.

Chapter Six

1. *Berliner Tageblatt* 9. March 1916. See also KA 3.1, p. 413f.

2. Klee. *Diaries*, 1912. See also Wolf-Dieter Dube, *The Expressionists*, p. 160f.

3. KA 1.1, 223, p. 166.

4. Marquardt, 1, p. 28.

5. These two paintings, *Die Gelbe Kuh* and *Die Grossen Blauen Pferde*, were among those exhibited by Walden in his first Sturm Gallery exhibition, "Der Blaue Reiter," in March 1912. *Die Gelbe Kuh* (*The Yellow Cow*) hangs today in the Solomon R. Guggenheim Museum in New York.

6. Marq 2, p. 30.

7. Schuster 1, p. 144.

8. *August Macke/Franz Marc Briefwechsel*. Dumont Schauberg Köln, 1964, pp. 146–149.

9. Maria Marc in *Botschaften...* Piper Verlag, 1954, p. 7.

10. Marq 9, p. 40.

11. The color blue for Lasker, as for Marc, had a deep significance. Ever since medieval times, blue has carried a heavy symbolic weight, originally inspired by alchemy, and amply illustrated in painting, through iconography. At different times it has taken on different connotations: to the German Romantics, like Novalis, the *blaue Blume* was a symbol of eternal yearning. Even closer in spirit to Lasker and Marc perhaps were the French Symbolists, Baudelaire and Mallarmé, who made blueness a quality in its own right rather than an attribute of some object.

12. Schuster 2, p. 86f.

13. Schuster 16, p. 94f.

14. *Briefe aus dem Feld*, p. 49. Marc quotes from *her* letter to him.

15. Marq 54, p. 82.

16. Schuster, p. 133. "The giving up of the strict cloisonné of her early drawings in favor of a soft, modulated, flaky contour, is a phenomenon that one finds in Kokoschka, who was attempting, at about this time, to imitate Baroque models." In general, Schuster sees Lasker's art as being more akin to the ornamental exoticism of Klimt than to Marc, whereas her linear style, in its expressiveness, may have been influenced by Kirchner.

17. Schuster, p. 133f. Marc's own drawings would evolve, over the course of their correspondence, into ever more abstract cubist color symphonies, influenced conceivably by Delauney—according, once again, to the art historian, Peter-Klaus Schuster.

18. Klabund, "Das Herz der Lasker," in *Revolution*, no. 1, 15 October 1913, pp. 3–4, as quoted in SB, p. 320f.

19. This painting once hung in the National Gallery of Berlin, but has been missing since the end of World War II.

20. See Schuster, p. 144f.

21. Franz Marc "Briefe aus dem Feld" 4 March 1916, p. 152f.

22. Elfriede Caro was the wife of Lasker's long-time friend and lawyer, Hugo Caro.

23. This was the reply of Ludwig Justi, Director of the Nationalgalerie.

24. For more details on these transactions, see Peter-Klaus Schuster, *Franz Marc-Else Lasker-Schüler. Karten und Briefe*, p. 137f.

Chapter Seven

1. Br I 44, p. 66.

2. KA 3.1, p. 189.

3. Br I 82, p. 104.

4. Ludwig Meidner. 1884–1966. Expressionist painter and writer. Founded Die Pathetiker, an anti–Impressionist group that exhibited at the Sturm Gallery. Subject of his painting was catastrophe—and the chaos of the metropolis. A regular at the Café des Westen. In 1939, with the help of Augustus John, he fled to England. In the 1920s better known as a writer than as a painter. See his memoir, *Dichter, Maler und Cafés*, p. 13f.

5. BKK, pp. 16, 17.

6. Schu 5, p. 88.

7. *Ibid.* 16, p. 94f.

8. In an essay about Benn she wrote: "He climbs down into the bowels of his hospital and cuts open the dead. Never sated, he is enticed by hidden things. He says, 'Dead is dead.' Despite his pious unbelief, he loves houses of prayer, dreamy altars, eyes that come from afar. He is an evangelical heathen, a Christ with a paganhead, vulturenose, and the heart of a leopard.... Each of his verses is a leopardbite, a wildanimal's leap. The bone is his pencil, with which he wakes the word to life." GWII, p. 227f.; KA3.1 p. 277.

9. Benn's dedication in his book of poems, *Söhne*, 1913. The phrase itself was hers. See "Mein Herz" GWII, p. 358; KA 3.1, p. 233 (Briefe nach Norwegen).

10. Schu 5, p. 88f.
11. *Ibid.* 6, p. 90f.
12. *Ibid.* 5, p. 89.
13. Benn's dedication to her in *Das Unaufhörliche*. Libretto for oratorio by Hindemith. 18 June 1931.
14. KA 1.1, 229, p. 172.
15. Gottfried Benn. "Hier ist kein Trost." Sämtliche Werke, Klett-Cotta, Stuttgart. Vol. III, p. 32.
16. KA 1.1, 385, p. 290.
17. Quoted by F.S. Grosshut in his book *Else Lasker-Schüler in der Emigration*. DD, p. 592.
18. Benn. "Else Lasker-Schüler." Commemorative address given at the British Center in Berlin. 23. Feb. 1952. Benn: Sämtl. vol.VI, Prosa 4, pp. 54–57.
19. Benn quotes last stanza of "Höre." *Ibid.*
20. His reply. *Ibid.*
21. Br I 17, p. 22f.
22. BKK, p. 50 (18 July 1912).
23. One of her epithets for Karl Kraus was "Herzog von Wien" ("Duke of Vienna"). Others were "Dalai Lama" and "Cardinal." She wrote of him: "Grown men and boys slink round his confessional, and confer secretly about how to grind down his grandiose cynic's skull to powder sugar.... Ineluctable, Karl Kraus towers over his city, a canny living monument." (GWII 225ff) KA3.1, p. 142ff.
24. BKK, pp. 51–53 (undated).
25. *Hebräische Balladen* A.R. Meyer, Berlin 1913. Gershom Scholem, who had heard her read from them the year they came out exclaimed, "Some of these are among her most beautiful and most unforgettable creations." (Scholem: "From Berlin to Jerusalem," pp. 42, 43).
26. BKK 21 August 1912, pp. 50, 51.
27. KA 1.1, 211, p. 158.
28. *Die Fackel.* 11 January 1913. Notice on back cover.
29. Holzmann. For a fuller account of the Holzmann story, see Walter Fahnders, *ELS und Senna Hoy* in "Meine Träume fallen ...," p. 55ff.
30. Ludwig Wittgenstein. 1889–1951. Viennese philosopher *sui generis*. Went to Cambridge, England, in 1908, where he became a leading member of the Bertrand Russell, G.E. Moore school of logical positivism. His famous last work, *Tractacus Logico-Philosophicus*, was a seminal effort in the new study of semantics.
31. Marianna von Werefkin (1870–1938). Daughter of the commanding general of the Peter and Paul Fortress in Saint Petersburg. (This is important in considering the role she played in ELS's effort to free Jakob Holzmann from Russian prisons.) Founding member (with Jawlensky and Kandinsky) of the Neue Künstlervereinigung München (New Artists' Alliance Munich: precursors of the Blaue Reiter group).
32. Br I, 26, p. 30f. Sir Ratcliff. Allusion to Heine's poem, "Ratcliff," in his *Buch der Lieder* (Book of Songs).
33. BKK 16 May 1914, p. 65ff.
34. *Ibid.*, p. 65ff.
35. "My daily piece of cake," she called it. (Br I 181, p. 147).
36. "Plumm-Pascha" KA 3.1, p. 368f.

Chapter Eight

1. "Friz Huf" KA 3.1, pp. 412, 413.
2. Gordon A. Craig. *Germany 1866–1945*, p. 339ff.
3. "Galakriegsschmuck." See Marq 5, p. 34. On the back of the envelope she had written, "Mein Galakriegsschmuck schon angeleget" ("My gala war decorations already in place").

Schu, p. 117: "In August 1914 she was arrested four times in Munich for flaunting Galakriegss-chmuck...." See also Wieland Herzfelde. "Fremd und Nah. Über meinen Briefwechsel und meine Begegunungen mit ELS," in *Marginalien, Blätter der Pirckheimer Gesellschaft*, 18. Heft, p. 6f (March 1965). Also, Herzfelde. "Begegnungen ..." in *Sinn und Form*, No. 6, 1969, pp. 1312–1325 (also SB, p. 37 plus note 36).

4. Emmy Ball-Hennings. "Ruf und Echo," pp. 38, 39.

5. Alvarez del Vayo. "Les Batailles de la Liberté," Paris 1963, p. 76.

6. *Mein Herz* GWII, p. 304; KA 3.1, p. 189 (Briefe nach Norwegen).

7. Walter Benjamin. "Berliner Chronik," vol. VI, Ges. Schr., pp. 480, 481.

8. Wieland Herzfelde in "Begegnungen mit der Dichterin" in *Sinn und Form*, 21, No. 6, 1969, p. 1311.

9. Franz Jung. "Der Weg nach Unten," p. 106.

10. ELS to Franz Jung. Br II 357, p. 66f.

11. About whether the poet Stefan George was a Jew, something she adamantly maintained after reading an erroneous entry in a guide to contemporary German literature. Believing that George was a Jew, and having taken offense at his bagatellizing her poetry, a second outburst followed. This one against the Jews, "because they don't honor my words...."

12. ELS to Martin Buber. Br I 97, p. 118.

13. *Ibid.*

14. Martin Buber. *Briefwechsel 1897–1918* no. 232, p. 354f.

15. George Grosz. "Ein kleines Ja," p182f.

16. Wieland Herzfelde in *Sinn und Form*, 21, No. 6, 1969, pp. 1311ff.

17. Kurt Hiller. "Begegnungen mit Expressionisten" in Paul Raabe *Expressionismus, Aufzeichnungen und Erinnerungen der Zeitgenossen*, pp. 243–245.

18. ELS to Karl Kraus. *Briefe an Karl Kraus*. 27 April 1915, p. 77ff.

19. Trakl, 1887–1914. Visionary poet given to morose suicidal speculation and "substance abuse." As a dispensing chemist, he had easy access to drugs. Trakl's poems appeared in the periodical, *Der Brenner*, edited by his friend and patron, Ludwig von Ficker. In August 1914, Trakl joined the Medical Corps of the Austrian army. The sight of war wounds, and his inability, as a dispensing chemist with insufficient supplies, to alleviate the misery, intensified his psychological imbalance. He was moved to Cracow for observation, but died of an overdose of cocaine on 3 or 4 November 1914. For more about Georg Trakl and his poetry, as well as poems in translation, see Michael Hamburger in *Lost Voices of World War I*, pp. 112–123.

20. ELS to v. Ficker. Br I 84, p. 105f.

21. Re her dream see Walter Mehring, *Berlin Dada*. Zurich 1959, pp. 18–20.

22. ELS to v. Ficker. Br I 87, p. 108.

23. Br I 88, 108f.

24. Br I 89, 109f.

25. *Ibid.*, 89, 109–110.

26. Br I 93, 114–115.

27. Br I 89, 110.

28. Louis Corinth. 1858–1925. German Impressionist painter. Traveled in France, Italy and Denmark. Painted Peter Hille's portrait. In 1915 was appointed president of the Berlin Secession.

29. ELS to v. Ficker. Br I 90, p. 110ff.

30. "I think I will go mad." see Br II note, p. 279, to Br I, 90.

31. Br I 91, p. 112f.

32. "Der alte Tempel in Prag." KA I. 235, p. 178.

33. "Trakl" KA I. 242, p. 180f.

34. Re Caro, see ELS to Herwarth. (Br nach Nor) KA 3.1, p. 189 (GWII, p. 304).

35. In 1918, Grosz made a drawing, "Lively Street Scene," depicting the vagabond poet Theodor Däubler and Else Lasker-Schüler on a street in Berlin. Lasker looks like Mary Poppins, with flowers in her hat. She, in turn, wrote a poem about Grosz (see Appendix 9).

36. Milly Steger. Sculptor about whom ELS wrote a poem. Steger designed public buildings in Hagen.

37. George Grosz. Sketchbook note, draft of letter to Milly Steger. quoted in Mar, p. 133f (source: AdK Berlin). Akad. der Künste. Hanseatenweg 10, 10557 Berlin.

38. Hans Richter. "Dada...," p. 67.

39. *Der Malik*, an oriental-fantasy novella (Paul Cassirer, 1919), was dedicated to the memory of Franz Marc, fictionalized in the tale as Ruben.

40. Abigail Jussuf in *Der Malik*, KA 3.1, p. 483.

41. The crowns. See KA 3.1, p. 461ff.

42. Today, her "Nicodemus," a drawing on the back of a telegram—one has to remember she went to the post office to keep warm—recently sold to a museum for about $30,000.

43. ELS to Hatzfeld: "My book is out." 1917, Klü, p. 57.

44. ELS to Hatzfeld "I am deadtired." August 9, 1917. p.c. Klü, p. 57.

45. ELS to Karl Kraus. BKK. 19 May 1917, p. 85ff.

46. ELS to Franz Jung. Br II 358, p. 67ff.

47. ELS to Hanns Hirt (undated, probably 1914.) Br I 113, p. 133.

48. ELS to Hanns Hirt Br I 123, p. 143ff.

49. Br I 117, pp. 137, 138.

50. Br I 118, 138ff.

51. Her letter to Franz Marc of 1912, apropos of her new love, Giselheer (Benn). She talks of sending him some gifts, along with this note: "Lieber König Giselheer, ich wollte, Du wärst aus Kristall, dann möchte ich Deine Eidechse sein, oder Deine Koralle oder Deine fleisch-fressende Blume." ("Dear King Giselheer, I wish you were made of crystal, then I would like to be your lizard, or your coral reef, or your flesh-eating flower.") 5. *Brief an Franz Marc*. Schu, p. 88f.

52. Br I 118, p. 138ff.

53. Br I 111, p. 130ff.

54. Br I 122, p. 143.

55. Br I 124, p. 146.

56. In a letter to Margarete Kupper, who edited the two-volume edition of Else Lasker-Schüler's letters in 1969 (Kösel Verlag), Hanns Hirt wrote, in 1966: "Despite this somewhat dramatic last letter, my relations with her remained very friendly." Br II, note to 124, p. 288.

57. ELS to Giselheer: "Come to Switzerland!" Between January and March 1918. Br II 360, pp. 70, 71.

Chapter Nine

1. BKK, p. 89.

2. Br II 375, p. 81f.

3. Helene von Nostitz (1978–1944) was the niece of Field Marshal von Hindenburg. She had close ties to Harry Graf Kessler, Hugo von Hofmannsthal, Rilke and Rodin. Her article "Welt der Auflösung" is quoted here from *Neue Zürcher Zeitung*, June 4, 1966.

4. Br I 180, 218f.

5. "Frau Durieux" KA 3.1, p. 126.

6. When she tried, two years later, to buy back the drawings, she found to her dismay that this was not possible. (She claimed she had only intended them as a loan.)

7. BKK. December 12, 1921, p. 90f.

8. Hugo Bergmann (1883–1975). Philosopher; first rector of Hebrew University, Jerusalem, and founder of the National-und Universitätsbibliothek (JNUL) in Jerusalem. Friend and colleague of Gershom Scholem and Ernst Simon.

9. Br II 384, p. 88.

10. Br II 388, p. 91f.

11. See note to 385 on p. 352 Br II, Einstein's letter of recommendation for Paul and a visiting card from him. Both in JNUL, ELS Nachlass, Jerusalem.

12. Her letter is written from Kolberg in Pommerania, on the Ostsee (Baltic Sea). Einstein appears to have been staying in a house five minutes away. 385, p. 89.

13. ELS to Kessler in Harry Graf Kessler, *Tagebücher*. DLA Marb.

14. Br II 359, p. 70.

15. Harry Graf Kessler. *Tagebücher*. DLA Marb quoted in Mar, p. 141.

16. *Ibid.*

17. Kessler Tagebuch entry for 21 December 1919, p. 205. Quoted in Mar, p. 152. Also Eng., Grove Press, 1999. *Berlin Lights: The Diaries of Count Harry Kessler (1918–1937)*, p. 114. "At Cassirer's the Lasker-Schüler woman pestered Däubler to introduce me to her. For four years I have tried to avoid this beastly person. Däubler behaved in such an elephantine way that I could not avoid the introduction. I said how-do-you-do and took my leave."

18. Kessler. *Tagebücher* p181. Also quoted in Mar, p. 145.

19. Bertolt Brecht. *Tagebücher 1920–1927*, p. 12.

20. Franz Blei. "Bestiarium," p. 46 and 146 (quoted in Mar, p. 167f).

21. KA 3.1, 21, p. 246f.

22. For a fuller treatment of the arts under Weimar, see John Willett, *Art and Politics in the Weimar Period*, Pantheon, 1978.

23. KA 1.1, 285, p. 215.

24. GWII p. 504; KA 4.1 p. 17. While "Der Wunderrabbiner" is set in medieval Spain, the figure of the miracle-rabbi himself is drawn from 18th century Hasidic lore: the Zaddik.

25. These were recently on display at the Jewish Museum in New York. "Berlin: Metropolis, 1898–1918." Exhibition Nov. 1999–Apr. 2000.

26. BKK (8 July 1921), p. 89.

27. Br II 382, p. 87.

28. Br II 383, p. 87.

29. Or so she was depicted by Else Lasker-Schüler. Fran Schwarzwald was a Viennese educator and a founder of such social services as soup kitchens.

30. BKK (17 December 1923), p. 91ff.

31. See "Herwarth Walden, The Conqueror" in Aktion. 5Jg. Nr. 51, Sp. 654. DLA marb and marmag, p. 131.

32. BKK (5 March 1924), p. 98ff.

33. Br II 382, p. 87.

34. ELS to Wollheim. Br II 375, p. 81f.

35. "Ich räume auf" GWII, p. 542; KA 4.1, p. 75.

36. *Ibid.*, p. 508; KA 4.1, p. 50.

37. *Ibid.*, p. 530; KA 4.1, p. 66.

38. *Ibid.*, p. 529; KA 4.1, p. 66.

39. *Ibid.*, p. 517; KA 4.1, p. 57.

40. "Du machst mich traurig" ("You make me sad") and "Hoer" ("Listen"), were both composed for voice and piano in 1917.

Chapter Ten

1. GWII, pp. 651ff; KA 4.1, p. 27ff. See note KA 4.2, p. 40. The Baltic resort Kolberg in Pommerania was a favorite summer destination for ELS. In the summer of 1930, anti-Semitic riots in German vacation spots were sharply on the rise. This fact was duly documented in articles and reports in a newspaper put out by the Central Organization of German Citizens of Jewish Faith. They noted an increasing number of Kolberg guest houses which could not be recommended, and requested that their readers write in about their experiences in resort towns.

2. "Paul Cassirer." GWII, p. 507; KA 4.1, p. 49.

3. Br I 128, p. 150ff.

4. *Prosa aus dem Nachlass*, p. 53.

5. GWII 787ff; KA 5, p. 11ff.

6. *Prosa aus dem Nachlass*, p. 51ff; KA5, p. 445ff.

7. "I was much in her disfavor following this conversation, and she referred to me as 'Herr Dispute.' I regarded her visions as fiction." Scholem to Benjamin, p. 104 in: WB/GS Correspondence 1932–1940. Schocken Books, New York.

8. StB Wup quoted in Mar, p. 200.

9. Br II Bachrach 401, p. 103.

10. StB Wup; Mar, p. 200.

11. In 1937, Goldscheider and his wife managed to escape to England, where he died in 1982.

12. Br I 140, p. 161f.

13. Paul Goldscheider. "Wo ich bin ..." in *Lasker-Schüler. Ein Buch zum Hundertsten Geburtstag*, ed. Michael Schmid, pp. 50–54.

14. Brecht was actually sued for plagiarism by Karl Klammer, whose translations of poems by François Villon he had used, "with some modifications, for a number of Threepenny Opera songs, leading Alfred Kerr and other critics to accuse him of plagiarism." Note to 157, p. 583. Bertolt Brecht, *Letters 1913–1956*.

15. Paul Goldscheider. "Wo ich bin ..." in *Lasker-Schüler. Ein Buch zum Hundertsten Geburtstag*, ed. Michael Schmid, p. 50–54.

16. *Ibid.*

17. *Rachmones* in Yiddish means *Barmherzigkeit* ("mercy"). It also refers to the eastern wall, that part of the synagogue in which the ark of the covenant is kept. See Heather Valencia, *ELS und A.N. Stenzel: Eine unbekannte Freundschaft*, p.61.

18. Heather Valencia. *ELS und Abraham Nochem Stenzel*. Campus Verlag, 1995, p. 84f.

19. *Ibid.*, p. 93.

20. *Ibid.*, p. 92.

21. *Ibid.*, p. 101.

22. See note (Anmerkung) Br II 156, p. 294.

23. Br I 143, p. 165f.

24. Br I 158, p. 187f.

25. Nachruf in *Berliner Tageblatt* 18 December 1927 and SB, p. 195 and note 7.

26. Br I 168, p. 203.

27. Br I 166, p. 200.

28. Br II, p. 299f: "Meine Bilder sind hier ausgestellt 75-ehrwürdige Monstrums, süsse wilde Juden—Kommen Sie bitte sofort. Meine Nerven werden verkauft von den Wänden. nehmen Sie sie alle. Ihr Bild—gegenüber Dehmel und die Angorakatzenblume Mechtild Lichnowsky—... der Malik von Theben ein Kaiserlich Krokodiltier betet für die Krieger im Krieg ... Kommen Sie, nehmen Sie sofort meine Bilder mit nach Wien...."

29. *Ibid.*

30. Br I 177, p. 214ff.

31. Br I 178, p. 216.

32. Br I 179, p. 217f.

33. Br I 180, p. 218f.

34. Br I 184, p. 224.

35. A letter from Freud to Else Lasker-Schüler is in the Else Lasker Schüler Nachlassarchiv in Jerusalem.

36. Br I 183, p. 223.

37. *Ibid.* #184 and Paul Goldscheider. "Wo ich bin," p53.

38. Benn. "Den Traum alleine ...," p. 71.

39. *Ibid.*, p. 73.

40. *Ibid.*, p. 74.

41. He died in a Soviet prison in 1941 during a Stalinist purge.

42. Br I 186, p. 225f.

43. *Ibid.*; Benn, p. 77.
44. KA 3.1, p. 87, line 35.
45. *Ibid.*, p. 180, line 21f.

Chapter Eleven

1. Mar, p. 241f Raas
2. *Ibid.*, p. 242.
3. Br I 215, p. 252.
4. Gottfried Benn. *Briefe. Band IV: Briefe an Tilly Wedekind. 1930–1955.* No. 62, p. 34.
5. Klaus Mann. *Der Wendepunkt*, p. 313.
6. Klaus Mann. *Tagebücher* v. 1, p. 183.
7. Br I 214, p. 251.
8. Mar, p. 242. Raas.
9. *Ibid.*
10. *Ibid.*, p. 241.
11. Br I 194, p. 233f.
12. Klaus Mann. *Tagebücher* v.2, p. 15.
13. Mar, p. 244 Raas.
14. Br II 459, p. 156ff.
15. Br II 460, p. 159.
16. Br II 464, p. 163.
17. Br II 475, p. 175ff.
18. See SB, p. 262. Source: Bulletin Leo Baeck Inst. 29 November 1965, p. 6.
19. Br I 226, p. 263.
20. GWII, p. 899; KA 5, p. 99.
21. *Ibid.*, p. 908; KA 5, p. 107.
22. *Ibid.*, p. 913; KA 5, p. 110.
23. Invited, one evening, to dinner at the home of Professor Hugo Bergmann, she mistakenly knocked on the door of his neighbor, who happened to be Scholem, "the renowned scholar of the cabala." When Scholem came to the door, she took the opportunity to engage him in a philosophical debate. He argued with her, hoping, she said, to convince her "with the poison of logic." Exasperated, she replied, "To marry the miracle with the schoolmaster's logic would be to make a misalliance" (GWII, p. 802).
24. GWII, p. 833ff; KA5, p. 48f.
25. *Ibid.*, p. 815; KA5, p. 32.
26. *Ibid.*, p. 902; KA5, p. 102.
27. *Ibid.*, p. 926; KA5, p. 120.
28. *Ibid.*, p. 919; KA5, p. 115.
29. *Ibid.*, p. 904; KA5, p. 104.
30. Heinz Politzer tells how the Palestinian poet, Kariw, was rebuffed when he offered to translate *Hebrew Ballads* into Hebrew. For a fuller discussion of the Hebrew-ness of her German, see Politzer, "Else Lasker-Schüler," in *Expressionismus als Literatur.* ed. Wolfgang Rothe. Franke 1969, pp. 219ff.
31. The correspondence of Walter Benjamin and Gershom Scholem 1932–1940. No. 47, p. 104.
32. *Ibid.*, 48, p. 108.
33. Br II 463, p. 162.
34. "But I *must* take on the Palestine book, that's so close to my heart. I would be a coward not to. I keep having to think of those being tortured in concentration camps, and am almost ashamed of my complaints." Letter to Jakob Job (18 March 1935). Br I 220, p. 256.

35. StA Zu Mar, p. 237f.
36. Raas. Mar, p. 247.
37. Raas. Mar, p. 290.
38. Klaus Mann *Tagebücher* v.2, p. 79f.
39. Kl Mann *Tagebücher* v.3. 1934–1935, p. 46.
40. *Ibid.*, p. 47.
41. Br I 225, p. 262.
42. *Ibid.*
43. Schalom Ben-Chorin, writer, co-founder of the work group, "Jews and Christians." He met Else Lasker-Schüler for the first time on her second trip to Jerusalem, in mid–May 1937.
44. Br I 249, p. 284.
45. SB, p. 43.
46. See Erika Klüsener, *Else Lasker-Schüler*, p. 114.
47. *Ibid.*
48. *Querschnitt.* Bd 6.1. 1926, p. 5.
49. *Ibid.* Bd 7.2. 1927, pp. 472–578.
50. Teo Otto in *Zum Hundersten ... FAZ* 10 February 1969 and Michael Schmid, Zum 100sten. Otto, p. 41ff.
51. DD, p. 614.
52. *Ibid.*
53. Raas. Mar, p. 261.
54. Apropos her handwriting: "For a calligrapher," she once wrote, "the content of his document is the mere pretext, just as for the painter the *subject* of his painting." Over her lifetime Else Lasker-Schüler "allowed" her letters to "burst into bloom." Her glyphs and rebuses are all expressive elements of her epistolary style. In his essay, "Aussicht ins Kinderbuch" ("A Close Look at Children's Books") (from *Angelus Novus*, WB. Ausg Schr 2, 156ff) Walter Benjamin comes very close in thought and feeling to her 1910 essay, "Handschrift" ("Handwriting"), for which the above statement served as motto. (KA 3.1, p. 158.)
55. Raas. Mar, p. 259f.
56. Adler, who had left Germany in 1933 like Lasker, and who died in London in 1949, only learned after the close of World War II that all nine of his siblings had perished in the Holocaust.
57. Br I 208. 244f.
58. KA 2., p. 80.
59. Br I 211, 247.
60. *Bulletin des Leo Baeck Instituts* 7, 1959.
61. Ben-Chorin. *Jussuf in Jerusalem*, p. 56.
62. *Ibid.*, p. 62.
63. Mie*srael* (Rotten*rael*) or, on occasion, Mi*srael* (Misery).
64. BSch., p. 44f ("Was soll ich hier?").
65. StA Zu, p. 292, Mar.
66. *Ibid.*, p. 297.
67. *Ibid.*, p. 302.
68. *Ibid.*
69. *Ibid.*

Chapter Twelve

1. Sigismund von Radecki: "Erinnerungen an E.L-S." DD, p. 575.
2. Br I 240, p. 277.
3. Br I 50, p. 75.
4. BSch 8, p. 49.

5. *Ibid.* 21, p. 61.

6. *Ibid* 22, p. 63f.

7. SB, p. 48.

8. Jehuda Amichai (1924–2000). Internationally acclaimed Hebrew poet. Born in Wurzburg, grew up in Palestine. After ELS's death, Amichai translated many of her poems into Hebrew.

9. Br I 289, p. 317.

10. Carl Sonnenschein (1876–1929). Theologian, founder and director of the Catholic-social(ist) student movement in Berlin.

11. With its coinage "Judenchristen," this letter touches on one of the poet's most deeply-held beliefs: namely, that Judaism and Christianity lie on a continuum, and are not inimical to each other. This idea finds its most eloquent expression perhaps in her play *Arthur Aronymus and his Fathers*. For a thorough-going exploration of the idea of "Judenchristen" with emphasis on its theological-historical roots, see Sigrid Bauschinger, "Judenchristen. Else Lasker-Schüler über die verlorene Brücken zwischen Juden und Christen." ELS: *Ansichten und Perspektiven*. Schürer und Hedgepeth.Tübingen, 1909.

12. Br I 107, p. 128.

13. For an extended discussion of *Ichundich* see Appendix II. See also Margarete Kupper in *Jahrbuch der DLA Marb 1970*, pp. 24–45 (*Anmerkungen*), and Heinz Thiel: "'Ich und Ich'—Ein versperrtes Werk?" pp. 123–159 in Michael Schmid, *Ein Buch zum 100*.

14. Br II 499, p. 199.

15. BSch 30, p. 71f.

16. *Ibid.*

17. She hoped to visit them in Haifa and read the play aloud in the presence of another guest, an important textile manufacturer, who she hoped would finance the play's publication. Nothing came of all this, however.

18. Br I 284, p. 313f.

19. In all there are 15 surviving letters from Ernst Simon to Lasker-Schüler. They date from January 1940 to summer 1943. See Ernst A. Simon, *Sechzig Jahre gegen den Strom. Briefe von 1917–1984 (Sixty Years Against the Stream: Letters 1917–84)* Hrsg. Leo Baeck Instituts Jerusalem. Mohr Siebeck, 1998.

20. ELS Archiv. Sig. 55:143 Bodenheimer, p. 104. This letter appears to have been mis-dated 1931, which led Bodenheimer and others to assume she had heard him deliver a sermon in Berlin.

21. *Ibid.*

22. Mar, p. 346f.

23. "Hamlet" Act III sc.1. Mar, p. 343.

24. Mar, p. 353.

25. *Ibid.*, p. 345.

26. KA 1.1, 396, p. 296.

27. KA 1.1, 469, p. 357.

28. KA 1.1, 471, p. 358.

29. Br II 518, p. 212.

30. SB, p. 273.

31. KA 1.1, 352, p. 267.

32. KA 2, p. 209 line 2.

33. KA 1.1, 406, p. 307.

34. "Mirra" was the then-eight-year-old Mira Bein, who later married an Israeli diplomat. She recalls the ageless face, the eyes, the bitter lines around the mouth, "but when she smiled she looked like an innocent child" (see Jürgen Serke, *Die verbrannten Dichter*, p. 33).

35. Br I 269, p. 300f.

36. Br I 288, p. 317.

37. See Ben-Chorin: "Jussuf in Jerusalem," p. 582f.

38. BrSch 15, p. 57.

39. Br I 50, p. 75
40. Br I 293, p. 318.
41. Mar, p. 359.
42. DD, pp. 594–598.
43. Mar, p. 317. Wolfskehl. *Briefwechsel aus Neuseeland 1938-48.* Bd 2, p. 673f (Luchter-hand) 1988. Karl Wolfskehl (1869–1948) was a leading member of the Stefan George Circle. An assimilated Jew, he was forced to emigrate and come to terms with his illusions about German culture. He died in New Zealand.
44. *Ibid.*
45. BSch 24, p. 67.
46. DD, p. 599. Ein Brief aus Jerusalem.
47. Mar, p. 318 (provenance unknown).
48. See Margarete Kupper in *Sämtliche Gedichte,* p. 310. Dr. Kurt Wilhelm went on to become chief rabbi of Stockholm. Writing to Lasker-Schüler's niece, Edda Lindwurm-Lind-ner, in 1947, he adds to the above that she was buried "in the section reserved for the most distinguished persons ..." and that "a very imposing tombstone was erected on the grave." He concludes, "I conducted the funeral and also the ceremony upon the unveiling of the stone."
49. Mar p. 318.
50. KA 1.1, 389, p. 292.
51. Three years after her death, by the division of Jerusalem, the Mount of Olives came under Jordanian jurisdiction. In 1967, when Israel reoccupied the territory, many gravesites were found to have been destroyed. The tombstone of Else Lasker-Schüler, which weighed several tons, lay crosswise over a newly laid road, as if a bulldozer had shoved it there. The grave itself had disappeared, possibly under the new asphalt surface. In 1976, with the help of a huge crane, the tombstone was moved to a new site. (See Erich gottgetreu. "Die letzten Jahre der Else Lasker-Schüler. Zum 100sten Geburtstag." *Die Zeit* 7 February 19679.)
52. Leopold Krakauer (1890–1954), architect and designer, born in Vienna, emigrated 1924 to Israel, where he designed many exemplary public and private buildings. He is renowned for his unadorned, sober style, reminiscent of 1920s Bauhaus.

Selected Bibliography

Adorno, Theodor W. and Walter Benjamin. *Briefwechsel 1928-1940.* Frankfurt am Main: Suhrkamp, 1994.

_____. *Philosophy of Modern Music.* New York: Seabury, 1973.

_____. *Prismen.* Frankfurt am Main: Suhrkamp, 1955.

Allen, Roy. *Literary Life in German Expressionism and the Berlin Circles.* Ann Arbor: UMI Research Press, 1983 (1972).

Appignanesi, Lisa. *The Cabaret.* New York: Universe Books, 1976.

Bab, Julius. *Die Berliner Bohème.* Paderborn: Igel Verlag, 1994.

Ball, Hugo. *Flight Out of Time.* New York: Viking, 1974.

Bänsch, Dieter. *Else Lasker-Schüler. Zur Kritik eines etablierten Bildes.* Stuttgart: Metzler, 1970.

Barron, Stephanie, ed. "Degenerate Art." Exh. Cat. Los Angeles: LACMA, 1991.

_____. "German Expressionist Sculpture." Exh. cat. LACMA. Chicago and London: University of Chicago Press, 1983.

Bauschinger, Sigrid. *Else Lasker-Schüler: Ihr Werk und ihre Zeit.* Heidelberg: Lothar Stiehm, 1980.

_____, ed. *Was soll ich hier? Exilbriefe.* Heidelberg: Lambert Schneider, 1986.

Ben-Chorin, Schalom. *Zwiesprache mit Martin Buber.* München: List, 1966.

Benjamin, Walter. *Angelus Novus. Ausgewählte Schriften, 2.* Frankfurt am Main: Suhrkamp, 1966.

_____. *Autobiographische Schriften. Gesammelte Werke, v. VI.* Frankfurt am Main: Suhrkamp, 1985.

_____. *Briefe, 2 v.* Frankfurt am Main: Suhrkamp, 1966.

_____, and Gershom Scholem. *The Correspondence of Walter Benjamin and Gershom Scholem, 1932-1940.* Ed. Gershom Scholem. New York: Schocken, 1989.

Benn, Gottfried. *Briefe. Band IV: Briefe an Tilly Wedekind. 1930-1955.* Hrsg v. Marguerite v. Schlüter. Stuttgart: Klett-Cotta, 1986.

_____. *Primal Vision. Selected Writings of Gottfried Benn.* Ed. E.B. Ashton. New York: New Directions. No date.

_____. *Sämtliche Werke, Die Stuttgarter Ausgabe.* 7v. Stuttgart: Klett-Cotta 1986-2001.

_____. *Den Traum alleine tragen.* Ed. Paul Raabe and Max Niedermayer. Wiesbaden: Limes, 1966.

Benson, Tim. *Raoul Hausmann and Berlin Dada.* Ann Arbor: UMI Research Press, 1987.

Bilski, Emily. "Berlin Metropolis." Jewish Museum Exh. cat. Berkeley: University of California Press, 1999.
Bithell, Jethro. *Modern German Literature 1880–1950.* London: Methuen, 1959.
Bodenheimer, Alfred. *Die Auferlegte Heimat. Else Lasker-Schüler's Emigration in Palästina.* Tübingen: Max Niemeyer, 1995.
Brecht, Bertolt. *Letters 1913–1956.* Transl. Ralph Manheim. London: Routledge, 1990.
Brod, Max. *Streitbares Leben.* München: Kindler, 1960
Bronner, Stephen Eric, and Douglas Kellner. *Passion and Rebellion: The Expressionist Heritage.* New York: Columbia University, 1987.
Buber, Martin. *Briefwechsel aus sieben Jahrzehnten. Geleitwort von Ernst Simon.* Heidelberg: Lambert Schneider, 1972–1976.
Craig, Gordon A. *Germany 1866–1945.* New York/Oxford: Oxford University Press, 1978.
Cross, Tim, ed. *Lost Voices of World War I.* Iowa City: University of Iowa Press, 1988.
Dahlhaus, Carl. *Schoenberg and the New Music.* Cambridge: Cambridge University Press, 1988.
Dick, Ricarda, ed. *Else Lasker-Schüler.* Schrift: Bild: Schrift. Bonn: August Macke Haus, 2000.
Döblin, Alfred. *Autobiographische Schriften.* Olten: Walter, 1980.
_____. *Briefe.* Olten: Walter, 1970.
_____. *Berlin Alexanderplatz.* Frankfurt am Main: S. Fischer, 1920; *Alexanderplatz* (Eng.). New York: Viking, 1931.
Dube, Wolf-Dieter. *The Expressionists.* London: Thames and Hudson, 1972.
Durieux, Tilla. *Eine Tür steht offen.* München: Herbig, 1964.
Dürrenmatt, Friedrich. *Theater-Schriften und Reden.* Zurich: Arche, 1966.
Easton, Laird M. *The Red Count: The Life and Times of Harry Kessler.* Berkeley: University of California, 2002.
Ehrenstein, Albert. *Gedichte und Prosa.* München: Luchterhand, 1961.
Elon, Amos. *The Pity of It All. A History of Jews in Germany, 1743–1933.* New York: Metropolitan Books, 2002.
Fischer, Grete. *Dienstboten, Brecht und andere.* Olten: Walter, 1966.
Gay, Peter. *Weimar Culture.* New York: Harper & Row, 1968.
Gilman, Sander and Jack Zipes, eds. *Yale Companion to Jewish Writing and Thought in German Culture 1096–1996.* New Haven: Yale, 1997.
Ginsberg, Ernst, ed. *Dichtungen und Dokumente.* München: Kösel, 1951.
Grass, Günter. *My Century.* New York: Harcourt, Brace, 2000.
Grosz, George. *A Little Yes and a Big No.* New York: Dial Press, 1946. German title: *Ein kleines Ja und ein grosses Nein.* Reinbek: Rowohlt, 1955.
Grunfeld, Frederic V. *Prophets Without Honor.* New York: Holt, Rinehart and Winston, 1979.
Gumpert, Martin. *Autobiography.* New York: Holle, 1962.
Hamburger, Michael. *Contraries.* New York: Dutton, 1970.
_____. *A Proliferation of Prophets.* London: Carcanet, 1986.
Hauptmann, Gerhart. *The Fool in Christ, Emanuel Quint.* New York: Viking, 1926.
Haxthausen, Charles W. *Berlin: Culture and Metropolis.* Minneapolis: University of Minnesota Press, 1991.
Heilbut, Anthony. *Thomas Mann.* New York: Knopf, 1996.
Hennings, Emmy. *Ruf und Echo, Mein Leben mit Hugo Ball.* Benziger: Einsiedeln, 1953.
Herald, Heinz. *Max Reinhardt.* Berlin: Felix Lehmann, 1915.
Herzfelde, Wieland. "Else Lasker-Schüler." *Sinn und Form,* 21 Jg. (1969) Heft 6.
_____. "Fremd und Nah. Über meinen Briefwechsel mit Else Lasker-Schüler." *Marginalien,* Blätter der Pirckheimer Gesellschaft, 18. Heft. März, 1965.
Hessing, Jakob. *Else Lasker-Schüler.* München: Wilhelm Heyne, 1985.
Heym, Georg. *Dokumente zu seinem Leben und Werk.* München: Beck, 1968.
Hille, Peter. *Dokumente.* Ed. Friedrich Kienecker. Essen: Ferdinand Schoningh, 1986.
_____. *Gesammelte Werke.* Berlin: Schuster & Loeffler, 1904, 1921.
Hiller, Kurt, ed. *Der Kondor, eine Anthologie.* Heidelberg 1912.
_____. *Leben gegen die Zeit.* Reinbek: Rowohlt, 1969–1973.

Hindemith, Paul. *Briefe*. Frankfurt am Main: Fischer Taschenbuch Verlag, 1982.

Hofmann, Werner. "Museum des 20.Jahrhundert: Hommage à Schoenberg." Nationalgalerie Berlin. Exh. cat. 1974.

Höxter, John. *So lebten wir. 25 Jahre Berliner Bohème*. Berlin, 1929.

Janik, Allan and Stephen Toumin. *Wittgenstein's Vienna*. New York: Simon and Schuster, 1973.

Jelavich, Peter. *Berlin Cabaret*. Cambridge: Harvard University Press, 1993.

Jentsch, Ralph. *Illustrierte Bücher des Deutschen Expressionismus*. Stuttgart: Cantz, 1990.

Kafka, Franz. *Letters to Felice*. New York: Schocken, 1967.

Kandinsky, Wassily, and Franz Marc. *The Blaue Reiter Almanac*. Ed. Klaus Lankheit. New York: Da Capo, 1989.

_____. *Concerning the Spiritual in Art*. Transl. and introd. By M. T. H. Sadler. New York: Dover Publications, 1977. Original title: *Über das Geistige in der Kunst* (1912).

Kessler, Harry. *Berlin in Lights. The Diaries*. New York: Grove, 1999. (German original: *Tagebücher 1918–1937*. Insel, 1961).

Kirsch, Sarah, Jürgen Serke and Hajo Jahn, eds. *Meine Träume fallen in die Welt. Ein Else Lasker-Schüler Almanach*. Wuppertal: Peter Hammer, 1995.

Klee, Paul. *Diaries*. Berkeley: University of California Press, 1968.

Klemperer, Victor. *Diaries*, 2 vols. New York: Random House, 1998.

Klüsener, Erika. *Else Lasker-Schüler*. Reinbek: Rowohlt, 1980.

_____. *Unveröffentlichte Briefe*. Leo Baeck Institut, Tel Aviv. v. 74. 1986.

_____, and Friedrich Pfäfflin, eds. *Marbacher Magazin* 71/1995, "Else Lasker-Schüler 1869–1945," DLA Marbach.

Kokoschka, Oskar. *My Life*. Transl. David Britt. New York: Macmillan, 1974.

Kraft, Werner. "Mein Blaues Klavier." *Deutsche Universitäts Zeitung* v.11, no. 23/24. 1956.

_____. *Spiegelung der Jugend*. Nachwort Jorg Drews. Frankfurt am Main: Fischer Taschenbuchverlag, 1996.

Krakauer, Siegfried. *From Caligari to Hitler*. Princeton: Princeton University Press, 1947.

Kraus, Karl. *Ausgewählte Werke in 3.v.* München: Langen-Müller, 1977.

_____. *Half-Truths & One-and-a-Half Truths*. Ed. & transl. Harry Zohn. London: Carcanet, 1986.

Kupper, Margarete. *Der Nachlass Else Lasker-Schülers in Jerusalem. II. Literaturwissenschaftliches Jahrbuch im Auftrag der Görres-Gesellschaft*. 10. Band, 1969.

Lankheit, Klaus. *Franz Marc im Urteil seiner Zeit*. Köln: DuMont Schauberg, 1960.

Laqueur, Walter. *Weimar*. New York: Putnam, 1974.

Linsel, Anne, and Peter von Matt, eds. *Deine Sehnsucht war die Schlange: Ein Else Lasker-Schüler Almanach*. Wuppertal: Peter Hammer, 1997.

Macke, August, and Franz Marc. *Briefwechsel*. Köln: DuMont Schauberg, 1964.

Mann, Heinrich, and Thomas. *Letters, 1900–1949*. Transl. Don Reneau. Berkeley: University of California Press, 1998.

Mann, Klaus. *Briefe und Antworten*, 2 vols. Edition. München: spangenberg, 1975.

_____. *Tagebücher. 1931–1933; 1934–1935*. München: spangenberg, 1989.

_____. *Der Wendepunkt*. München: spangenberg, 1976. This autobiography appeared first in English in 1942 under the title, *The Turning Point. Der Wendepunkt* is an expanded version, written by the author himself in German, and first published by Nymphenburger Verlagshandlung, München, 1969.

Marc, Franz. *Botschaften an den Prinzen Jussuf*. Piper, 1954.

_____. *Briefe aus dem Feld*. Ed. Klaus Lankheit and Uwe Steffen. München: List Taschenbuch, 1982 (originally Rembrandt Verlag, 1941).

_____. *Franz Marc / Else Lasker-Schüler. Karten und Briefe*. Ed. Peter-Klaus Schuster. München: Prestel, 1988.

Meidner, Ludwig. *Dichter, Maler und Cafés*. Zurich: Arche, 1973.

Mühsam, Erich. *Tagebücher (1910–1924)*. München: DTV, 1994.

Muschg, Walter. *Von Trakl zu Brecht*. München: Piper, 1961.

Nostitz, Helene. *Aus dem alten Europa*. Leipzig: Insel, 1926.

Or, Gala Bar. *Miron Sima/From Dresden to Jerusalem*. Mishkan le Omanut, Museum of Art, Ein Harod. Jerusalem 1997 (Hebrew and English).

Paret, Peter. *The Berlin Secession*. Cambridge: Harvard University Press, 1980.

Phelar, Anthony. *The Weimar Dilemma*. Manchester, 1985.

Pinthus, Kurt, ed. *Das Kinobuch*. 1913. Zurich: Arche, 1963.

_____. *Menschheitsdämmerung*. Reinbek: Rowohlt, 1919, 1959.

Politzer, Heinz. "Else Lasker-Schüler" in *Expressionismus als Literatur*. Ed. Wolfgang Rothe. Bern: Francke, 1969.

Raabe, Paul, ed. *Espressionismus: Aufzeichnungen und Erinnerungen*. Olten: Walter Verlag, 1965.

Richter, Hans. *Dada, Art and Anti-Art*. New York: Oxford University Press, 1978.

_____. *Dada, Kunst und Anti-Kunst*. Köln: DuMont Schauberg, 1964.

Rosenthal, Mark. *Franz Marc*. München, New York: Prestel, 1989.

Ruckaberle, Axel, ed. *Text + Kritik*. Heft 122. *Else Lasker-Schüler*. April 1994. München: edition text + kritik, 1994.

Sabarsky, Serge. *George Grosz, The Berlin Years*. New York: Rizzoli, 1985.

Schmid, Michael (also Schmid-Ospach), ed. *Else Lasker-Schüler. Ein Buch zum 100. Geburtstag der Dichterin*. Wuppertal: Peter Hammer, 1969.

_____, ed. *Mein Herz–Niemandem: Ein Else Lasker-Schüler Almanach*. Wuppertal: Peter Hammer, 1993.

Schoenberg, Arnold, and Wassily Kandinsky. *Letters, Pictures and Documents*. London: Faber, 1984.

Scholem, Gershom. *Walter Benjamin, The Story of a Friendship*. Transl. Harry Zohn. Philadelphia: Jewish Publication Society, 1981.

Schorske, Carl. *Fin de Siècle Vienna*. New York: Putnam, 1974.

Schrader, Bärbel, and Jürgen Schebera. *The "Golden" Twenties*. New Haven: Yale University Press, 1988.

Serke, Jürgen. *Die Verbrannten Dichter*. Basel: Beltz & Gelberg, 1977.

Shedletsky, Itta, ed. "Else Lasker-Schüler's Jerusalem." Ex. Cat., JNUL, Jerusalem, 1995.

Shepard, Jim. *Nosferatu*. New York: Knopf, 1998.

Sichelschmidt, Gustav. *Berlin! Berlin!* Berlin: Edition Erdmann, 1980.

Simon, Ernst. *Sechzig Jahre gegen den Strom. Briefe von 1917–1984*. Leo Baeck Institut, Mohr Siebeck, Jerusalem, 1998.

Sokel, Walter. *The Writer in Extremis*. Stanford: Stanford University Press, 1959.

Spiel, Hilde. *Vienna's Golden Autumn*. London and New York: Weidenfeld, 1987.

Starke, Ottomar. *Was Mein Leben Anbelangt*. Berlin: F. A. Herbig, 1956.

Stern, Fred. B. *Auftakt zur Literatur des 20. Jahrhunderts. Briefe aus dem Nachlass Ludwig Jacobowski*. Heidelberg: Lothar Stiehm, 1974.

Stuckenschmidt, Hans Heinz. *Musik des 20. Jahrhunderts*. München: Kindler, 1969.

Taylor, Ronald. *Berlin and its Culture, A Historical Portrait*. New Haven: Yale University Press, 1998.

Valencia, Heather. *Else Lasker-Schüler und Abraham Nochem Stenzel*. Frankfurt, New York: Campus, 1995.

Walden, Nell Roslund. *Herwarth Walden. In Memoriam*. Berlin: Kupferberg, 1963.

_____, and Lothar Schreyer. *Der Sturm: Ein Erinnerungsbuch an Herwarth Walden*. Berlin: Woldemar Klein, 1954.

Whitford, Frank. *Expressionist Portraits*. New York: Abbeville, c 1987.

Willett, John. *Art and Politics in the Weimar Period*. New York: Pantheon, 1978.

_____. *Expressionism*. London: Weidenfeld, 1970.

Yudkin, Leon I. *Else Lasker-Schueler*. Science Reviews Limited: Northwood, Middx, 1991.

Zuckmayer, Carl. *Als wärs ein Stuück von mir*. Frankfurt: S. Fischer, 1966.

_____. *A Part of Myself*. Transl. Richard and Clara Winston. London: Secker & Warburg, 1970.

Works by Else Lasker-Schüler

Main Editions of Works by Else Lasker-Schüler

Kritische Ausgabe (Critical Edition), Suhrkamp: Jüdischer Verlag.

Werke und Briefe. Kritische Ausgabe im Auftrag des Franz Rosenzweig Zentrums der Hebräischen Universität Wuppertal und des Deutschen Literaturarchiv Marbach am Neckar hrsg. Norbert Oellers, Heinz Rolleke and Itta Shedletzky.

Band 1.1; 1.2 *Gedichte. Anmerkungen.* Bearbeitet von Karl Jurgen Skrodzki unter Mitarbeit von Norbert Oellers, 1996.

Band 2. *Dramen.* Bearbeitet von Georg-Michael Schulz, 1997.

Band 3.1; 3.2 *Prosa 1903–1920. Anmerkungen.* Beabeitet von Ricarda Dick 1998.

Band 4.1; 4.2 *Prosa 1921–1945.* Nachgelassene Schriften. Anmerkungen. Bearbeitet von Karl Skrodzki und Itta Shedletzky 2001.

Band 5. *Prosa.* Das Hebräerland. Bearb. Skrodzki und Shedletzky, 2002.

The main body of available letters (Briefe), are currently contained in two volumes:
- *Liebe gestreifte Tiger* and *Wo ist unser buntes Theben?* Hrsg.: Margarete Kupper. Kösel Verlag Munchen, 1969.

The letters to Karl Kraus, *not* included in these volumes, are to be found in a separate edition:
- *Briefe an Karl Kraus.* Ed: Astrid Gehlhoff-Claes. Berlin: Kiepenheuer & Witsch Koln, 1959.

The letters to Salman Schocken, edited and with commentary by Sigrid Bauschinger, *Was soll ich hier? Briefe aus dem Exil,* appeared in the Lambert Schneider Verlag, 1986.

When the next volumes of the Critical Edition appear (in summer 2003), numerous hitherto unpublished letters will be added to the above.

Gesammelte Werke in Drei Banden:
- Band I. *Gedichte.* Hrsg. Friedhelm Kemp. Kösel, 1961.
- Band II. *Prosa und Schauspiele.* Hrsg. Friedhelm Kemp. Kösel, 1962.
- Band III. *Prosa aus dem Nachlass.* Hrsg. Werner Kraft. Köhn, 1961.

Gesammelte Werke in 8 Banden. Deutscher Taschenbuch Verlag (DTV), 1986.

Some Else Lasker-Schüler Works Available in German Editions, Other Than the Above

Hebräische Balladen. Bibliophile facsimile. Hrsg. und Nachwort, Norbert Oellers. Suhrkamp: Jüdischer Verlag, 2000.

Mein lieber, wundervoller blauer Reiter. Privater Briefwechsel Else Lasker-Schüler/Franz Marc. Hrsg. Ulrike Marquardt und Heinz Rolleke. Artemis & Winkler, 1998.

Werke in einem Band: Lyrik. Prosa. Dramatisches. Edited with Afterword, Commentary and Chronology by Sigrid Bauschinger. Artemis & Winkler, 1991.

Ich suche allerlanden eine Stadt. Gedichte, Prosa, Briefe. Hrsg. Silvia Schlenstedt. Reklam, 1988.

Ich sel dich anseh'n Gedichte und Bilder. Nachwort Elfriede Friesenbiller. Brandstatter, 1986.

Books by Else Lasker-Schüler Available in English

Concert, translated by Jean Snook. Lincoln, NE, and London: University of Nebraska Press, 1994.

Hebrew Ballads and Other Poems, translated by Audri Durchslag and Jeanette Litman-Demestere. Preface by Jehuda Amichai. Philadelphia: Jewish Publication Society, 1980.

Star in My Forehead, Selected Poems, translated by Janine Canan. Duluth, Minnesota: Holy Cow! Press, 2000.
Your Diamond Dreams, poems, translated and with an introduction by Robert P. Newton. Chapel Hill: University of North Carolina Press, 1982.

Books About Else Lasker-Schüler Available in English

Else Lasker-Schüler: The Broken World. Hans Werner Cohn. London: Cambridge University Press, 1974.
Else Lasker-Schüler: Inside This Deathly Solitude. Ruth Schwertfeger. New York Oxford: Berg Publishers, 1991. (Schwertfeger's book offers a brief biography, as well as interpretations of the poems she translates.)
Else Lasker-Schüler: A Study in German Jewish Literature. Leon I. Yudkin. Science Reviews Limited, Northwood, Middlesex, England, 1991.

Selected Essays and Chapters Devoted to Else Lasker-Schüler in Books, Periodicals and Catalogs Available in English

Avery, George C. The unpublished correspondence of Herwarth Walden and Karl Kraus. *Expressionism Reconsidered*. Houston German Series. V.1, 1979.
Bauschinger, Sigrid. "Else Lasker-Schüler and Café Culture." *Berlin Metropoplis*, Exhcat Jewish Museum. New York: University of California Press and Jewish Museum 1999, 58ff.
Flimm, Jürgen. "On Filming Else Lasker-Schüler's *Die Wupper*." *Theater Heute* (4) 1985, 16–17.
Grunfeld, Frederic V. "An Angel at the Gate: Else Lasker-Schüler. Erich Mühsam, Ernst Toller." *Prophets Without Honor*. Holt, Rinehart, New York 1979, pp. 96–145.
Guder, G. "The Meaning of Colour in Else Lasker-Schüler's Poetry." *German Life and Letters*, xiv. 1960/1961, 175ff.
Lorenz, Dagmar. "Else Lasker-Schüler Becomes Permanently Exiled in Jerusalem." *Yale Companion to Jewish Writing and Thought*. Ed. Gilman and Zipes. 1997, 563–570.
Politzer, Heinz. "The Blue Piano of Else Lasker-Schüler." *Commentary* 9 (1950) no. 4, pp. 335–344.
Robertson, Ritchie. "The Imposed Homeland: Else Lasker-Schüler in Palestine." *Modern Language Review* 93, April 1998, 583–585.
Tyson, Peter. "Else Lasker-Schüler's *Die Wupper*: Between Naturalism and Expressionism." *A.U.M.L.A.* (*Journal of the Australasian Universities Language and Literature Association*). New Zealand. MLA November 1985, 144–153.
Webb, Karl E. "Else Lasker-Schüler and Franz Marc: A Comparison." *Orbis Literarum*, no. 33, 1978, pp. 280ff.
Zimroth, Evan. "The Black Swan of Israel." *Tikkun* v. 5 no. 1, pp. 35–39.
Zohn, Harry. "Poet and Scarecrow." *TLS* Oct. 16, 1981, p. 1207.

Selected Essays and Articles in German About (or Relating to) Else Lasker-Schüler

Bodenheimer, Alfred. "Else Lasker-Schüler's Briefe an Emil Raas." *Zeitschrift für Deutsche Philologie*. 116(4) 1997. 588–602.
Carr, G.J. "Zu den Briefen Else Lasker-Schülers an Karl Kraus." *Literatur und Kritik* (4) 1970, Heft 49. 549–556.
Gottgetreu, Erich. "Näher heran an Else Lasker-Schüler." *Neue Deutsche Hefte*. 1980.
Hessing, Jakob. "Dichterin im Vakuum." *Text + Kritik* 122, 1994. 3–17.
Kesting, Marianne. "Zur Dichtung Else Lasker-Schülers." *Rodopi*. Amsterdam, 1982.

Kraft, Werner. "Erinnerungen an Else Lasker-Schüler." *Hochland* 43, no. 6. 1951. 588–592.
Kupper, Margarete. "Materialien zu einer kritischen Ausgabe der Lyrik Else Lasker-Schülers."
  Literaturwissenschaftliches Jahrbuch. im Auftrage der Görres-Gesellschaft. Neue Folge,
  Bd.4 1963. 95–190.
Pazi, Margarita. "Verkünderin west-östlicher Prägung: Else Lasker-Schüler in Jerusalem." *Text*
  + *Kritik* 122, 1994. 65–74.
Sprengel, Peter. "Else Lasker-Schüler und das Kabarett." *Text* + *Kritik* 122, 1994. 75–86.
Thiel, Heinz. "'IchundIch'—ein versperrtes Werk?" in *Lasker-Schüler: Ein Buch zum Hundertsten
  Geburtstag der Dichterin.* Hrsg. Michael Schmid. 1969. 123–159.

Partial Listing of Documentary Films About Else Lasker-Schüler

Else Lasker-Schüler, A Portrait. WDR/WDF (Westdeutsche Rundfunk/Fernsehen). 1968.
Ich Räume Auf. A film celebrating the fiftieth anniversary of Else Lasker-Schüler's pamphlet
  by the same name. WDR/WDF. 1979.
Approaches to Else Lasker-Schüler. A film by Ludwig Brundiers. WDR/WDF. 1985.
Jussuf, Prinz von Theben. A film about Else Lasker-Schüler by Nina Fischer. WDR/WDF. 1993.
Der Schwarze Schwann (The Black Swan). A film about Else Lasker-Schüler. WDR/WDF,
  Dortmund. 1995.
Else Lasker-Schüler figures as a character in novels and films. Two recent examples are *Nos-
  feratu,* a novel by Jim Shepard (Knopf, 1998), and *Berlin/Jerusalem* (France-Israel), a film
  by Amos Gitai, 1989.

Plays by Else Lasker-Schüler, Televised, and Available on Film

Die Wupper; Arthur Aronymus und seine Väter; IchundIch: Käthe Gold liest Else Lasker-Schüler.

Some Musical Settings to Poems by Else Lasker-Schüler

Hildemann, Wolfgang. *Drei Gesänge.* (Three Songs): "Weltende" (World's End), "Mein Volk"
  (My People), and "Gebet" (Prayer).
Leyendecker, Ulrich. *Hebräische Balladen: 7 Lieder für Mezzosopran und Kammerensemble*
  (Hebrew Ballads: 7 songs for mezzo-soprano and chamber ensemble).
Lombardi, Luca. *Ein Lied für Sopran, Flöte, Klarinette und Klavier nach Texten von Else Lasker-Schüler*
  (A Song for soprano, flute, clarinet, and piano with texts by Else Lasker-Schüler). All of the
  above were performed on "Workshop Neue Musik," WDR3, Tuesday, September 27, 1994.
Hindemith, Paul. "Weltende" (World's End), for soprano and orchestra, Op. 9, 1917; "Ich
  bin so allein" (I am so alone), no opus #, 1917, from *Zwei Lieder für Alt und Klavier,* no.
  1 (Two songs for alto and piano, no. 1), B. Schott's Söhne, Mainz 1983; "Traum" (Dream),
  "Du machst mich traurig" (You make me sad), from *Acht Lieder mit Klavier* (Eight songs
  with piano) Op. 18, 1920, B. Schott's Söhne, Mainz-Leipzig.
Previn, André. "Ein Liebeslied" (A Love Song) for soprano, alto flute and piano. In *From
  Ordinary Things,* Selections. Recorded in Osawa Hall, Tanglewood July 17–19, 1997. Sony
  CD #7867.
Stern, Robert. "My Blue Piano." Song Cycle for soprano, tenor and piano. Recorded at the
  New Music Festival, Northampton, MA, 1997.
Walden, Herwarth. "Weltflucht" (Retreat from the World), "Verdamnis" (Damnation),
  1910–1914. Sturm Verlag.
Windt, Herbert. "Gebet" (Prayer). In *Das dramatische Theater.* 1.Jg. H3/4 (1924), pp. 193–196.

Index

Index